Covenants without Swords

Covenants without Swords

IDEALIST LIBERALISM AND THE SPIRIT OF EMPIRE

Jeanne Morefield

PRINCETON UNIVERSITY PRESS

PRINCETON AND OXFORD

Copyright © 2005 by Princeton University Press
Published by Princeton University Press, 41 William Street,
Princeton, New Jersey 08540
In the United Kingdom: Princeton University Press,
3 Market Place, Woodstock, Oxfordshire OX20 1SY

Library of Congress Cataloging-in-Publication Data

Morefield, Jeanne, 1967–
Covenants without swords : idealist liberalism and the spirit of empire /
Jeanne Morefield
p. cm.
Includes bibliographical references and index.
ISBN 0-691-11992-9 (alk. paper)
1. Liberalism. 2. Internationalism. 3. Equality. 4. Hierarchies. I. Title.

JC574.M67 2005
320.51—dc22   2004041749

British Library Cataloging-in-Publication Data is available.

MR This book has been composed in Sabon

Printed on acid-free paper. ∞

www.pupress.princeton.edu

Printed in the United States of America

10 9 8 7 6 5 4 3 2 1

For Paul, Anna, and Niko

And covenants, without the sword, are but words and of no strength to secure a man at all.

—Thomas Hobbes, *Leviathan*, ch. XVII

Contents

Acknowledgments

THIS BOOK HAS BEEN A LONG TIME in the making. Many people have contributed their support, advice, and input to its creation. Thanks are due to the chair of my dissertation committee, Isaac Kramnick, both for his comments along the way and for instilling in me a love of Laski. The other members of the committee, Mary Katzenstein, Anna Marie Smith, and Susan Buck-Morss, also commented extensively on the earliest version of this manuscript and helped to fundamentally shape the final product. Thanks to Henry Shue for his comments and essential advice about publishing. Benedict Anderson also deserves recognition for inadvertently guiding my work toward the interwar era.

Many of my colleagues at Whitman College have read and commented on various chapters of this book. Special thanks are due to Timothy Kaufman-Osborn, Lynn Sharp, David Schmitz, Julia Davis, Tom Davis, Susan Fergusson, and Bob Tobin, both for their invaluable insights and for their willingness to put up with my fascination with liberalism. Thanks also to Shampa Biswas and Bruce Magnusson for their last minute International Relations lessons and a steady stream of helpful information about all things global. I would also like to express my appreciation to Whitman College for funding my two trips to Oxford and for my sabbatical. Finally, thanks to all the members of the Whitman College Politics Department for their generous spirit, openness of mind, sense of community, and intellectual curiosity, which have made it a jewel within the discipline and a lovely place to call home.

Many thanks to the outside readers from Princeton University Press, Peter Wilson and Michael J. Smith, for their invaluable insights. This book would not look as it does had not Professor Smith's suggestions prompted me to recast its central premise in an infinitely more coherent manner. Thanks also to my editor at the press, Ian Malcolm, for his consistent advice and support throughout the revision process.

The efforts of a number of talented research librarians also enormously helped the book. At Whitman, special mention goes to Henry Yaple and Lee Keene. Thanks also to Julie Morefield for her help with the index. Thanks to the Bodleian Library for allowing me access to the Gilbert Murray and Alfred Zimmern papers. The entire staff at the Bodleian was extremely helpful, but particular mention goes to Colin Harris for his tireless (sometime transatlantic) efforts to help me locate, copy, and correctly cite the papers.

I am grateful to those individuals who have inspired me to write through their being in the world: to Tony Perlstein, whose commitment to labor justice is matched only by the joy he takes in the struggle; to Anthony Arnove, the hardest working anti-imperialist I know; to Karim Dharamsi, who lives philosophy more honestly and naturally than the rest of us breathe; and to John Morefield and Kathy Morefield, who embody social justice for me.

A number of other people deserve recognition. Thanks to those friends, including Libbie Rifkin, Juliet Williams, Elisabeth Nishiura, Rich Clayton, Fernanda Zullo, and James Buchwalter-Arias, who have listened patiently to my ideas about this project from its germinal stages. And finally, the greatest thanks of all are due to Paul Apostolidis who, more than anyone else, has read and commented on various versions of the manuscript since its inception. Without his suggestions, insights, support, childcare, patience, and inspired conversation, this book would not be.

Covenants without Swords

Introduction

IN 1921, CLASSICS SCHOLAR, liberal activist, and League of Nations advocate Gilbert Murray looked around at a Europe still reeling from the effects of World War One and boldly pronounced that "nothing but the sincere practice of liberal principles will save European society from imminent revolution and collapse."[1] And yet Murray also maintained that European society should not apply these same liberal principles universally, that the post-war world needed a reestablishment of "World Order," organized around extant relations of imperial power, in which all understood the differences between "leaders and led, governors and governed."[2]

Just three years earlier, Alfred Zimmern, Murray's friend and colleague and committed League activist, had applied liberalism to world politics, reaching similarly odd conclusions. Finding a solution to international conflict, he argued, meant making sure "of the foundations of our liberal faith."[3] But the key to maintaining this faith was not to be found in any liberal commitment to equality on a global scale or in the Wilsonian notion that all nations had a "right" to "self determination." Rather, for Zimmern Europeans could best serve the goals of internationalism by approaching nationality first as a "spiritual possession."[4] Once understood in these terms, Zimmern argued, creating a just international society did not require a radical transformation of the world's political landscape. Instead, the League of Nations and internationally minded statesmen simply needed to ensure that the spiritual and cultural needs—as opposed to the political demands—of these "families of mankind" were taken seriously.[5]

As two of the most powerful intellectual influences on both the League of Nations Covenant and the developing discipline of International Relations (IR), Murray and Zimmern successfully folded these seemingly contradictory understandings of liberalism into the theory and practice of

---

[1] Gilbert Murray, *The Problems of Foreign Policy* (Boston: Houghton Mifflin, 1921), v.

[2] Gilbert Murray, *Satanism and the World Order* (London: George Allen and Unwin, 1920), 40.

[3] Alfred Zimmern, *Nationality and Government* (New York: Robert M. McBride and Company, 1918), xv.

[4] Ibid., 31.

[5] Alfred Zimmern, "German Culture and the British Commonwealth," in *The War and Democracy*, eds. R. W. Seton Watson, J. Dover Wilson, Alfred E. Zimmern, and Arthur Greenwood (London: Macmillan and Co., 1928), 380.

British international relations between the wars. Despite the long-term influence of their thinking on what has come to be known as "liberal internationalism," however, since the Second World War most accounts of Murray and Zimmern have taken their cue from E. H. Carr's profoundly influential critique of the interwar period, *The Twenty Years Crisis*, and dismissed their work as largely incomprehensible and hypocritical. Indeed, even many of their liberal contemporaries didn't know what to make of them. The editors of *The Nation*, for instance, entitled a 1918 review article of Zimmern's *Nationality and Government* simply "A Liberal in a Muddle."[6]

This book is a sustained critical engagement with that liberal muddle. It springs from an intellectual commitment not to dismiss Murray's and Zimmern's liberalisms as simply hypocritical. Rather, it argues that a closer examination of their work can provide political theorists with the perfect opportunity to journey down the road that connects liberalism with its antithesis, to explore one of the most philosophically interesting moments when liberal thinkers and activists engaged in the politics of hierarchy and paternalism. From justifications of empire, to nineteenth-century bourgeois paternalism, to contemporary debates about welfare, liberals have frequently advocated a politics that both proclaims an ideological commitment to human equality and relegates sections of the population to the status of children. A closer examination of Murray's and Zimmern's liberal internationalisms not only supplies us with a means to investigate this phenomenon on a global scale but also offers us a particularly stark example of liberalism at its most philosophically and politically fraught.

The main goal of this book, then, is to investigate the dense ideological matrix that made Murray's and Zimmern's simultaneous commitment to an international politics based on the "Fraternity of Mankind" and their conservative attachment to a language of social stasis, nationhood, and empire appear coherent. It seeks to illuminate the internal logic that made it possible for these men to fancy themselves apostles of a radically transformative approach to world politics that required little to no change in the global status quo. It focuses on that space between global visions that logically should not align but seem, in practice, to do so—the space between liberal universalism and hierarchical world order.

This book departs most dramatically from Carr's precedent-setting critique of liberal internationalism in its analysis of what *kind* of political theory occupied this space. The book is in complete agreement with Carr's political portrayal of the internationalism that thinkers like Murray and Zimmern developed between the wars as utopian on the one hand and

---

[6] "A Liberal in a Muddle," *The Nation* (London), November 23, 1918, 228.

obdurately conservative on the other. For Carr, the liberal internationalists' dogmatic insistence that the world should look a particular way—what he referred to as the "utopian edifice"—prevented them from seeing the world as it actually was, as characterized by the competing interests of states. Their inability to come to terms with this reality, Carr claimed, locked utopian thinkers into a slavish nostalgia for "a century past beyond recall—the golden age of continuously expanding territories and markets of a world policed by the self-assured and not too onerous British hegemony."[7] This book does not take issue with these traditionally overlooked Marxist overtones of Carr's analysis. Rather, the disagreement with Carr centers on his simplification of the liberal paradigm. For Carr, the ideological glue that made utopianism and the status quo cohere was liberalism at its most orthodox, embodied in the "harmony of interests" doctrine. First articulated by Adam Smith, this doctrine proffered a vision of good society generated by the self-interested actions of individuals. According to Carr, the doctrine also justified economic greed and political domination in the name of the social good. In contrast, this book insists that the "harmony of interests" served as a kind of doctrinal straw man for Carr (one easily toppled by a Marxist critique of power) whose expeditious demise allowed Carr to elide the much more complicated political-theoretical tradition that informed Murray's and Zimmern's approaches to international politics: liberal reformism.

In essence, this book argues that the ideological tradition of liberalism is much more capacious than Carr gives it credit for, and that Murray and Zimmern were not dyed-in-the-wool laissez-faire liberals who uncritically threw their weight behind an eighteenth-century doctrine. Rather, both men were products of a nineteenth-century philosophical movement to reform liberalism, to free liberal theory from the "harmony of interests" and from its dependence on self-interested individualism, to move liberal politics in a more social—what we would now call communitarian—direction. And yet in their attempts to theorize liberal society, Murray and Zimmern produced an approach to international politics characterized by a perennial disconnect between liberal universalism and a vision of international morality replete with imperial and political hierarchies. Indeed, the world as described in Murray's and Zimmern's political philosophies was so redolent with conservative longings for tradition, family, and order that even Filmer—that ardent defender of the divine right of kings—no doubt would have found himself quite at home there.

Thus, what is ultimately most striking about the international theories of both Murray and Zimmern was their failure to speak to the liberal

---

[7] Edward Carr, *The Twenty Years Crisis, 1919–1939: An Introduction to the Study of International Relations*, 9th ed. (London: Macmillan, 1961), 287.

muddle that they and their philosophical progenitors had set out to solve; they failed to define community in liberal terms without sacrificing these terms themselves. And yet ironically, neither man was drawn toward anti-liberal understandings of the social order by a simple, clandestine conservatism. Rather, Murray's and Zimmern's turn toward the conservative was generated by their very liberal unwillingness to challenge free trade economics and imagine state authority—or, in this case, "world state" authority—in anything other than repressive terms. The institutional result of this unwillingness was the creation of a League of Nations Covenant "without the sword," a form of international governance fortified by the moral authority of international society alone that had the advantage of sounding revolutionary even as it required the Great Powers to sacrifice little of their sovereignty and relinquish virtually none of their economic and colonial assets.

From the standpoint of intellectual history, a closer examination of the contradictory impulses at work in the creation of this first, full-fledged experiment with international organization has much to tell us about the origins of twentieth-century internationalism. As two of the contemporary proposals that most closely favored the status quo, Murray's and Zimmern's approaches to internationalism and to the League of Nations ultimately occluded other liberal and more radical alternatives under consideration, schemes for international organization committed to a much more rigorous critique of international capital and the concept of sovereignty. Cracking open the intellectual edifice that congealed and then hardened around Murray's and Zimmern's understandings of sovereignty prompts us to challenge the ossified conception of statehood that still occupies the heart of both the liberal and realist approaches to international politics. Such an endeavor may then invigorate efforts to reimagine and reinvent some of these forgotten alternatives.

From the standpoint of political theory, if, like Carr, we ignore that Murray and Zimmern began their political project from a place of reform and not orthodoxy, we miss gaining critical insight into liberalism's ability to theorize community. In other words, it was liberalism *reformed* not liberalism *unmodified* that failed to imagine a world community simultaneously equitable *and* able to address what Carr termed the "intensity and complexity of the international crisis."[8] Taking a closer look at Murray's and Zimmern's muddle has much to teach us about how far we can stretch liberalism before it breaks, how hard we can push liberalism in a social direction before it doubles back on itself, how much of liberalism we can reject without vitiating everything worth saving. Their decades-long attempt to make liberalism and world society speak to one another

[8] Ibid., 39.

offers us an unprecedented glimpse into the liberal project at its most embattled and potentially transformative. Perhaps most importantly, during an intellectual era in which political theorists are used to neatly dividing concern for the individual and concern for the social into the descriptive categories of liberalism and communitarianism, Murray's and Zimmern's work speaks not only to the sustained yet unarticulated presence of community within liberalism but also to the urgent need for contemporary liberals to develop their own independent language of the social. At the same time, it demonstrates all too clearly just how difficult it is to find this language—to reform liberalism—without jettisoning the fundamental belief in equality that makes the liberal polity coherent in the first place.

THE HARMONY OF INTERESTS AND ITS LIBERAL CRITICS

The bulk of this book engages in a critical exegesis of Murray's and Zimmern's internationalism, following their liberalism from its reformist origins to its hierarchical conclusions. Some contemporary liberal scholars may find it puzzling that I consider Murray and Zimmern liberal at all given the largely communitarian, idealist, and even reactionary impulses of their work. And yet both men were self-proclaimed liberals and members of the Liberal Party; both insisted on a commitment to individual rights, and both harbored a liberally conceived wariness of state authority. At the same time, Murray and Zimmern claimed that their political theories transformed traditional conceptions of liberality into a worldview that took the good of the social whole as seriously as it did the well-being of the individual. Thus, they argued, their liberalisms were uniquely able to reconcile the divergent and contradictory political impulses of international society, and to combine a serious regard for global community with all that was redeemable about the liberal commitment to individual freedom.

Even though this book opposes Carr's characterization of Murray's and Zimmern's liberalisms, it takes a key methodological point from *The Twenty Years Crisis* in treating their political theories as coherent bodies of work—that is, in tracing their developing visions of liberal society from the domestic to the international realm. For Carr, the weaknesses associated with inter-war internationalism arose not from the peculiarities associated with forcing a political framework developed within the state upon the international sphere but rather from problems internal to liberalism itself, problems he associates with the harmony of interests. Similarly, this book assumes that to truly understand the complexities, promises, and limitations of liberal reformism as it was practiced internationally, it is also necessary to critically examine the dense configuration of philosophical lacunae and political tensions that constituted its earlier life within the state.

This approach runs counter to many contemporary analyses of the relationship between political theory and international relations. For thinkers like Hidemi Suganami and Charles Beitz, the problems political theorists confront when they begin to theorize the international are largely problems of translation, problems associated with transcribing what Suganami calls the "domestic analogy" into a context and a discipline that has, in Beitz's words, neither "so rich a theoretical tradition nor so well defined or recurrent a set of political issues."[9] This book acknowledges that translation presents political theorists (who are primarily used to thinking within the context of the state) and internationalists alike with a real conundrum. How does one theorize rights or the rule of law on an international level when state authority—that which makes political liberalism possible in the domestic realm—does not currently exist on a global scale? For this reason, a pantheon of much less theoretically savvy realists than Carr have referred to the inter-war thinkers and subsequent generations of internationalists not only as liberal but as "idealists," a term they use in a colloquial rather than a philosophical sense to denote an international politics based on an ideal rule of law rather than, in Morgenthau and Thompson's words, "the concrete circumstances of time and place."[10] In contrast, I maintain that despite the very real problem of translation, many of the political vagaries and philosophical inconsistencies that arise when liberals theorize the international also have something to do with liberalism itself.

Again, however, the book also argues that rather than viewing these inconsistencies as part of liberalism's complex ideological heritage, Carr dramatically reduced all liberal theory to the inherent belief that "highest interest of the individual and the highest interest of the community naturally coincide" as long as these individuals were in engaged a process of economic production based on the division of labor.[11] When applied to international politics in the nineteenth century, Carr argued, liberal inter-

---

[9] Hidemi Suganami, *The Domestic Analogy and World Order Proposals* (Cambridge: Cambridge University Press, 1989); Charles Beitz, *Political Theory and International Relations* (Princeton: Princeton University Press, 1970), 5. Beitz also does a stellar job of exploring the many obstacles facing anyone interested in thinking through a normative international theory, ranging from the general perception that it is inappropriate to make normative judgments about world affairs to the lack of empirical data concerning international politics.

[10] Hans Morgenthau and Kenneth Thompson, *Politics Among Nations*, 6th ed. (New York: Alfred A. Knopf, 1985), 12.

[11] Carr, 42.

nationalists committed to this same belief in a natural "harmony of interests" assumed a similar "division of labor between nations." Thus, for thinkers like Mazzini, each nation had a unique role to play on the world stage and peace would naturally prevail when each performed its special task to perfection.[12]

Carr's response to this vision of the good was deeply incredulous. On both domestic and international levels, the harmony of interests doctrine, he argued, served to obscure power relationships between classes and among states. For Carr, what liberal theorists had historically assumed to be universally desirable was merely "the ideology of a dominant group concerned to maintain its predominance by asserting an identity of interests with the community as a whole."[13] As Carr's cutting analysis of Henry Ford illustrates, assuming that what led most naturally to increased production was also most beneficial to society served the economic interests of eighteenth-century liberals and their industrial offspring. Carr maintained that at the bottom of liberalism's (and capitalism's) presumed harmony of interests lay economic and political domination disguised as universal good. Once you exposed the harmony of interests doctrine at the heart of inter-war utopianism, Carr argued, you were left with what amounted to a true picture of international power politics at work.

Because of the popularity of *The Twenty Years Crisis*, Carr was immensely successful at convincing future generations of International Relations (IR) scholars that the harmony of interests was the *most* suspect doctrine at the heart of all inter-war thought. Even Hedley Bull, whose sympathies lay with both the inter-war thinkers and with Carr, insisted that "this doctrine, despite the battering it had received in the late nineteenth century at the hands of Hegelians, Marxists, Social Darwinists, and others, had been given a new lease on life by the accession of United States to world leadership and had been applied to twentieth century international politics, which were quite unable to bear any such description."[14]

And yet the picture was never this simple. Bull gestures in the right direction by mentioning Hegelian, Marxist, and Social Darwinist critiques of liberalism. He fails to account, however, for the number of liberals who not only took these criticisms to heart but used their insights to address liberalism's role in fostering the massive economic and social disparities that distinguished their world. In other words, liberalism was never the largely monolithic, unreflecting ideology that Carr's analysis

---

[12] Ibid, 44. Carr uses Mazzinian nationalism as an example of a particularly nineteenth-century approach to the "harmony of interests" doctrine.

[13] Ibid.

[14] Hedley Bull, "The Twenty Years' Crisis Thirty Years On," *The International Journal* 24(4) (1969): 625.

implies and Bull's comments overlook, an ideology whose core interests were passed down in a similar form from "the eighteenth century rationalists to Bentham and from Bentham to the Victorian moralists."[15] For Carr, all liberals looked pretty much the same; those who did not espouse an untroubled vision of the harmony of interests he positioned outside of the canon. Most significantly for our purposes, Carr called the liberal reformer and Oxford scholar T. H. Green an "English Hegelian" who only "tempered the doctrines of his master with concessions to British nineteenth-century liberalism."[16]

In fact, T. H. Green never described himself as a Hegelian nor did he believe that he was somehow making concessions to liberalism. Instead, Green was a self-described liberal who drew upon what Charles Taylor has termed an "oddly transposed variety of Hegelianism" to help him address a crisis in liberal social theory; a crisis generated by the tension between laissez-faire individualism and the needs of "an absolute and common good."[17] And Green was not alone in this endeavor. An entire generation of thinkers educated primarily at Oxford during the 1860s, '70s, and '80s also sought to address the contradiction between individual desires and the needs of the community by theorizing, through Hegel, a more social (what Green called "constructive") liberalism.[18]

Adherents to Green's particular blend of German idealism and constructive liberalism such as Bernard Bosanquet, David Ritchie, and John Muirhead (hereafter referred to as idealist liberals), developed a liberal politics and philosophy that embraced Hegelian commitments to "Spirit" (Geist) and an organic theory of community. Here was a cluster of likeminded thinkers who tried—not very successfully, as this book will argue—to couple liberalism's emphasis on individual autonomy with a richer and more interdependent notion of community. In its essence, this was a philosophical movement that used idealism to save liberalism from itself. Ironically, in the process of also trying to retain liberalism's historic wariness toward state interference, many idealist liberals turned to the language of organicism—the use of the body as a metaphor for political society—as a way of disassociating the state from the ambit of social relations. These thinkers then coupled this approach to organicism with a vision of moral community read through the lenses of Social Darwinism and a Victorian commitment to the sanctity of the monogamous family.

---

[15] Carr, 44.

[16] Ibid., 45.

[17] Charles Taylor, *Hegel* (Cambridge: Cambridge University Press, 1975), 537; Thomas Hill Green, *Prolegomena to Ethics* (Oxford: The Clarendon Press, 1884), par. 218.

[18] Thomas Hill Green, "Letter to the Editor," *Oxford Chronicle* 4 (January 1873): 3 [i.c., Peter Nicholson, *The Political Philosophy of the British Idealists* (Cambridge, 1990), 283].

Thus, in the process of trying to make their liberal theory more communal, these thinkers reinstated the kind of social hierarchies against which the most orthodox of their liberal brethren argued. In the end, the "common good" depicted here looked much less like Adam Smith's society of small producers and much more like the medieval chain of being, a place where family relations—rather than a liberal equality of citizenship—governed the political order.

This book makes the potentially controversial historical claim that as "Oxford men," schooled in the tradition of this Greenian approach to liberal reformism, Murray and Zimmern drew upon idealist and organic conceptual motifs similar to those of an earlier generation in their attempts to make liberalism speak the language of community. In the process, both men rearticulated on a global scale many of the same pre-liberal political prescriptions of their intellectual progenitors. In essence, Murray's and Zimmern's understandings of the communal order that held liberal international society together were ultimately modeled after the hierarchies of classical Athens, the fixity of the medieval body politic, and the holistic workings of nature.

MURRAY, ZIMMERN, AND THE "TWENTY YEARS CRISIS"

In its historical capacity, this book takes great inspiration from the recent movement within IR to rethink the inter-war period, or, in Carr's words, the "twenty years crisis." Thanks to scholars such as Peter Wilson, David Long, Brian Schmidt, and Andreas Oslander, we now know that inter-war British internationalism was much more diverse than Carr originally portrayed it. In particular, these recent works suggest that the term "idealist" (which has been applied to this period by IR scholars since World War Two) is not rich enough to describe the breadth and depth of inter-war thinking on international politics. Indeed, these authors all conclude that the indurate division between "realism" and "idealism" falls apart when one begins to examine the work of many of these so-called idealists in detail.[19] Wilson complicates the picture still further when he rightly points out that Carr's analysis of utopianism during this period was couched largely as an attack on liberalism. As Wilson notes, that many

---

[19] As Andreas Oslander points out, it was G. Lowes Dickinson, one of the leading figures of the British League of Nations Movement, who coined the term "international anarchy," a phrase which has now become the stock and trade of modern "realism." [See Andreas Oslander, "Rereading Early Twentieth Century IR Theory: Idealism Revisited," *International Studies Quarterly* 42 (1998): 413].

(if not most) of these thinkers were liberals cannot be denied.[20] But the *variety* of liberal plans for international organizations was much more expansive than traditional interpretations (taking their cue from Carr) have assumed, ranging from Norman Angell's international public sphere, to J. A. Hobson's international government, to Harold Laski's call for a serious reconsideration of the entire idea of sovereignty.

In this context, the book's focus on two of the period's most mainstream, quintessentially idealist thinkers (in the IR sense of the word) may seem a bit counterintuitive and slightly out of step with the overall spirit to rethink the inter-war period. Murray and Zimmern embraced all of the stereotypical attributes of this era, everything that inter-war idealism has been derided for ever since: a utopian faith in international law, an overestimation of the role of the League in world politics, a nervous commitment to the imperial and economic status quo, a basic belief in the power of international "Spirit" or "mind" to change global politics in fundamental ways, and a naive acceptance of collective security as an almost evolutionary development in the progress of international politics. In particular, perhaps because he actually became an IR scholar (as opposed to Murray, who remained a professor of classics throughout his career), numerous accounts of idealism continue to see Zimmern's texts as definitive. Martin Hollis and Steve Smith go so far as to label Zimmern's 1933 book, *The League of Nations and the Rule of Law*, "the best example of Idealist writing."[21] And yet it is precisely because they *were* so mainstream, because their works were so stereotypical, that we ought to be concerned with them. Murray and Zimmern played an enormous role in erecting the intellectual edifice that made this account of the world—an account based on reconciling liberal universalism with the global status quo—not only predominant between the wars but also in later accounts of the period. Perhaps, then, the greatest "crisis" of that critical twenty years was not that utopianism briefly ascended to the level of policy in Europe but that this form of internationalism (whether one calls it "idealist," "liberal," or "utopian") so successfully silenced alternative internationalist voices that, eighty years later, many of them have yet to be reheard.

While neither Murray nor Zimmern was present at the 1919 meetings in Paris to draft the League Covenant, and while neither had an illustrious diplomatic career, both wielded an immense amount of behind-the-scenes intellectual power from their complementary institutional orbits. Murray, who has been called the "principle architect of the League of Nations

---

[20] David Long and Peter Wilson, *Thinkers of the Twenty Years Crisis* (Oxford: Oxford: The Clarendon Press, 1995), 3.

[21] Martin Hollis and Steve Smith, *Explaining and Understanding International Relations* (Oxford: The Clarendon Press, 1990), 217.

Union" (LNU), successfully purged this powerful voluntary organization of what he termed "pacifist faddists" in mid-1918.[22] He went on to transform the LNU into one of the most powerful intellectual and political influences on the League Covenant largely through his personal contacts with powerful delegates at the Peace Conference, namely Sir Robert Cecil. Following the war, Murray helped push the emerging discipline of IR in Britain in a pro-League direction by participating in a process that both defined and filled key academic positions at Oxford, the University of London, and elsewhere.

Zimmern (to whom Hans Morgenthau once referred as "the most influential representative of our field" during the inter-war era) had a tremendous impact on IR circles in Britain both before and after the First World War. As a young Fellow at New College before 1910, he influenced a number of students who would go on to play key roles in British international politics, including Arnold Toynbee, Reginald Coupland, and several future members of the pro-imperialist Round Table Society.[23] As the first professor of IR in the world (at the University of Wales, Aberystwyth), the first Montague Burton Professor of International Relations at Oxford, and one of the founding members of both the Institute of International Affairs in London and the Geneva Institute for International Relations, Zimmern was intimately involved with the formation of the discipline during its earliest days.[24] Like Murray, he exercised a formidable impact on the League Covenant (and thus the practice of League internationalism between the wars) from his position within the Foreign Office during World War One.

Readers familiar with this period might be surprised to find that this book does not discuss the work of other inter-war internationalists in greater detail, particularly that of Arnold Joseph Toynbee, the other unfortunate whipping boy of Carr's critique, whose name, along with Zimmern's, is practically synonymous with inter-war utopianism. One could argue that although Toynbee would go on to profoundly influence foreign policy and IR in Britain (particularly in the 1930s when he was editor of Chatham House's *Survey of World Affairs* and during World War Two when his team dominated the Foreign Office), he did not have the kind

---

[22] Duncan Wilson, *Gilbert Murray OM 1866–1957* (Oxford: The Clarendon Press, 1987), 254; Bodl. MS Gilbert Murray (adds. 11) fol.3 (*Gnoman*, 1957.) Thanks to Professor Alexander Murray for the permission to cite the Murray Papers. Thanks also to the owners of the papers, the Bodleian library at Oxford.

[23] See Toynbee's account of Zimmern in *Acquaintances* (Oxford: Oxford University Press, 1967), 48–61. Also, Carroll Quigley, *The Anglo-American Establishment: From Rhodes to Clivenden* (New York: Books in Focus, 1981), 89.

[24] D. J. Markwell, "Sir Alfred Zimmern Revisited: Fifty Years On," *Review of International Studies* 12 (1986): 280.

of initial impact on the League Covenant that Murray and Zimmern had. But the decision not to include Toynbee in this book was prompted less by the fact that he was not as influential as Murray and Zimmern toward the beginning of the inter-war period and more by the fact that his work did not emerge out of the same philosophical tradition to reform liberalism from within an idealist framework that inspired the work of the other two men.

Readers familiar with Toynbee's lineage might be equally confused by this assertion. Of the three, Toynbee had the most direct genealogical connection to the first generation of idealist liberals to come up at Oxford through his uncle, also named Arnold Toynbee, who was a student and colleague of T. H. Green. The first Arnold Toynbee's tireless commitment to liberal social reform prompted his fellow idealist liberals to establish Toynbee Hall in London's East End after his early death in 1883; Toynbee Hall would subsequently become a focal point for Oxford-generated liberal reformism in late nineteenth-century Britain. But Arnold J. Toynbee's social theory did not reflect this tradition largely because, at ten years Zimmern's junior, he was much more affected by World War One then were either Murray or Zimmern. Indeed, from the first sentence of the first paragraph in his memoirs, Toynbee referred to World War One as the pivotal event of his life. "Half my contemporaries at school" he recounted, "were killed before they turned twenty-seven. Ever since 1915 I have been surprised at being still alive."[25] Before the war, the young Toynbee's work on international politics closely mirrored that of his mentor, Alfred Zimmern.[26] But the war profoundly changed not only his approach to IR but his entire worldview. The post-war approach to IR which he developed over years of working with Chatham House, was characterized less by an idealist commitment to create a morally righteous international liberalism than by a scientific desire to catalogue and even predict the cataclysmic rise and fall of civilizations. While equally concerned with matters of Spirit, Toynbee's internationalism (caught up as it was in his cyclical theory of history) lacked the ethical intensity of Murray's and Zimmern's work, and perhaps because of this, he never maintained the same kind of fierce commitment to the League of Nations that Murray and Zimmern would display throughout their careers.

By contrast, while the Great War was a pivotal topic of Murray's and Zimmern's writings on international politics, it seemed to have little to no effect on the *substance* of their liberalisms. In other words, both men applied the same brand of reformist liberalism they had developed before

---

[25] Arnold J. Toynbee, *Janus at Seventy Five* (New York: Oxford University Press, 1964), 1.

[26] See in particular, *Nationality and the War* (London: J. M. Dent and Sons, 1915).

the war in response to domestic issues to the post-war world, a liberalism largely shaped by the spiritually infused, "oddly transposed" Hegelian sensibilities of nineteenth-century Oxford.

In making this claim this book bucks a number of historical assumptions about both Murray and Zimmern and the political significance of Hegel to British liberalism. Scholars of liberal reformism in late nineteenth- and early twentieth-century Britain tend to focus their work on either those nineteenth-century thinkers associated with Green and the Scottish universities *or* on the "new liberals" who came to prominence during the Edwardian era. Even though most of the thinkers identified with Green's Oxford-led movement (including Bosanquet, Ritchie, Edward Caird, and John Muirhead) considered themselves liberal, the majority of scholars who focus on this period refer to them simply as "idealists."[27] My decision to refer to these thinkers as "idealist liberals" emphasizes the liberal half of their political and theoretical agenda: to transform liberalism by combining liberal and idealist sensibilities and conceptual categories. In addition, even though most "new liberals" (such as L. T. Hobhouse, J. A Hobson, Delisle Burns, and A. D. Lindsay) looked to Green as their philosophical and political inspiration, historians usually treat these thinkers as largely distinct from the idealist liberals at Oxford.[28] Finally, scholars of both British idealism and new liberalism have taken most liberals' vociferous rejection of all German metaphysics after World War One as a sign that the influence of Hegelian idealism ended abruptly in the 1920s. In Peter Robbins' words, "British Hegelianism, like the British Empire, was mortally wounded by the First World War: unlike the Empire, Hegelianism did not linger long. . . . It is still regarded as something of a period piece."[29]

This book makes three novel claims in this regard. First, it argues that Murray and Zimmern do not fall neatly into the distinction between the British idealists of the late nineteenth century and the "new liberals" of the early twentieth century and, in fact, confounded these distinctions by continuing to evoke markedly idealist, even quasi-Hegelian conceptions of the social as a way to enrich liberalism's paucity of thinking on community. As classical scholars, they inherited these idealist motifs largely through their experience with Oxford's *Literae Humaniores* (or Greats Curriculum), which by the 1880s was thoroughly saturated with the Hegelian interpretations of Green and his senior colleague, Benjamin Jowett.

---

[27] See for instance the works of Sandra Den Otter, David Boucher, Andrew Vincent, Raymond Plant, and Peter Robbins.

[28] For more on British "new liberalism," see the works of Michael Freeden, Richard Bellamy, and Steven Collini.

[29] Peter Robbins, *The British Hegelians* (London: Garland, 1982), 102.

Second, Murray and Zimmern deployed these idealist motifs even as they were ostensibly rejecting the entire German philosophical tradition, thus inoculating themselves from the career-wrecking taint of Prussianism that haunted thinkers like Ritchie both during and after the war. Third, while many scholars assume that British idealism lost its political cachet following World War One, this book argues that, thanks to thinkers like Murray and Zimmern, key aspects of this school of thought continued to influence international politics even after they had been explicitly rejected by most British liberals. Thus, Murray's and Zimmern's internationalisms not only mimicked the general philosophical trajectory by which their nineteenth-century forebears had used idealism to make liberalism more socially responsible, they also replicated many of political and philosophical contradictions that drove these thinkers toward organicism and paternalism.

In arguing that the implicit idealism of thinkers like Bosanquet and Green largely structured Murray's and Zimmern's liberalisms, this book also works to complicate the picture of inter-war idealism still further. Taking their cue from American realists like Morgenthau, most mainstream accounts of inter-war internationalism have traditionally used the term "idealist" interchangeably with "liberal" or "liberal phase" to describe the period. From a realist perspective, this slippage makes sense in that both terms imply a belief in something beyond power relations, whether it be the rule of law or international organizations like the League of Nations.[30] From a philosophical standpoint, however, the conflation of these terms is incoherent since "liberalism" and "idealism" apply to two separate philosophical traditions. And yet, ironically, Murray and Zimmern were *both* liberal and idealist in the philosophical sense. Oddly, then, the realists' dismissive decision to use these terms interchangeably is more accurate than they themselves could have anticipated. Simply put, Murray's and Zimmern's inter-war internationalisms represented an attempt to fuse liberalism and idealism in a manner already developed by nineteenth-century intellectuals. Their internationalism was thus both liberal and idealist, not in the colloquial sense in which realists employ the term (as in being about ideas rather than power) but in the historical, philosophical sense. In many ways, the tensions found within their internationalisms were the inevitable tensions to arise from the merging of these two traditions.

And Murray's and Zimmern's works were, above all else, alive with tensions. For both men, the Great War had demonstrated beyond a shadow of a doubt that the biggest problems in international politics

---

[30] The post-war triumph of realism within the American Academy helped ensure that this conflation of "liberalism" and "idealism" continues to exert itself today in IR textbooks and introductory classes aimed at an overall survey of the discipline.

arose from forces of economic production and trade growing more international while political and social forces remained local, grounded in the selfish, often nationalist and expansionist, interests of states. In the idealist tradition of the Oxford liberals, Murray and Zimmern approached such discrepancies as crises of Spirit. Thus, just as Green and his colleagues had argued that the only way to make the liberal economy moral was to foster a deeper appreciation among citizens of the spiritual bonds that connected them to the social whole, so too did Murray and Zimmern maintain that the only way to save the world from regressing once again into the chaos of war was to make it, in Zimmern's words, "as interdependent in its spiritual relations just as it is in its economic relations." The project of internationalists and the League of Nations in particular, they argued, was to encourage citizens and statesmen to participate in the movement of what Murray termed "Liberal Spirit" in the world, to take their bonds of duty to one another as seriously as they took those to their fellow nationals. Their highly watered down, "oddly transposed" version of the Hegelian dialectic made this kind of international interdependence possible by reconciling what both Murray and Zimmern argued were the unnecessary contradictions between affiliation for one's national communities and participation in the rapidly developing international society.

But like their Victorian counterparts, Murray and Zimmern were faced with the similarly liberal, albeit radically altered, problem of statehood. Unwilling to conceive of a League of Nations with any of the coercive authority of a state—authority that might be used by Bolsheviks and "non-adult races" to challenge the sovereignty of the Great Powers—they threw their political and philosophical weight behind the idea of an organic, international social order conditioned at once by an enduring commitment to empire, a *pre-liberal*, family-centered approach to nationhood and sovereignty, and a rejection of democratic, international governance. Their dependence on this strikingly conservative understanding of international order became a kind of supplement, the book argues, for their liberal unwillingness to imagine political alternatives to sovereignty, to envision a global economy regulated by workers, and to theorize a democratic form of international governance with real political (not just moral and symbolic) power.

At the same time, historical circumstances ensured that these conservative impulses were exacerbated on an international level in a way no longer possible within the British state. Thus, in a domestic context, nineteenth-century idealist liberals like Bosanquet supported a philanthropic movement that consistently violated the private lives of working-class people and pushed the emerging welfare state in Britain to recognize families, rather than individuals, as the fundamental bearers of rights.

With the expansion of the franchise in 1918, however, and the emergence of a more democratic political system in Britain, the paternalism of the nineteenth-century reformers would be countered by the increasingly powerful Labour Party (a movement attested to by the spectacular decline of the Liberals in the early 1920s). This was not the case, however, internationally, where liberal and conservative heads of states and their intellectual supporters (including Murray and Zimmern) worked hard to ensure that the League of Nations would have no autonomous power of its own. This complete absence of any kind of democratic authority meant that thinkers like Murray and Zimmern were able to push successfully for the continuance of a paternalistic global politics based on organic conceptions of nationhood and the supposedly natural relationship between imperial and colonized societies. Even as working-class activists within liberal democratic states challenged Victorian paternalism, Murray and Zimmern played a critical role in ensuring that it lived on in the international realm.

This is not to say, however, that the power of Murray's and Zimmern's arguments alone convinced the British government and Conference participants to enact their particular approach to international organization in 1919. The book makes no such directly causal claim. Rather, it suggests that Murray's and Zimmern's particular blend of internationalism happened to dove-tail with the economic and political goals of key liberals. Given the great tide of public opinion in favor of a League of Nations immediately following the war, Prime Minister Lloyd George was well aware that his Liberal government had to support *some* kind of post-war international organization of states to promote peace. Murray, Zimmern, and the internationalism they and their colleagues developed held out the promise of world organization without dramatic political commitments or sacrifices, conveniently relieving the British of the need to cut back or disarm their navy.[31] In addition, its calls for a tempered but reinvigorated return to free-trade liberalism supplied the ideological fodder for Britain's symbolic war against Bolshevism.[32] In addition, Zimmern's emphasis on nationhood seemed to satisfy the Wilsonian imperative that all nations had a right to self determination while simultaneously insisting that international politics continue to be shaped and implemented by the colonial powers.[33] In essence, Murray and Zimmern argued for an internation-

[31] Max Beloff, *Britain's Liberal Empire: 1897–1921*, 2nd ed. (London: Macmillan, 1987), 272–73.

[32] Konni Zilliacus, *Mirror of the Past: A History of Secret Diplomacy* (New York: Current Books, 1946), 239.

[33] For more on the political deployment of the term "national self-determination" during World War One and its subsequent effects on European ethnic conflict, see Allen Sharpe, "The Genie that Would Not Go Back Into the Bottle; National Self Determination and the

alism that embraced precisely what power brokers in Britain wanted most: to safeguard British military capability, protect free trade and colonial expansion, exclude the Soviet Union, and, in the words of Lloyd George, "offer Europe an alternative to Bolshevism."[34] The most powerful aspect of their approaches to international politics, then, was the way they called for very few institutional and political changes in the global order even while claiming to revolutionize the world.

ORGANIZATION OF THE BOOK

This book deepens our understanding of how Murray and Zimmern could begin theorizing international society as liberal reformers and end up defining that social sphere in conservative terms, terms brimming with the naturalistic, hierarchical, familial images of the pre-liberal world. In a basic sense, then, the book is genealogical in its desire to follow the philosophical and political logic of Murray and Zimmern's internationalism from its roots in nineteenth-century Oxford through the inter-war period. This inquiry does not assume, however, that when we return to the source of Murray and Zimmern's liberalism their work will immediately appear more coherent. Rather, it rejects the possibility of discovering philosophical and political origins that are in any way untroubled and seamless. Indeed, disparities ran deep throughout the palimpsest of Oxford liberalism, disparities that continued to weave their way through Murray's and Zimmern's works. What finally emerges from a prolonged consideration of both these nineteenth- and twentieth-century approaches to liberal reformism is a constellation of conflicting political ideologies, some gesturing toward liberal universalism, others toward spiritual idealism, some toward an equality of human beings and nations, others toward Social Darwinism and imperial union. The ultimate product of Murray's and Zimmern's internationalist imaginings was indeed hierarchical, based on the politics of the colonial and economic status quo—but as a truly genealogical investigation of its origins reveals, the theory itself was more than a monolithic "utopian edifice," more than a liberal apology for conservatism. Rather, Murray's and Zimmern's works were striated with a multitude of liberal, conservative, and even socialist political visions, visions that ran parallel to one another in a largely unarticulated fashion.

Legacy of the First World War and the Peace Settlement," *Europe and Ethnicity*, eds. Seamus Dunn and T. G. Fraser (London: Routledge, 1996), 10–29.

[34] Lloyd George, "Some Considerations for the Peace Conference before They Finally Draft their Terms," *Mirror of the Past: A History of Secret Diplomacy*, ed. Konni Zilliacus (New York: Current Books, 1946), 224.

The book delves into these unarticulated spaces by puncturing the integument that houses these conflicting logics in one body, and by exploring the complex ideological structure within. As Uday Sing Mehta cautions regarding John Stuart Mill's longtime rationalization of empire, the complexities that emerge from the "extended link" between liberalism and its hierarchical opposite cannot not be shrugged off as hypocritical or incomprehensible but rather must be taken "as an invitation" to explore the political realm that spans these two logics.[35] Mehta suggests that when we follow the strands of the political contradictions that wove together nineteenth-century liberalism and imperialism, we can begin to think through the potentially long-term theoretical significance of empire to contemporary liberalism. This book not only sets the stage for a similar examination of the long-term obfuscating effect of Murray's and Zimmern's conflicting political theories on contemporary internationalism but also maintains that a critical unearthing of their work has much to tell us about the complicated relationship between liberalism writ large and its concealed assumptions about the social world.

Chapter 1 begins the investigation by examining the social theory developed by Oxford idealist liberals during the 1870s and '80s. It demonstrates how Green and Bosanquet turned to Hegelian idealism to help them develop a liberal theory of moral interdependence and community. It argues that while these thinkers supported a Hegelian notion of universal Spirit, they were reluctant to unequivocally endorse Hegel's dialectical theory of the state. This decision to diverge from Hegel's dialectic led to a basic, philosophical incoherence in their social theory, an incoherence rooted in their inability to reconcile the individual with the state and the state with the community. The chapter goes on to argue that this philosophical tension prompted a number of key idealist liberals, particularly Bosanquet, Ritchie, and Muirhead, to turn to organicism and Social Darwinism. As a result of this move toward scientific and naturalistic explanations, these thinkers arrived at a political theory that retreated to an almost pre-liberal, pre-Hegelian notion of the state as family. The chapter concludes by demonstrating that on a political level, this dual commitment to both liberalism and a vaunted sense of the nuclear family as the generator of moral righteousness led to a deeply paternalistic set of policy prescriptions.

Chapter 2 shifts the analysis toward the interpolation of many of the most conflicting and politically conservative tendencies of the Oxford idealist liberals into Murray's and Zimmern's developing liberal social theories. The chapter begins by focusing on the controversial historical claim

---

[35] Uday Sing Mehta, *Liberalism and Empire* (Chicago: University of Chicago Press, 1992), 8.

that Murray and Zimmern (who attended Oxford in the 1880s and '90s) were influenced by the "mystics or transcendentalists" associated with the preceding generation.[36] Indeed, because of Hegel's supposedly inherent authoritarianism and the rather hazy connection Murray and Zimmern drew between the entire tradition of German philosophy and Marxism, both men, like so many of their contemporaries, were vocal in their rejection of all things German. But, chapter 2 contends that despite their protestations Murray and Zimmern absorbed many of the most idealist and indeed quasi-Hegelian tendencies of the Oxford school, largely through their association with the *Literae Humaniores*. The chapter goes on to demonstrate how two key idealist liberal motifs resurfaced in Murray and Zimmern's shared perspective on ancient Greece, a preoccupation with the spirituality of Greek culture and a reverence for the Athenian commitment to preserve individual freedom through duty to the polis. Murray and Zimmern each blended these dual concerns for spirituality and community into their liberalisms and in the process evoked many of the same political and philosophical antinomies of their Oxford progenitors, particularly with regard to theorizing state power. Ultimately, through an examination of both men's published and unpublished writings, this chapter concludes that Murray's and Zimmern's liberalisms were shot through with conservative, pre-liberal longings for communal order. In addition, both men overcompensated for their emphatic commitment to make liberalism spiritual by rejecting all analysis of power in political theory as vulgarly materialist.

Chapters 3 and 4 focus on a detailed analysis of Murray's and Zimmern's internationalisms as expressed primarily through their published writings. Chapter 3 is concerned with how the underlying notion of Spirit played out in both men's approaches to international politics. The chapter demonstrates how Murray and Zimmern responded to a nihilistic unraveling of the pre-war international order by calling for a radical unification of the world through Spirit. For Murray, this approach was best encapsulated in the relationship between "Liberal Spirit" and the transformation of the world into "One Great City of Men and Gods." For Zimmern, it occurred in the more specifically global conception of "international mind." Although distinct, both ideas claimed to resolve the thorny but putatively unnecessary opposition between individual freedom and global federation, and thus nudge states and individuals alike to take the good of the international whole—as opposed to the competitive principles of orthodox liberalism or the "materialism" of socialism—as their moral

---

[36] J.A.K. Thomson, *Proceedings of the British Academy*, vol. XLIII (Oxford: Oxford University Press, 1957), 257. See also Francis West's biography, *Gilbert Murray: A Life* (New York: St Martin's Press, 1984).

compass in world affairs. The chapter examines both Murray's and Zimmern's approaches to global spirituality and details how these notions responded to and were shaped by the domestic expansion of British working-class politics, the Bolshevik Revolution, and both men's anxious perception of an international system potentially dominated by the world's "simple races." The chapter concludes by examining how these notions of spirituality were ultimately at odds with themselves and thus sets the stage for the central conflict in chapter 4 between Murray's and Zimmern's idealistically oriented emphases on Spirit and their equally emphatic liberal intolerance for state power.

Chapter 4 maintains that it was Murray's and Zimmern's liberalisms that ultimately kept them from supporting a state-like League of Nations. Thus, this chapter begins by examining the conflict between their understandings of Spirit and their refusal to imagine international government as anything other than a super-state. It then explores how both men (in the idealist liberal tradition) supplemented for this lack of institutional power by grounding all of the transformative and reformist impulses of their liberalisms in an organically conceived notion of international community. For Murray, this community was shaped by the movement of the world toward "cosmos," an organic ordering of international relations characterized by the natural distinction between leader and led. Zimmern found the equally natural origins of international society in the warm, sheltering qualities of nations, which he termed the "families of mankind."

Chapter 5 focuses on the implications of Murray's and Zimmern's internationalisms more generally. It begins by taking a close historical look at how Murray and Zimmern transformed their liberal social theories into their profoundly influential approaches to international organization. It thus focuses on the origins of the League of Nations movement in Britain, Murray's and Zimmern's connections to this movement (and ultimately, to the League Covenant), and both men's impact on the disciplinary development of IR in Britain between the wars. The chapter goes on to examine the implications of this influence by making the somewhat novel claim that, despite the supposedly idealist compulsion to undermine sovereignty, Murray's and Zimmern's unflagging rejection of a super-state and their refusal to examine the relationship between state sovereignty and capital ultimately helped take the issue of sovereignty completely off the table at the Paris Peace Conference and thus significantly contributed to its current status within the discipline. At the same time, by developing a form of liberal internationalism that alleviated the need for a critique of sovereignty, Murray's and Zimmern's internationalisms occluded the work of more radical scholars like Harold Laski who were actively calling for the abrogation of sovereignty as a necessary step toward world peace. The chapter suggests that an active reconsideration of the ossified form of sovereignty that remains embedded in both the discipline and practice of international relations will help contemporary democratic theorists, international ethicists, and IR scholars to address some of today's more intractable problems associated with economic integration and to reimagine truly global, democratic responses to them.

Chapter 6 critically explores the lessons that contemporary liberals can draw from Murray's and Zimmern's failure to theorize international society in a way that retained a liberal commitment to equality. It argues that in the blatant idealism of their project to socialize liberalism without a state, to craft a "covenant without the sword," both Murray's and Zimmern's works reveal something essential about liberalism. For Thomas Hobbes, political covenants without force "are but words and of no strength to secure men at all" because, in the absence of political authority, society would devolve into atomistic chaos. Murray and Zimmern thought differently.

For both men, liberalism on a global scale could survive without a state because it was, first and foremost, grounded on a preexisting notion of the social. Thus, by stripping the state away from liberal theory, Murray's and Zimmern's works expose the unarticulated, communal underbelly of liberalism itself. All liberalism, in this sense, is idealist in that it assumes the presence not only of a stable state but also of a naturally coherent culturally and nationally bounded community within which its principles make sense and because of which the state's claims to power appear both legitimate and natural. The complete absence of a state in Murray's and Zimmern's internationalism forces to the surface liberalisms' dirty little secret—its dependence on some untheorized form of legitimizing community—and at the same time demonstrates just how densely paternalistic, hierarchical, and pre-liberal such a community can be. This suggests that perhaps liberal theorists need to more closely examine the already existing yet unexamined communal—largely national—assumptions at the heart of the liberal polity. Are these assumptions based on universal notions of equality or are they rooted, as was Murray's understanding of "world order," in forms of social organization that rely on practices of racial and cultural domination and exclusion? To what extent do these assumptions depend on the same kind of symbolic conflation of nation and family that Zimmern so explicitly laid out for us?

Ironically, then, this book is also a call to take Murray's and Zimmern's project seriously, to escape from the easy dualism that allows liberals to delegate all thinking about the social to communitarians, and to rest comfortably on the assumption that their theory is grounded in a people's voluntary yet tacit consent to be "the people." Murray's and Zimmern's utopianism not only forces us to think about the forms of nationhood and community that lurk below liberalism's placid surface but also makes perfectly clear the need for contemporary liberals to artic- ulate alternative visions of the social that are explicitly committed to liberalisms' fundamental assumption of equality. Thus, Murray's and Zimmern's work speaks pointedly to contemporary liberals who are try- ing to do precisely this—who are breaking down the intellectual divide between liberalism and communitarianism, and wrestling with the prob- lem of how liberal theory ought to approach the relationship between the liberal state and its citizens, and between citizens and their cultural communities. It suggests that these liberal thinkers (scholars such as Yael Tamir and Will Kymlicka) might do well to examine how an earlier gener- ation of liberals also sought to push their social theory in a more commu- nitarian direction and ended up sacrificing liberalism itself. The chapter concludes with a critique of four post–September 11 "new imperialists," Michael Ignatieff, Robert Cooper, Robert Kagan, and Farid Zakaria, whose work echoes some of the most distressing and anti-egalitarian im- pulses of Murray's and Zimmern's liberalisms. While all of these authors claim allegiance to some configuration of liberal ends—equality, human rights, democracy—they are ultimately willing to sacrifice them at the altar of world order. At the same time, as with Murray and Zimmern, it is precisely the manner in which they articulate their liberalisms that allows them to elide the tight knot of hierarchies that constitutes the very essence of this order.

The final point of the book, however, is not to argue that Murray's and Zimmern's experiences demonstrate the inevitable failure of the liberal reformist agenda, that all liberal reformism is doomed because of an inter- nal flaw that always, in every circumstance, compels it to advocate a pa- ternalistic understanding of the social. Rather, it reveals the intensity of the temptation to compensate for liberalism's own lack of communal lan- guage by drawing upon the putatively more authentic qualities of the pre- liberal world. Indeed, ever since Locke first gestured toward the existence of a self-sustaining state of nature, liberals have looked toward the pre- liberal for moral and communal consolation to fill the void left by their tradition's faltering attempts to speak of social responsibility. If nothing else, unearthing the deeply contradictory political and philosophical vi- sions at the heart of Murray's and Zimmern's logic of community demon- strates the difficulty of defining community in liberal terms without falling back on the hierarchies of tradition, the intimacies of family life, and the comforting solidity of the natural world. At the same time it also demonstrates that if liberalism is to survive as a viable political alternative to nationalism, to an ever expanding corporate culture, to emerging forms of global governance based on the dictates of non-democratic institutions such as the World Trade Organization, and to the political siren's call of a "new imperialism"—indeed, if it is to be saved from itself—contemporary liberals must avoid these pitfalls, look power politics in the face, and boldly commit themselves to a radically egalitarian understanding of global community.

CHAPTER ONE

Oxford Liberalism and the Return of Patriarchy

IN 1938, GILBERT MURRAY ARGUED IN *Liberality and Civilization* that liberalism was "not a doctrine; it is a spirit or attitude of mind . . . an effort to get rid of prejudice so as to see the truth, to get rid of selfish passions so as to do the right."[1] Murray had suggested something similar fifty years earlier, while a young fellow at Oxford in 1888. In an unpublished speech to the Russell Club, he suggested that the foundational logic of what he described as the "new liberalism" was an emerging consensus that something other than self-interest—something other than what Murray then called "that negative way the old Liberals got their enthusiasm"—must motivate liberal social theory.[2] Murray's consistency on this matter demonstrates the profundity of his belief that liberalism ought to be understood as an essentially spiritual and deeply selfless approach to politics and to life, an antidote, in fact, to almost all the problems of modernity. In the final analysis, it was this faith in liberalism as essentially transformative (a faith shared by Zimmern) that would map out the contours of Murray's political theory and shape his approach to internationalism. It would also lead to future charges of utopianism.

And yet Murray's particular formulation of liberalism was hardly particular. It was, rather, conditioned by a reformist tradition within British liberalism, associated most directly with T. H. Green and his students and colleagues at Oxford, a tradition that arose out of what these earlier thinkers perceived as a deep crisis within liberal theory. For scholars such as Green, Bernard Bosanquet, Edward Caird, David Ritchie, John Muirhead, and Henry Jones, the kind of economic and political liberalism long associated with the Locke, Smith, Ricardo, and Bright had, by the mid-nineteenth century, brought about positive political change only at the cost of generating massive economic disparities, widespread poverty, and appalling working conditions for millions. These disparities had themselves led not only to class conflict but also to the rise of socialism and its "absolute negation" of the individual.[3] For Green and his colleagues, liberalism could weather this crisis only if it were rearticulated in "con-

---

[1] Gilbert Murray, *Liberality and Civilization* (New York: Macmillan, 1938), 33.
[2] Bodl. MS Gilbert Murray (489) fol.4 ("Liberalism Old And New," 1888).
[3] Edward Caird, "Individualism and Socialism," *The British Idealists*, ed. David Boucher (Cambridge: Cambridge University Press, 1997), 179.

structive" terms.[4] Such a constructive, new liberalism would seek to combine an appreciation for individualism and laissez-faire economics with a theory of moral responsibility. It would stretch liberal political theory to encompass both a notion of freedom and a commitment to the common good. Ultimately, it would explain why individuals in a liberal society should care about one another and about their community.

And in this quest, the Oxford liberals were not alone. Many of their contemporary liberal brethren (including John Stuart Mill and the American Progressives) also sought to move liberalism in a more social direction. What distinguished the first generation of Oxford liberals (those who had worked and studied with Green) both from a slightly later cohort of "new liberals" and from other socially oriented liberals in Britain (particularly those associated with Cambridge at the turn of the century) was their explicit decision to look for philosophical remedies to a perceived liberal crisis within Hegelian idealism.

While the extent to which nineteenth-century liberals embraced Hegel has been disputed, historians have long acknowledged the presence of what Charles Taylor has termed an "oddly transposed variety" of Hegelianism in the social theory of thinkers like Green, Bosanquet, and Ritchie.[5] Many contemporary scholars of this particular form of idealist liberalism argue that these thinkers drew upon Hegelian logic specifically to theorize a more proactive role for the state in a liberal society.[6] Likewise, these scholars see the turn of many idealist liberals toward organicism in the later half of the nineteenth century as a means through which idealistically inclined liberal theorists could naturalize the moral state, and, in essence, smuggle Hegel into liberal political thought.

This chapter takes a slightly different approach to the relationship between Hegelian state theory and the social philosophy of the idealist liberals, and, in so doing, casts a different light on some of the more fundamental discrepancies at work in the Murray's and Zimmern's liberalisms. I maintain that what motivated the Oxford liberals' move toward the organic was not merely a philosophical need to justify Hegel's state theory but, more importantly, a liberal desire to avoid excessive state authority. Organicism, in this context, provided a terminology for imagining an alternative social organism beyond the state, one animated by a Hegelian inspired notion of Spirit. The language of the organic thus

---

[4] Green, "Letter to the Editor," 3.

[5] Taylor, Hegel, 537; Frederick Philip Harris, The Neo-Idealist Political Theory (New York: King's Cross Press, 1944), 2.

[6] For examples of contemporary scholars who view liberal Hegelianism in this light, see in particular Andrew Vincent and Raymond Plant, Philosophy, Politics, and Citizenship (Oxford: Basil Blackwell, 1984); Michael Freeden, The New Liberalism: An Ideology of Social Reform (Oxford: The Clarendon Press, 1978); Robbins, The British Hegelians.

allowed these scholars to theorize a moral community and yet avoid the totalizing implications of state as the "ultimate expression of Spirit in the world." But through the process of embracing Hegel, rejecting his state theory, and evoking the organic, many of these scholars were caught in an ironic philosophical cycle that ultimately brought them to a vision of society that looked both pre-liberal and pre-idealist, a place where family relations—rather than a liberal equality of citizenship—governed the political order.

The bulk of this chapter critically examines the tensions between liberalism, Hegelianism, and organicism in the work of some key nineteenth-century idealist liberals to set the stage for a closer analysis of a similar disquiet that haunted the social theories of their intellectual legatees, Murray and Zimmern. In its historical capacity, this chapter highlights the particularities of the liberal social theory that still dominated Oxford (and specifically the *Literae Humaniores*) while Murray and Zimmern attended New College in the 1880s and '90s. It is most concerned, however, with developing the unique theoretical argument that thinkers like Bosanquet both accepted key ideas from Hegel and then rejected his state theory in favor of a more organic approach to community, and that this philosophical turn helps explain many of the idealist liberals' support for a paternalistic—indeed, almost pre-liberal-looking—politics. Establishing the historical and philosophical foundations of this liberal turn toward the organic and the paternal ultimately provides us with the critical perspective necessary to trouble Murray's and Zimmern's own unarticulated linkage between liberalism, spirit, and the hierarchical social whole.

But this chapter should not be read simply as a template for understanding Murray's and Zimmern's internationalisms; both liberal reformism and the Oxford movement would go through a variety of changes toward the end of the century, ultimately resulting in an overall purging of Hegelian thought from liberal social theory more generally. And yet as chapter 2 demonstrates, despite these changes the liberalism of their youth still influenced Murray and Zimmern, an influence that compelled them to articulate their own visions of the liberal polity in terms remarkably similar to those of an earlier generation. Specifically, Zimmern's emphasis on nationality as primarily spiritual and familial reflects the tendency of some idealist liberals to read state and national communities through the lenses of the Darwinian family. Likewise, Murray's belief in a fixed, paternalistic world order mirrors a similar philosophical move made by the earlier idealist liberals, one that ultimately jettisoned liberal equality and replaced it with hierarchical holism.

Thus, in asking similar questions about the relationship of liberalism to the global community that an earlier generation had asked about the relationship of liberalism to the social whole, Murray's and Zimmern's internationalisms evoked many of the same ideological stresses endemic to nineteenth-century Oxford liberalism, stresses that clustered around the disconnect between liberal universalism and patriarchy. In many ways, Murray's and Zimmerns' internationalisms widened this political fissure by projecting it outward, toward the world.

THE ORIGINS OF LIBERALISM AND HEGELIANISM AT OXFORD

Scholars have historically most closely linked nineteenth-century idealist liberalism as a philosophical school with the works of T. H. Green. While Green's works and teachings were fundamental to the development of this philosophy in Britain, however, and while Green is perhaps the best known of these scholars, he was part of a much larger intellectual community that included (among others) Edward Caird, F. H. Bradley, Henry Jones, and Green's students, Bernard Bosanquet, John Henry Muirhead, and David George Ritchie. Most of these men were associated with Balliol and New Colleges at Oxford (hence the decision to sometimes refer to them as "Oxford liberals") and the Scottish universities. They shared a vision of themselves as emphatically public intellectuals and as strong supporters of nineteenth-century liberal causes. In fact, the connections between these scholars, their academic institutions, their voluntary and political organizations, and their relationships with various factions of the Liberal Party from the 1860s through the 1906 election, trace a spider web of complex intellectual, political, and personal linkages.[7]

Liberalism at Oxford began its rise to prominence in the 1830s and '40s, perhaps most significantly because many of the colleges moved away from institutional preference and toward competition in entrance examinations.[8] During this period, the number of liberal faculty gradually increased such that by 1865 Charles Roundell could claim that a generation of liberal fellows was now "in possession" of the colleges.[9] At the same time, the influence of philosophical and political liberalism also increased at Cambridge. The unique characters of the two universities, however,

---

[7] For some excellent historical analyses of nineteenth-century idealist liberalism as a living complex of relationships continually challenged and influenced by the politics of the day, see Eugenio Biagini, *Citizenship and Community: Liberals, Radicals, and Collective Identities in the British Isles, 1865–1931* (Cambridge: Cambridge University Press, 1996); Sandra Den Otter, *British Idealism and Social Explanation: A Study in Late Victorian Thought* (Oxford: The Clarendon Press, 1996); Vincent and Plant, *Philosophy, Politics, and Citizenship*; Freeden, *New Liberalism*; Melvin Richter, *The Politics of Conscience: T. H. Green and His Age* (Cambridge: Harvard University Press, 1964).

[8] Christopher Harvie, *The Lights of Liberalism* (London: Allen Lane, 1976), 56.

[9] Ibid. 52.

ensured that the particular type of liberalism that flourished at Oxford differed significantly from its collegial counterpart. While Cambridge was historically associated with rationalism and scientific inquiry, Oxford was known for its commitment to philosophy and classical studies, to the "sovereignty of Aristotle and the Authority of Antiquity."[10] The Oxford honors course of study, the *Literae Humaniores* (also known as the Greats curriculum) helped institutionalize this belief in the eternal lessons of antiquity.[11] In turn, the emphasis of the *Literae Humaniores* on ancient and classical philosophy combined with the university's longstanding interest in theology led many of its most powerful liberal-minded scholars to stress the importance of moral philosophy in their curriculum and in their politics. And it was this concern with moral philosophy that initially propelled a number of these same thinkers toward the work of G.W.F. Hegel.[12]

Classics scholar Benjamin Jowett is largely responsible for bringing Hegelianism to Oxford. Jowett's interest in Hegel centered on his interpretation of Plato's "unity of difference," a concept he read as a direct precursor to Hegel's own notion of unity through Spirit.[13] Jowett drew upon this Platonic-Hegelian conception of Spirit to criticize radical liberal individualism and utilitarianism, a critique that came to have considerable influence over his students, T. H. Green and Edward Caird. After Caird left Oxford for Glasgow University in 1866, Green rose to prominence as the leading moral philosopher on campus and, eventually, more greatly inspired a generation of Oxford students than did Jowett. Indeed, throughout the 1870s until his death in 1882, Green exercised at Oxford

---

[10] Ernst Barker, quoted from V. R. Mehta, "The Origins of English Idealism in Relation to Oxford," *Journal of the History of Philosophy* 13(2) (1975): 178.

[11] Frank M. Turner, *The Greek Heritage in Victorian Britain* (New Haven: Yale University Press, 1981), 6.

[12] While Oxford scholars' incorporation of Hegelian thought into nineteenth-century liberalism marked the apex of German influence on British philosophy, it was certainly not the only instance of this kind of intellectual borrowing. The first half of the century is widely regarded as an era of cultural and intellectual exchange between Britain and Germany. [Paul Kennedy, *The Rise of the Anglo-German Antagonism, 1860–1914* (London: Allen and Unwin, 1980), 110]. This atmosphere of open cultural exchange prompted a number of scholars, such as Sir Walter Scott, to become interested in the work of Immanuel Kant. At hotbeds of this newfound interest in Kant, such as the University of Edinburgh, students learned German, formed German literary societies, and made extended visits to Germany itself. [Den Otter, *British Idealism*, 22]. An interest in Hegel followed in the 1850s with the publication of James Hutchison Stirling's *The Secret of Hegel, Being the Hegelian System in Origin, Principle, Form and Matter*, widely considered incomprehensible. As one Oxford professor was rumored to have put it, "If Mr. Hutchinson Stirling knew the secret of Hegel he had managed to keep it to himself." [John Muirhead, *The Platonic Tradition in Anglo Saxon Philosophy: Studies in the History of Idealism in England and America* (New York: Macmillan, 1931), 171].

[13] Benjamin Jowett, *Dialogues of Plato*, vol. 3 (Oxford: The Clarendon Press, 1871), 353.

what Richard Bellamy has described as an "influence of almost Parisian dimensions" over his students.[14] In contrast, while Jowett sympathized with liberal causes, his politics tended to be more reserved and his focus on institutional (rather than societal) reform. And yet in many ways the institutional reforms begun by Jowett—primarily, his insistence that the *Literae Humaniores* be pushed to engage modern writers and contemporary issues—set the stage for Green's own transformation of both the Greats curriculum and liberalism on campus.[15]

Through Green's efforts, the *Literae Humaniores* introduced an essay on Kant in 1875. During that same year, it required a paper on logic that, for the first time, asked candidates to comment on Hegel's notion of the "real" and the "rational."[16] By the mid-1870s, a knowledge of German philosophy, as interpreted through the Classics, had become an established feature of the Greats curriculum, precisely at a time when a young generation of thinkers like Bosanquet, Ritchie, and Muirhead were beginning their studies with Green. For these thinkers (and for others who were to come up at Oxford's more progressive colleges in the following decades), the study of ancient philosophy, contemporary liberal ethics, and German idealism were deeply intertwined even after the specifically "German" character of this idealism had etiolated significantly.[17]

This fusion of contemporary ethics and philosophical inquiry prompted Green and his students to develop a profoundly *public* ideology, one that called on its adherents to actively live their philosophical commitments.[18] As R. G. Collingwood later noted in his autobiography, "The school of Green sent out into public life a stream of ex-pupils who carried with them the conviction that philosophy, and in particular the philosophy they had learnt at Oxford, was an important thing and that their vocation was to put it into practice."[19] In this spirit, Green founded the Cooperative Society at Oxford in 1872 to encourage students and fellows to establish greater links with the community by extending educational opportunities to the poor.[20] Out of the cooperatist movement grew a number of

[14] Richard Bellamy, "T. H. Green and the morality of Victorian Liberalism," *Victorian Liberalism*, ed. Richard Bellamy (London: Routledge, 1990), 133.

[15] Harvie, *The Lights of Liberalism*, 34.

[16] Mehta, "The Origins of English Idealism in Relation to Oxford," 183.

[17] This tradition continued into the twentieth century, prompting one observer to note in 1932 that Oxford students exhibited "a tendency to study the classics not in and for themselves, but in relation to modern thought and modern life." [Turner, *The Greek Heritage in Victorian Britain*, 6].

[18] Ken Dyson, *The State Tradition in Western Europe* (Oxford: Oxford University Press, 1980), 191.

[19] R. G. Collingwood, *An Autobiography* (London: Oxford University Press, 1939), 44.

[20] Den Otter, *British Idealism and Social Explanation*, 194.

influential liberal associations, including the University Extension Movement and the Workers Educational Association (WEA).[21] In true Oxford liberal style, one of the key educational goals of the University Extension Movement and the WEA was to expose the working class to what these thinkers argued were the deeply unifying standards of moral citizenship.[22]

Green and Jowett began a school of thought at Oxford that quickly transformed itself into a movement of scholars and activists who eventually—according to a growing number of contemporary historians—had a profound effect upon the development of the welfare state in Britain.[23] These thinkers' social theories were by no means identical, and in fact differed considerably from one another in terms of their levels of commitment to liberal individualism, German idealism, organicism, nationalism, and Social Darwinism. On a philosophical level, however, despite these differences, a common goal united the idealist liberals at Oxford: each sought to theorize a more collectivist liberal society through the Hegelian notion of Spirit.

A LIBERAL PREDICAMENT

For Green and his students, orthodox liberalism clearly placed too great an emphasis on the individual, resulting in a kind of hyper-subjectivism, a general disregard for morality among both politicians and philosophers, and economic disparities. And yet as committed political liberals and firm believers in laissez-faire economics, these thinkers intended neither to call the entire legacy of liberalism into question nor to develop a theory that might provide ammunition for Tory politicians and their Burkean longing

---

[21] Richter, *The Politics Of Conscience*, 361.

[22] See Bernard Bosanquet, "Three Lectures on Social Ideals," *Social and International Ideals* (New York: Books for Libraries, 1917), 1967. As Richard Bellamy, Jeffrey Weeks, and others have argued, these supposedly transcendent standards were often simply rearticulated middle-class Victorian values, which stressed the power of individual "character" over structural critiques of the capitalist economy. Note too that the WEA and other educational societies (including the educational projects sponsored by the Fabians) that the elite organized for the benefit of the working class emerged *after* many working-class organizations and trade unions had established their own schools and reading rooms in the 1840s and '50s. [Neville Kirk, *The Growth of Working Class Reformism in Mid-Victorian England* (Urbana: University of Illinois Press, 1985), 211]. It is perhaps not unfair to speculate then that much of the emphasis that middle-class reformers in the mid- to late nineteenth century placed on working class education was in response to what they saw as the revolutionary potential of class consciousness as taught in schools run by trade unions and Chartists.

[23] Martin Pugh, *The Making of Modern British Politics* (New York: St. Martin's Press, 1982), 136–37.

for tradition.[24] At the same time, Green and his colleagues viewed socialism with dread as "the reduction of the individual under the control of society."[25] In the end, they hoped to achieve the creation of a philosophical "middle way" between these alternatives.

To do so, these scholars argued that liberal theory needed an infusion of publicly oriented thinking, a new perspective that would simultaneously champion individual responsibility and transcend class politics. Green and his colleagues turned to German idealism, and in particular to the works of Hegel, to help them imagine this theory. In this context, the conceptual language of Hegel's *Geist* allowed these scholars to theorize the existence of an objective good found in both individuals and in the universal realm beyond. Green, for instance, argued for the existence of an explicitly Hegelianized "Spiritual Principle," and Bosanquet a "world consciousness."[26]

Because idealist liberals emphasized the ability of the Spiritual Principle to unite the individual with both a higher intelligence and the broader social whole, many of them ultimately elaborated a core political philosophy that emphasized social relationships rather than abstract individualism. In the words of Green, men "in detachment from social relations . . . would not be men at all."[27] Likewise, for Henry Jones, "an individual has no life except that which is social."[28] These thinkers believed that the atomistic individuality of orthodox liberalism was actually contrary to the very nature of humanity. This critique was itself informed by Hegel, who in *The Philosophy of Right* had accused liberalism of conflating that which was "fundamental, substantive, and primary" with the "will of a single person."[29] In following Hegel on this point, idealist liberals called into question one of the key assumptions at the heart of liberalism, namely, that human beings are fundamentally constituted by a hypothetical genesis in a *pre-social* era and that their rights as individuals can be traced back to these origins. Instead, they argued that the rights as well as the duties of individuals originated in, and ought to be directed toward,

[24] Thomas Hill Green, "Liberal Legislation and Freedom of Contract", *The Works of Thomas Hill Green*, ed. R. L. Nettleship (London: Longmans, Green, 1906.) In Green's view, the abuses of the capitalist system (e.g., poverty and child labor) directly resulted from liberalism's *uneven* emphasis on the private as opposed to the public good, rather than something inherent in the free-market approach itself. Competition was not, according to Green, inherently bad and could have a moralizing influence on the individuals involved.

[25] Caird, "Individualism and Socialism," 179.

[26] Green, *Prolegomena to Ethics*, par. 141. Bernard Bosanquet, *Science and Philosophy* (New York: Macmillan, 1927), 379.

[27] Green, *Prolegomena*, par. 288.

[28] Henry Jones, "The Social Organism", *The British Idealists*, 9.

[29] G.W.F. Hegel, *Philosophy of Right*, trans. T. M. Knox (Oxford: Oxford University Press, 1967), par. 33.

the community or "the public good."[30] Green and his colleagues differed from Hegel, however, in their often contrary attitudes toward the relationship between this public good and the state.

For Hegel, a clear, dialectical connection linked this unfolding of Spirit in the world and the modern state. As articulated in *The Philosophy of Right*, *Staat* embodied two meanings. On the one hand, it referred to the practices of governmental institutions in relation to civil society; on the other, to the holistic workings of *Sittlichkeit* or the ethical system of Spirit working through individuals and social institutions. *Staat*, as understood in this first context, looked almost liberal insofar as it contained "pluralist" institutions to which individual citizens devoted themselves not out of feeling (as in the family) but out of rational thought.[31] In its second manifestation, however, *Staat* appeared both transcendent and organic, ultimately based on the primacy of communal bonds.[32] Hegel believed that it was within this latter notion of *Sittlichkeit*—of the state as holistic ethical system—that the subjective wills of individuals and the objective will of Spirit were dialectically reconciled and found their "concrete meeting point."[33] Thus, the state in this form was "an end in itself . . . the actuality of the ethical idea."[34]

The state made this actualization possible by systematically breaking down society into three autonomous but interrelated spheres: the family, civil society, and the legalistic state apparatus. For Hegel, within these separate realms the subjective and objective wills were nurtured, revealed at their most contradictory, and, ultimately, dialectically resolved. Hence, in the family, human beings understood themselves as *members* rather than individuals and, correspondingly, loved blindly. To become a free, thinking individual, however, the male citizen had to leave the family and

[30] Bernard Bosanquet, *The Philosophical Theory of the State*, 8th ed. (London: Macmillan, 1889), 102.

[31] A number of contemporary Hegel scholars argue that, in contrast to the widely held nineteenth-century view of Hegel as an apologist for modern totalitarianism, Hegel's practical state was perfectly compatible with modern ideas of individual autonomy and liberal constitutional politics. See, for instance, Allen Wood's comparison of Hegel's state theory to John Stuart Mill's notion of "collective good" [Allen Wood, *Hegel's Ethical Thought* (Cambridge: Cambridge University Press, 1990), 29].

[32] Communitarian thinkers like Charles Taylor tend to emphasize this reading of Hegel's state. Taylor, for instance, argues that Hegel's community-oriented notion of "*Sittlichkeit*" provides an alternative interpretation of traditional, liberal notions of atomistic individuality. For Taylor, the doctrine of *Sittlichkeit* "is that morality reaches its completion in a community." This, Taylor argues, "is the point where Hegel runs counter to the moral instinct of liberalism then and now." [Taylor, *Hegel*, 377].

[33] G.W.F. Hegel, *Introduction to the Philosophy of History*, trans. Leo Rauch (Indianapolis, IN: Hacket, 1988), 26.

[34] Hegel, *Philosophy of Right*, par. 257.

become a participant in civil society.[35] In contrast to the family, civil society was conditioned by particularity and movement, by economic and social relationships. Within the "complexity" of these relationships and "social ties," Hegel argued, male individuals strove to have their autonomy "recognized" by others.[36] But the very "complexities" of these social and economic interactions created the need for an external organization to protect individual interests. Hegel conceived of this external organization (*Staat*, in its first, legalistic manifestation) as more than the protector of individual interests; it also came to embody the reconciliation of universal and particular wills. Human relationships were defined in this moment in terms of membership, but membership was based on a rational self-consciousness and a knowledge of the state's laws and constitution rather than on love, the guiding principle of the family.[37]

At times, liberal proponents of Hegel spoke a language of statehood remarkably similar to Hegel's second conception of *Staat* as an ethical unity. In these instances they argued for a more complex, ethical approach to the state that could provide a moral alternative to orthodox liberalism's detached "night watchman." Because they agreed with Hegel that rights originate within society rather than in an imaginary state of nature, idealist liberals sometimes shared Hegel's commitment to a state that acted as the embodiment of self-consciousness.[38] For Henry Jones, this meant that "no State can be alien to the individuals that compose it."[39] In this context, the state became a moral extension of society and an expression of the public good or the Spiritual Principle.[40] Likewise, many idealist liberals were also critical of liberal individualistic accounts of state coercion. According to Green, the liberal obsession with the state's coercive power resulted from a faulty logic that dualistically pitted a "supreme coercive power on the one side" and the "individuals, to whom natural rights are ascribed, on the other."[41] For Bosanquet, the state itself was an essential "organ of the community" that must have the coercive power to maintain "the external conditions necessary to the best life."[42]

---

[35] Hegel's exclusion of women from civil society will be discussed later.

[36] Hegel, *Philosophy of Right*, par. 214, 219.

[37] Ibid., par. 257.

[38] Schlomo Avineri, *Hegel's Theory of the Modern State* (Cambridge: Cambridge University Press, 1972), 181.

[39] Jones, "The Social Organism," 24.

[40] In Bosanquet's words, "the end of the State . . . is the end of Society and of the Individual—the best life, as determined by the fundamental logic of the will." [Bosanquet, *The Philosophical Theory of the State*, 173].

[41] Green, *Lectures on Political Obligation*, par. 114.

[42] Bosanquet, "The Function of the State in Promoting the Unity of Mankind," *The British Idealists*, 271.

Perhaps the best-known aspect of idealist liberal social theory was this belief that the state had a commitment to make these "external conditions" a reality through some level of social and economic intervention.[43] "Our ideal state," Muirhead argued, "must provide that free scope for individuality which is the most modern feature of modern politics."[44] The state was thus obliged to expand possibilities for human freedom by creating equality of opportunity (as opposed to equality of experience) through such programs as universal education and national healthcare. As Green argued, the state had a moral responsibility to use its power "on the part of the citizens as a body to make the most and best of themselves."[45]

Despite this holistic account of the relationship between the individual, society, and the state, most of the Oxford liberals were unwilling to follow Hegel's dialectic to the moment of resolution, when the individual and the universal concerns of the ethical state became one. At this point, many of these thinkers abandoned what they had initially found attractive in Hegel's notion of *Sittlichkeit* and instead evoked a more liberal and legalistic sense of the state—that stood apart from both individuals and the social good—a state with the potential for tyranny.

The relationship of private property to the state offers an interesting example of this parting of ways. Hegel and the many of the Oxford liberals agreed that in the context of civil society the movement of a free market economy allowed individuals to develop and refine their moral autonomy through competition and recognition. Thus, both opposed the idea of state-managed, collectivized economies. In the context of *Sittlichkeit*, however, Hegel argued that private property was inherently social and contained no innate ethical qualities besides those that accrued to it when it came in contact with ethical institutions.[46] Green used similar language when he argued that the "right to property" made sense in society alone.[47] Hegel maintained, however, that because private property was so intimately linked to the realization of freedom in civil society, some redistribution (although not an equal distribution) was necessary.[48] In contrast, Green argued that the "uncontrolled" and unequal accumulation of property was not necessarily anti-social, and that when such accumulation

[43] A number of contemporary scholars argue that this notion of a proactive state best represents the idealist liberal legacy. [See, for instance, Pugh, *The Making of Modern British Politics*, 136–37].

[44] Muirhead, *The Platonic Tradition*, 195.

[45] Green, "Liberal Legislation and the Freedom of Contract," 372.

[46] In particular, property and capital became ethical within the context of the family. [See Hegel, *Philosophy of Right*, par. 170].

[47] Green, *Political Obligation*, par. 216.

[48] Hegel, *Philosophy of Right*, par. 49A.

came about through hard work and a respect for the property of others, the result would be the betterment of society as a whole.[49] Thus Green's "ideal state" required no redistribution of property. Bosanquet voiced a similar opinion when he argued that "absurdity results" if the distribution of private property "is transferred to functions of the State."[50]

Both Green and Bosanquet finally backed away from Hegel's vision of the state as a holistic, ethical system. In other words, while they might have envisioned a state that was, in Bosanquet's words, "the guardian of the whole moral world," they also seemed to believe that the state could behave immorally (as in the case of slavery). Likewise, while these thinkers often argued for a state that was more than a "night watchman," more than a coercive power dualistically pitted against the interests of self-serving individuals, they also clearly believed that the redistributive state could illegitimately stand in opposition to the individual's right to own property.[51] As a result, while support for a moral, interventionist state is perhaps the best known of all the idealist liberal principles to emerge from the Oxford school, it was also perhaps the least philosophically consistent. This inconsistency would reemerge with renewed vigor in Murray's and Zimmern's liberalisms.

The central irony here is that while Green and his colleagues initially turned to Hegelian theory as, in Peter Robbins' terms, a "metaphysical consolation" for liberalism's lack of a unifying center, their simultaneous rejection of Hegel's *Sittlichkeit* on liberal individualist grounds gave rise to a critical question that remained unanswered in their theory: Is the state an instrumental political formation somehow dissociated from the individuals who compose it, or is it a holistic, spiritual, and moral community? Hegel resolved these problems by declaring the state both, the latter ultimately taking precedent over the former.[52] In the final analysis, the state as an ethical whole—as Spirit actualized—superseded the state as mere externality.[53]

Liberals sympathetic to idealism could not support Hegel's decisive elevation of one form of state over another. In effect, they wanted it both ways. In some instances they were drawn toward a theory of the state as ethical whole; in others, toward an anti-statist politics of liberal individualism. While Hegel addressed both of these impulses by positing them as

---

[49] Green, *Political Obligation*, par. 221. Green also argued that the only form of property to pose a true danger to society was property generated from landed estates, whose owners lived off the "unearned increment" of the soil.

[50] Bosanquet, *The Philosophical Theory of the State*, 242.

[51] Ibid., 302.

[52] Hegel, *Philosophy of Right*, par. 157.

[53] Wood, *Hegel's Ethical Thought*, 29.

moments in the dialectical movement of Spirit toward its final manifestation, most Oxford liberals were never completely comfortable with this, and thus never seemed to make up their minds about the exact relationship between the individual, society, and the state. As a result, their works are filled with unresolved antinomies. For many idealist liberal authors, these frayed ends were immensely troubling, and their writings reflected this underlying note of anxiety as if they were frantically trying to pull together the loose threads of a theoretical fabric that they themselves had unraveled. In the end, several sought to address this predicament by re-imagining the social, reconstituting a more coherent philosophical framework on the terra firma of the natural world.

AN ORGANIC SOLUTION: THE SOCIAL BODY

Ironically, while some of the fundamental contradictions in nineteenth-century idealist liberal thought resulted from the decision *not* to follow in the direction of Hegel's state theory, many of these thinkers (most prominently Bosanquet and Ritchie) nonetheless drew largely upon a Hegelian notion of the organic to address these contradictions. Although English philosophers had made analogies between the human body and the body politic for centuries, the notion lost favor in Britain during the late eighteenth and early nineteenth centuries with the ascendancy of liberal individualism. It reemerged in mid-nineteenth-century Britain via a variety of routes. The influential social theorist Herbert Spencer made explicit comparisons between modern industrial societies and animal organisms.[54] In addition, an increased interest in the writings of Plato encouraged philosophical support for the notion of holism, or the unity of different parts.[55] Finally, like so many of the ideas fundamental to the social theory of the idealist liberal school, the notion of organic unity was reintroduced through a heightened fascination with Hegelian philosophy.[56]

For Hegel, the utility of the body metaphor lay in its capacity to express both the significance of society's individual parts and their inability to function without the animating presence of the whole. As Hegel argued,

---

[54] For Spencer, societies, like natural organisms, were subject to the same laws of evolution as were individuals. Thus, he argued, as they evolved toward higher levels of industrial development, these societies also became more internally differentiated, complex, and interdependent. See Herbert Spencer, *The Evolution of Society; Selections from Herbert Spencer's Principles of Sociology* (Chicago: University of Chicago Press, 1967).

[55] Den Otter, *British Idealism and Social Explanation*, 45.

[56] Ibid., 156.

the "limbs and organs . . . of an organic body are not merely parts of it; it is only in their unity that they are what they are and they are unquestionably affected by that unity, as they also in turn affect it."[57] The ethical unity of the state *writ large* (*Sittlichkeit*) was a "dependent organism" and, like "the so called 'parts' of an animal organism," members of a state were "moments in an organic whole whose isolation and independence spell disease."[58] This notion of ethical unity, however, not only implied a relationship between individuals and society but also insisted upon the organic relationship between social institutions. Hegel referred to institutions such as families and corporations as the "cells" within which the "actuality of the ethical idea" was first developed.[59] Thus, the concept of organic union necessitated an interdependence between these "cells" and the ethical whole of the state.

Many idealist liberals, including Ritchie, Bosanquet, and Jones, were explicit in their debt to this Hegelian notion of a complex, ethical organicism. Spencer's notion of the social whole, they argued, never amounted to more than an aggregate entity, life-like rather than alive, a collection of individuals and economic practices with no ethical end. In contrast, Ritchie and Jones in particular argued for a Hegelian notion of social embeddedness. For these thinkers, not only must a deeper notion of the universal good guide the social organism but, in addition, individuals had to come to know themselves as part of that universal good through participation in social institutions, what Jones termed their "stations." In contrast to Plato's holism, they argued, Hegel's organicism addressed both ethical relations and freedom of movement, and thus, in Ritchie's words, gave "the completest expression to that organic conception of human society."[60]

And yet while these thinkers embraced an organicism inspired by Hegel, their particular approach differed from Hegel's in its attitude toward the state. Whereas Hegel repeatedly described the individual moments that composed the ethical system of the state (e.g., family, civil society, and "external" or legalistic state) as united in one organic body, these idealist liberals took a much more Spencerian approach when they employed images of the living, dead, or diseased body to describe *society*

---

[57] Hence, he argued that the organs and limbs of the body "become mere parts, only when they pass under the hands of the anatomist, whose occupation, be it remembered, is not with the living body but with the corpse." [G.W.F. Hegel, *Logic*, trans. William Wallace, 3rd ed. (Oxford: The Clarendon Press, 1989), par. 135].

[58] Hegel, *Philosophy of Right*, par. 276, 278.

[59] Ibid., par 276 (add.), par. 257.

[60] David Ritchie, *The Principles of State Interference* (London: Swan Sonnenschein, 1891), 156.

in distinction from the state. In making this argument, this chapter parts
ways with many scholars of nineteenth-century British liberalism and idealism, most of whom maintain that idealistically inclined liberals of this
period used the notion of the organically linked social whole primarily
to expand the role of the state in liberal society. For these scholars, the
conceptual framework of the organic allowed many idealist liberal thinkers to root their vision of a more interventionist state within the intricate
workings of the social body.[61] But something distinctly *anti-statist* lurked
in the lure of the organic. In other words, nineteenth-century scholars like
Ritchie, Muirhead, Jones, and Bosanquet might have used the language
of organicism to describe those moments when it was appropriate for the
liberal state to intervene in society, but they also used the same language
to indicate clearly when state intervention was *not* appropriate. Contrary
to establishing the life of a state as existing prior to its members, organicism allowed some Oxford liberals to theorize a social whole distinct from
the state. In essence, rather than smuggling an interventionist state into
liberal theory via idealism, organicism made it possible for these thinkers
to vacate idealism of the totalizing state to liberalize it, to address their
discomfort with parts of Hegel's theory and still imagine a moment of
quasi-Hegelian resolution separate from, and prior to, the political state.
Instead of unfolding within the overall rubric of *Sittlichkeit*, as in Hegel's
system, the moment of resolution between the universal and the particular
manifested itself within the organic body of society. The state could potentially interact with this social body in such a way that it too became a
holistic extension of the organic community, but the prior existence of
that community ultimately bestowed legitimacy upon the state itself.

In this manner, Bosanquet excused himself from liberal critics' charges
that his notion of the moral state was implicitly authoritarian by grounding his state theory in the existence of a "social whole" whose origins
predated the state and whose members constituted the "parts or organs
of a living body."[62] The state was thus moral insofar as it reflected this
social whole. In the introduction to the second edition of *The Philosophical Theory of the State*, Bosanquet spoke directly to his critics on this
issue by setting himself apart from presumably Hegelian theories in which

---

[61] For example, Vincent and Plant argue that the new liberals' organicist approach to
society assumed that the state was "deeply involved" in the body politic as a kind of nerve
center or brain, a "responsible repository of stimuli." [Vincent and Plant, *Philosophy, Politics and Citizenship*, 91]. Freeden echoes this argument, noting that new liberal organicism
primarily regarded the state as *prior* its members. [Freeden, *The New Liberalism*, 94]. For
Robbins, many British followers of Hegel ultimately espoused the analogy of organic
growth in order to explain history's progression toward the "rational state."[Robbins, *The
British Hegelians*, 11].

[62] Bosanquet, *The Philosophical Theory of the State*, 20.

the social is subsumed by the state.[63] Instead, according to Bosanquet, the relationship of society to the state "is like that by which a tree makes its wood, or a living body deposits its skeleton. The work of the State is *de facto* for the most part . . . setting its *imprimatur,* the seal of its force, on what more flexible activities or the mere progress of life have wrought out in long years of adventurous experiment or silent growth."[64] These organic processes occurred before the state and beneath the state, and explained both the "co-operation" of human beings and state power itself. Ritchie made a similar argument in which he maintained that society, as separate from the state, was no mere aggregate of individuals but rather a "spiritual body animated by that love which is the highest religious conception of Deity."[65]

Ultimately, for Bosanquet, Ritchie, and others, it was this holism that explained the need for human self-sacrifice and charity. Isolation resulted in the death of the social organism and the reduction of the individual to a bloody stump of flesh, a "mutilated fragment" for Bosanquet, a "severed limb" for Jones, and "a hand cut off from a living body" for Caird.[66] For these thinkers, the social whole was analogous to a "living body, and not . . . a dead body" precisely because it was animated by a unifying spirit that was present only when all "tissues," "currents," and "organs" were responding to one another.[67]

In sum, the move to embrace organicism helped Bosanquet, Ritchie, and many of their cohorts address some of the indurate tensions embedded in their particular idealist liberal ideology, tensions that accumulated around the relationship of the autonomous individual to the state. Organicism spoke to these tensions by removing the unity of community from the realm of the state and relocating it within the organic body of the social. It was society, then, and not the state, that naturally called for human duty and sacrifice. And yet, however different this social vision was from Hegel's, these Oxford liberals up until this point had drawn upon a tradition of organicism inherited from Hegel himself that used the natural realm *metaphorically.* These thinkers truly parted company with Hegel in their more explicit borrowings from the biological sciences, and in particular from theories of evolution. In so doing, they were both reflecting and challenging one of the most dominant intellectual influences of the nineteenth century: Social Darwinism.

---

[63] Ibid., xxxvii.

[64] Ibid.

[65] David Ritchie, "Darwin and Hegel," *Proceedings of the Aristotelian Society* 1 (1891–92): 73.

[66] Bosanquet, *Science and Philosophy,* 42; Jones, "The Social Organism," 9; Caird, "Individualism and Socialism," 183.

[67] Jones, "The Social Organism," 13.

An Organic Solution: The State, Natural Selection, and the Family

The idea that Darwinian laws of biological evolution could be used to explain social, political, and economic phenomena was a dominant theme in mid- to late nineteenth-century British thought. For the Social Darwinists, Darwin's notion of the "survival of the fittest" both explained and justified the economic inequalities of industrial society and gave credence to a kind of laissez faire social theory.[68] Social Darwinists argued for the inevitability of human evolution and insisted that the natural laws of competition and individualism be allowed to function freely. In this context, any kind of "artificial" state intervention in society or in the economy necessarily tampered with the rhythms of evolutionary progress by disrupting natural selection and thus encouraging the survival of those weaker members of the species.[69] True social and ethical progress, according to Herbert Spencer (who actively embraced Darwinism in the 1850s), could occur only once the strongest and cleverest of individuals, the "highest type" of human beings were allowed to "live more in the presence of [their] fellows."[70]

For many nineteenth-century new liberals, this approach to evolution lacked both a moral purpose and a sense of spiritual cohesion. As Ritchie argued in *Darwinism and Politics*, Spencer's focus on individual adaptability disentangled human beings from their social matrix, resulting in an amoral, individualized vision of society where "nothing succeeds like success."[71] And yet his criticism of Spencer led him not to reject Social Darwinism outright but to couple it with a Hegelian understanding of Spirit. Thus, Ritchie took seriously Hegel's adage that the "real is the rational" by arguing that "reality" was more than a mere reflection of current conditions—it was, moreover, an expression of the Spiritual Principle itself.[72] In Hegel's teleological vision, Spirit harbored within it the divine idea of the world in its totality.[73] In like manner, Ritchie identified a similar force of reason behind the natural development of the species, a movement toward an ethical and moral universe that became clearer as time progressed. Ritchie also argued that the Darwinian concept of natu-

---

[68] Harold Vanderpool, *Darwin and Darwinism: Revolutionary Insights Concerning Man, Nature, Religion, and Society* (Lexington, MA: Heath, 1973), xxi.

[69] Ibid.

[70] Herbert Spencer, *Data of Ethics* (New York: William Allison, 1879), 31.

[71] Ritchie, *Darwinism and Politics*, 13.

[72] Ritchie, "Darwin and Hegel," 68.

[73] Hegel, *Philosophy of History*, 21.

ral selection provided the historical contingencies and variety of experience necessary for Spirit's journey through time. Therefore, according to Ritchie, "natural selection is a perfectly adequate cause to account for the rise of morality," a point on which Bosanquet agreed.[74]

Ritchie and Bosanquet, however, were also faced with the same logical dilemma that dogged most proponents of Social Darwinism: how does a particular social vision come to fruition in the absence of state intervention? How does the social engineer encourage some members of society to thrive while still insisting that the evolutionary struggle for existence be allowed to play itself out, unencumbered by the state? Some idealist liberals responded to this tension by making a distinction between universal social reform and state interference in the *individualized* process of natural selection. Bosanquet, for example, argued that the moral state should facilitate the common good by creating universal programs that intelligent individuals could take advantage of, rather than providing poor relief for the weakest members of society whose poverty was attributable to their failure to participate in the "social mind."[75] Similarly, for Ritchie, state interference was justified if it was *nonspecific*.[76] In many ways, this universalism masked what was often an erratic approach to state intervention by wrapping it in the mantle of an overall scientific vision of human progress.

Finally, some idealist liberals argued that Darwinism offered an explanatory framework in which the ultimate direction of the Spiritual Principle was conclusively *knowable* through scientific investigation. Just as the science of evolution exposed the processes of the natural world, so too could it expose the logic of reason working through nature. For Ritchie, "knowing a system of nature" and discovering the will of the Spiritual Principle were one in the same.[77] Reason, in this context, was observable within the workings of the natural, within "our apprehension of a single object and our view of nature as a whole."[78] This belief that the "real"

[74] Ritchie, "Darwin and Hegel," 63; Bosanquet, "Socialism and Natural Selection," *The British Idealists*, 54, 57.

[75] Bosanquet, "Charity Organization and the Majority Report," *International Journal of Ethics* 20 (1910): 397.

[76] Ritchie, *Darwinism and Politics*, 29.

[77] Ibid., 115.

[78] Bosanquet, *Philosophical Theory of the State*, 275. By grounding their theories of reason and the Spiritual Principle in scientific naturalism, Ritchie and Bosanquet moved in a distinctly different direction from both Green's and Hegel's approaches to the universal. Green, in fact, had explicitly rejected both evolutionary theory and naturalistic social explanations in a series of articles published in 1878 entitled "Mr. Herbert Spencer and Mr. G. H. Lewes: Their Application of the Doctrine of Evolution to Thought." [*The Works of T. H. Green*, 373–541]. According to Green, scientific naturalism obscured real knowl-

was the "natural" (and that the closer to nature a political or social phenomenon was, the more it had to tell us about the true course of Spirit in
the world) became a kind of unifying logic for the more Darwinian-ori-
ented of the idealist liberals. In the end, this faith in nature supplied the
philosophical groundwork for these thinkers' particular fascination with
the family.

For Hegel, the family was both historical and naturally timeless.[79]
While the family *form* may have developed and changed historically,
Hegel maintained that the reproductive process so integral to the family
remained rooted in a timeless, natural shell.[80] Thus, Hegel referred to the
bonds of the father-mother and parent-child relationships as the "natural
unity of the family," or as that moment when "ethical mind is in its natural or immediate phase."[81] Hegel argued that this natural immediacy was
necessary because only through an instinctual knowledge of blood ties,
rather than civic ones, could a male citizen experience the first moment
of the dialectic.[82] Thus, the "natural ethical community" of the family
played a crucial role in Hegel's system as both the source and protector
of the developing individual.[83]

Those idealist liberals most sympathetic to German idealism, particularly Bosanquet, Jones, and Ritchie, borrowed extensively from Hegel's
theory of the family. They too argued that the family was closer to nature
than any other social institution, that it stood "nearest to the natural
world, and has taken, so to speak, the minimum steps into the realm of
purpose and consciousness."[84] The chrysalis of the family was thus rooted
in the preconscious, in the spontaneous acts of kindness and love that
Hegel himself described as Mind in its immediate phase. Muirhead argued
that human beings first developed their "social qualities" within the fam-

---

edge by dividing the world into discrete, observable pieces, which amounted to a mere "aggregate" of consciousness rather than a singular, rational conscience capable of resolving
the particular and the universal [Green, "Mr. Spencer on Subject and Object," 407].

[79] To be sure, Hegel was well aware that this particular form of family organization was
an historical development rather than a fixed biological formation. In fact, he insisted that
the historical withering away of older forms of familial cohesion—such as families or
clans—enabled the full, dialectical development of the individual. At the same time, however, despite its historical existence, the institution of the nuclear family—with "the husband
as its head"—was closer to nature than any other social realm. [Hegel, *Philosophy of
Right*, 171].

[80] Mary O'Brien, "Hegel: Man, Physiology, and Fate," *Feminist Interpretations of G.W.F.
Hegel*, ed. Patricia Jagentowitz Mills (University Park: Pennsylvania State University Press,
1997), par. 187.

[81] Hegel, *Philosophy of Right*, par. 157, 175.

[82] Ibid., par. 167.

[83] Rudolf Siebert, *Hegel's Concept of Marriage and the Family* (Washington, DC: University Press of America, 1979), 5.

[84] Bosanquet, *The Philosophical Theory of the State*, 250.

ily.[85] These thinkers agreed that because the family embodied that first moment of total and unconscious obligation and sacrifice, it was both precious to and necessary for the moral development of society. In Bosanquet's words, "the co-operative individual, as demanded by civilized life, can only be produced in the family."[86]

This belief in the uniqueness of the family as an ethical realm led both Hegel and the Oxford liberals to a seemingly similar conclusion about the relationship between the family and society, and the family and the state. To maintain its socializing and moralizing qualities, they argued, the integrity of the family must be upheld in distinction from both the state and civil society. But while both Hegel and the idealist liberals could agree that, by virtue of its very naturalness, the family required protection from the public realm, their assumptions about nature itself led them to somewhat different conclusions about the family's social role.

Thus, Hegel argued that the second moment of the dialectic—the male individual's development of an autonomous, self-conscious will—depended on the first: that is, it required the individual's prior and total immersion in the natural, ethical immediacy of the family. While for Hegel Spirit might sometimes work through nature, it was never reducible to nature itself.[87] In contrast, for many idealist liberals, nature was not inherently irrational. In evolutionary terms, they argued, nature was a fully rationalized, scientific engine of progress, capable not only of promoting the movement of the Spiritual Principle in the world but of improving the species and the race as well. As that social unit most closely attached to the natural, the family became for them the undisputed terrain of evolutionary development. Bosanquet reasoned that "being thus 'natural,' the idea of the family has a hold like no other upon the whole man."[88] The primeval struggle to "realize the conditions of true family life," he argued, pushed humankind toward perfection. Interfering in this struggle would result in the "extinction of the stock" or in a population riddled with disease and dominated by the mentally feeble.[89] But for Bosanquet it was not just the struggle to achieve "true family life" that ultimately improved the species but also what happened within the monogamous nuclear family unit itself. As that social sphere closest to the "very animal roots of life," the evolutionary cradle of the family gave rise to a healthy

---

[85] John Henry Muirhead, "The Family," *Ethical Democracy: Essays in Social Dynamics*, ed. Stanton Coit (London: Grant Richards, 1900), 112.

[86] Bosanquet, "Socialism and Natural Selection," 61.

[87] Hegel, *Philosophy of Right*, par. 146.

[88] Bosanquet, *The Philosophical Theory of the State*, 279.

[89] Bosanquet, "Socialism and Natural Selection," 61, 63. Here Bosanquet invokes the famous Jukes family. An example often cited by eugenicists and Social Darwinists, the socially deviant Jukes supposedly gave rise to 1200 "mentally feeble" and criminal descendants.

population and to ethically and morally pure individuals. Evolutionary principles present in the family, he argued, aided in the process of "soul molding" by which individuals not only became ethically autonomous but also learned their responsibilities to the common good.[90] Thus, social interaction with others in the natural community of the family created socially conscious individuals. Perhaps Muirhead put it best when he argued that "society depends for the strength of its tissue on the health and strength of the cells that compose it, and especially of the primeval cell we call the family."[91]

This underlying dependence on the family as the natural source of evolutionary progress led a number of idealist liberals to reinsert a kind of family morality writ large into society by proposing it as a model for both the political state and the cultural nation. In so doing, these thinkers ultimately evoked a social theory that in key ways began to look not only pre-liberal but also pre-Hegelian in its approach to the state. For instance, Hegel argued that the family was essential to both the male individual's quest for self-fulfillment and the unfolding of Mind in the world. Nevertheless, he also maintained that to be resolved dialectically with the universal, the family and its natural foundations must first be transcended in favor of reason and the competition of individuals in civil society, and then actively dissolved into civil society once the male children "have been educated to freedom of personality."[92] In this sense, Hegelian idealism and classical liberalism were in full agreement. John Locke, for instance, argued that political legitimacy was constituted through the explicit or tacit consent of free and equal (male) individuals rather than through any notion of a divine "paternal right" based ultimately on family loyalty.[93] While for Hegel the transcendence of the family was necessary for the eventual resolution of the individual with the state, for Locke the family had to be carefully circumscribed to avoid the abuses of a capricious monarchy. Despite this fundamental difference, however, both of these thinkers argued that mapping the morality of the family onto the "external world" evoked an earlier, historical phase in the development of the mature state.

For many idealist liberals, however, the natural origins of the family were never dissolved in favor of civil society. Rather, their writings on the subject suggest that precisely because of the family's closeness to nature—and because nature itself was identical with the evolutionary progress of

[90] Bosanquet, *Principle of Individuality and Value* (London: Macmillan, 1912), 91. [i.c., Den Otter, *British Idealism and Social Explanation*, 100].

[91] Muirhead, "The Family."

[92] Hegel, *Philosophy of Right*, par. 119.

[93] John Locke, "Second Treatise on Government," *Locke: Political Essays*, ed. Mark Goldie (Cambridge: Cambridge University Press, 1997), 70.

reason—the nuclear family ought to serve as a kind of permanent social laboratory for evolutionary and moral progress. In this sense Bosanquet, Ritchie, Muirhead, Caird, and others allagreed that, as Caird noted in 1897, "a pure domestic life and the sanctity of the home are the indispensable basis of the moral as well as the economic organization of society.[94] Because of the "*permanent* utility of the family as the unit of social life," these thinkers supported a social vision that shuttled between the sanctity of the home and the larger society, a society that included other social communities, such as voluntary organizations, trade unions, and schools.[95] Thus, rather than transcending the intimacy of the family, as Hegel insisted participants in civil society do, idealist liberals stressed that an ethically mature citizen actively take the lessons learned in the family and apply them to their interactions with the community. In a paradoxical manner, then, these thinkers simultaneously saw the family as "cell" in the healthy social body—that is, a permanently enshrined social institution—and as a source of moral and civic energy that influenced both the community at large and the state itself.

The philosophical and political results of this osmosis took different forms in the various social theories of idealist liberal scholars. Ritchie, for instance, argued that the state "must be regarded as one with the family."[96] For Ritchie, the naturally moral, evolutionary power of the nuclear family not only provided the individual citizen with the critical social lessons necessary for the creation of a good state but also acted as a *model* for that state through a dehiscence of the "ethics of the family" into the public realm. In explicit opposition to liberal individualism, Ritchie argued that family ethics provided a better foundation for the state than the disinterested image of the "night watchman." "The family ideal of the State," he argued in 1891, "may be difficult of attainment, but, as an ideal, it is better than the policeman theory. It would mean the moralization of politics."[97] Ritchie's family ideal of the state ultimately rejected "any abstract principle of equality" and replaced it with the hierarchies of the family, resulting in a social theory that treated working-class and colonial peoples as children under the tutelage of their benevolent state parent.[98]

[94] Caird, "Individualism and Socialism,"181; Muirhead, "The Family," 112.

[95] Muirhead, "The Family," 116 (emphasis added). As Caird argued, an ideal society ought to be constructed out of the "round of duties that seem commonplace and secular—these family ties, this college companionship." [Caird, *Lay Sermons and Addresses* (Glasgow: James Maclehouse and Sons, 1907), 70].

[96] David Ritchie, *Natural Rights: A Criticism of Some Political and Ethical Conceptions*, 3rd ed. (London: George Allen and Unwin, 1916), 262.

[97] Ritchie, *Darwinism and Politics*, 73.

[98] Ritchie, *Natural Rights*, 262. Also see Ritchie on colonialism in "Ethical Democracy."

Other thinkers—namely, Bosanquet, Caird, and Muirhead—explicitly rejected the more authoritarian themes apparent in Ritchie's vision of the family state. For these thinkers, differentiating between the political state and the spiritual, organically conceived *nation* to which the state was closely related was essential. As "the highest really organic society," the nation embodied both the power of blood origins and the same kind of feelings of good will as those generated by the nuclear family but did not carry the totalitarian overtones of the family state.[99] Thus, according to Bosanquet, "in a modern nation the atmosphere of the family is not confined to the actual family. The common dwelling place, history, and tradition, the common language and common literature, give a colour of affection to the every-day citizen-consciousness, which is to the nation what family affection is in the home circle."[100] Feelings of intimacy and affection generated within the family, which Hegel believed to end at the door of the home, for Bosanquet "colored" the everyday interactions within the nation, creating what Muirhead and Hetherington called "common sentiment."[101] Patriotism itself, which Bosanquet described as "an immense natural force, a magical spell," arose first and foremost from "family and kindred—the tie of blood."[102] Like family love, patriotism was natural and thus both rational and inherently unifying. Thus, states must wrap themselves around the authentic core of the national family to be truly legitimate. In the end, communal unity itself could be achieved through "nationality alone."[103]

Writing during an era of intense nation-making activities in Europe and throughout a period when British nationalism was defining itself vigorously in opposition to the expanding colonial empire, the Oxford liberals' choice of the term "nation" to describe the natural, ethical community is hardly surprising. What is surprising in a political sense is how much this notion differs from the nationalism more common to British liberals of the time, a nationalism grounded in the concept of self-determination. According to this liberal imaginary, a "people" became a coherent nation in that moment when they voluntarily claimed themselves as such and not because of any a priori, natural existence.[104] In contrast, by explicitly drawing out the prepolitical, organic qualities of the nation, idealist liber-

---

[99] Caird, "The Nation as Ethical Ideal", *Lay Sermons*, 111.

[100] Bosanquet, *Philosophical Theory of the State*, 273.

[101] Hetherington and Muirhead, *Social Purpose*, 262.

[102] Bosanquet, "The Teaching of Patriotism," *Social and International Ideals*.

[103] Bosanquet, "The Function of the State in Promoting the Unity of Mankind," *Social and International Ideas* (Freeport, NY: Books for Libraries, 1967 [1917]), 294.

[104] For an excellent example of this type of nineteenth-century liberal nationalism see John Stuart Mill, "Considerations on Representative Government."

als like Bosanquet evoked a much more Germanic notion of a national community knit together by blood relations.

And yet while this notion of a blood-based or family-based nation might have more closely resembled the German notion of *Volk*, it was emphatically *not* Hegelian. Hegel had argued in the *Philosophy of Right* that "nations" (the standard English translation of "*Völker*" or "peoples") begin as families, as extended kinship groups.[105] Hegel was also clear, however, that the inchoative links between the family and the nation were not enough to legitimate statehood. Instead, he argued, the transition from *Volk* to *Staat* required the realization of the ethical idea of state. In this context, nations were simply proto-states, whose mere existence was not, in itself, a reason for sovereignty.[106] For Hegel, then, no such thing as a dialectically realized "nation state" existed because such a state could not become the "actuality of the ethical idea"; it merely reflected the national community.[107] For Bosanquet, in contrast, the familial idea of the nation was the moral foundation upon which the state justified its actions. It not only naturalized the need for social cooperation, it naturalized the form of the nation-state and explained why "men are distinguished into separate adjacent political bodies instead of forming a single system over the whole earth's surface."[108] In contrast to Hegel's belief that *Staat* superseded *Volk*, Bosanquet thus argued that *Volk* predetermined *Staat*. In the end, the family was not just incidentally related to the national community in a symbolic, Andersonian sense as part of the "deep, horizontal comradeship" that characterizes nationalist imaginaries.[109] It was the central, organizing principle of the national community and justified the existence of the state itself.

Ultimately, however, this theoretical coupling of the family with society at large—whether Ritchie's family-state or Bosanquet's family-nation—did not always blend seamlessly with these thinkers' liberal political commitments. Because they had rooted their theory of organic community in the loving shelter of the nuclear family and the familiarized nation, the

---

[105] "Hegel, *Philosophy of Right*, par. 181. Note that Hegel rarely used the German word "*Nation*." When he did so, it was almost always in reference to a more limited notion of "customs" rather than an organic sense of "peoples." [See, for instance, par. 339 of *Grudlinien der Philosophie des Rechts* (Leipzig, 1911)].

[106] Hegel, *Philosophy of Right*, par. 279.

[107] In this instance, Knox's translation of "*Das Völk als Staat*" as "nation state" is extremely misleading [i.c. par. 331]. A more appropriate translation would be "the people *as* state," that is, a people who have reached that historical moment when the realization of State as "Mind" is possible, rather than a state that exists as a mere reflection of a national community.

[108] Bosanquet, "The Function of the State in Promoting the Unity of Mankind," 275.

[109] Benedict Anderson, *Imagined Communities*, 2nd ed. (London: Verso, 1991) 7.

nineteenth-century controversy over the increased movement of middle-
and working-class women (seeking employment, education, and the vote)
away from the family now placed these thinkers in an awkward position.
On the one hand, they were drawn toward a vision of society with inherently conservative undertones, a vision composed of cohesive nuclear
families that required fulltime domestic maintenance. On the other hand,
these thinkers were also politically aligned with a liberal politics that supported expanded economic, educational, and political opportunities for
women. In the end, idealist liberals like Bosanquet and Ritchie chose the
more conservative response. Their social theory in this regard required a
sustained level of interference by charity organizations in the lives of
working-class families and a policy agenda based on the perceived needs
of families rather than of individual citizens.

THE POLITICS OF LIBERAL PATERNALISM

Both Hegelian idealism and classical liberalism argued for a separation
between the family and the state, but the theoretical shape and depth of
this separation was quite different. On the surface, for liberals like Locke,
the nuclear-family form was important not so much for its particular qualities as for its *absence* from public life. While feminist historians and political theorists have rightly demonstrated that Locke's vision of the family
was riddled with untheorized, gendered assumptions about the emerging
dominance of the nuclear-family form in European society and the leadership role of husbands and fathers within this family, these assumptions
were not linked expressly to an overall vision of liberal society.[110] Historically, Lockean liberalism, and liberalism more generally, has thus held out
the possibility of an equality-based politics for women—a possibility that
Mary Wollstonecraft and John Stuart Mill drew upon extensively—while
at the same time assuming that men, as the "abler and stronger" of the
two sexes, would dominate both family relations and politics.[111]

Hegel, by contrast, avoided this contradiction by theorizing both the
necessity of the monogamous nuclear family to the evolution of the modern state and the essential differences between the sexes that grounded
women permanently in the home. According to Hegel, only through making a monogamous commitment—when a man and a woman consented

---

[110] See, for instance, Linda Nicholson, *Gender and History: The Limits of Social Theory
in the Age of the Family* (New York: Columbia University Press, 1986), 133–166; Carol
Pateman, *The Disorder of Women: Democracy, Feminism, and Political Theory* (Stanford:
Stanford University Press, 1989), 118–40.

[111] Locke, *Second Treatise of Government*, par. 82.

"to make themselves one person"—did the male citizen obtain the "substantive self-consciousness" he needed to enter civil society.[112] Women, however, never developed "substantive self-consciousness" themselves because of their "intellectual and ethical differences" from men.[113] Echoing the Western philosophical conviction that women were intimately linked to feeling rather than rationality and to nature rather than history, Hegel concluded that woman "has her substantive destiny within the family."[114] This rootedness of women in the family, however, was hardly incidental. Instead, women's inherent association with the family played a critical role in Hegel's overall dialectical system by providing the family with a permanent connection to nature. Women ensured the constancy and "natural immediacy" of family life that the male citizen was born into, moved away from, and ultimately resolved with at a higher level of universal Spirit. Women were the heart, the essence of life, the fixed, natural objects that the maturing male citizen consumed as, in Judith Butler's words, "self-consciousness eats its way through the world."[115]

The philosophical underpinnings of Oxford liberalism provided its proponents with a slightly different set of theoretical and political problems with regard to women. Thus, their explicitly Hegelian-influenced belief in the nuclear family as an essential component in the overall health of the social body led them to a rather conservative set of assumptions about women's relationship to the family. And yet these thinkers associated themselves politically with the more progressive elements in the Liberal Party, elements that actively lobbied for women's suffrage throughout the late nineteenth and early twentieth centuries and contributed an average of 68 percent of the total suffragist vote in Parliament during this period.[116] As a result, while most of these thinkers supported a more liberal individualist approach to both women's suffrage and women's education, they tended to undercut this support with an insistence on women's fundamental connection to the home.

To their credit, thinkers like Bosanquet and Ritchie did attempt to correct Hegel's unconditional relegation of women to the family sphere. Bosanquet, for instance, consciously added women to his description of Hegel's civil society in *The Philosophical Theory of the State.*[117] For Bosanquet, sexual difference did not necessarily mean difference of mind.

---

[112] Hegel, *Philosophy of Right*, par. 162.

[113] Ibid., par. 166.

[114] Ibid.

[115] Judith Butler, *Subjects of Desire: Hegelian Reflections in Twentieth-Century France* (New York: Columbia University Press, 1987), 39.

[116] Brian Harrison, *Separate Spheres: The Opposition to Women's Suffrage in Britain* (New York: Holmes and Meier, 1978), 39.

[117] Bosanquet, *Philosophical Theory of the State*, 253.

Instead, in the liberal tradition of Wollstonecraft and Mill, he argued that education played a large part in determining social role.[118] Bosanquet and most idealist liberals agreed that women should be granted access to both education and the same political and property rights as men.[119] Nevertheless, they also believed that it was the exceptional woman who would not or could not be married. Such women should be allowed to find "in the life of the school mistress or the government clerk, an attractive alternative" to marriage.[120] Such an alternative would prevent unmarriageable girls from turning into "sour old maids."[121] Most women, they assumed, should remain in the home as mothers, the role for which they were biologically and evolutionarily suited.[122]

And yet in reality, by the mid-nineteenth century, unmarried middle- and working-class women were leaving the home in record numbers to work for wages.[123] At the same time, female literacy rates and school attendance increased sharply.[124] Accompanying these two phenomena was the emergence of an entirely new public role for some women, the "suffragette," whose militancy and outspokenness inspired untold amounts of anxiety amongst both Liberal and Conservative "antis."[125] Likewise, during this period working-class women began to organize publicly through trade unions.[126] By the late nineteenth century, the emergence of women into the public sphere resulted in a liberal theory and politics profoundly at odds with itself. John Stuart Mill, for instance, argued for women's full enfranchisement and equal access to economic and educational opportunities but drew the line at the prospect of married women working outside the home.

While Mill believed that full-time mothers were essential to child rearing, his discussion of the issue in "The Subjection of Women" was suggestive rather than alarmist. By contrast, for liberals of a more idealist bent like Bosanquet, Ritchie, and Muirhead, the specter of married women working outside of the home raised the possibility of not only familial

---

[118] Bosanquet, "The English People: Notes on National Characteristics," *International Monthly* 3 (Jan. 1901): 91.

[119] Ritchie even stretched this notion of equal opportunity to include military service. [*Darwinism and Politics*, 74].

[120] Muirhead, "The Family," 120.

[121] Bosanquet, "The English People," 92.

[122] See Ritchie's discussion of women, motherhood, evolution, and Malthusian logic in *Darwinism and Politics*, 73–82.

[123] Steven Mintz, *A Prison of Expectations: The Family in Victorian Culture* (New York: New York University Press, 1983), 16.

[124] Mintz, *A Prison of Expectations*, 16.

[125] Harrison, *Separate Spheres*, 27.

[126] Sonya Rose, *Limited Livelihoods: Gender and Class in Nineteenth-Century England* (Berkeley: University of California Press, 1992), 181.

but social collapse. "Undoubtedly the family idea has been threatened by the long hours of factory work, and the working of married women," argued Bosanquet in 1901. This "weakening hold of the family," he continued, resulted in higher rates of alcoholism, juvenile crime, and a general "failure to form the mind to the notion of a social place."[127] Likewise, for Muirhead, the fact that women's employment was "bound to act unfavourably on the health, cleanliness, and moral influence of the home needs no proof."[128] For these thinkers, the movement of large numbers of women into the workplace would necessarily have antisocial and unnatural consequences. As a result, dire warnings of social chaos tempered the call of these Oxford liberals for some measure of sexual equality. For instance, Ritchie argued that the "responsibility of the husband" could not be compromised without wreaking havoc on the evolutionary drive to improve the species.[129] The patriarchal family was, he insisted, the "chief bond of cohesions" found amongst "all those peoples that have developed high civilizations."[130]

Some of the idealist liberals were driven by a fundamental fear that the movement of large numbers of women away from the home would lead inevitably to social disease and the death of the society as a whole. Bosanquet concluded that when "family responsibility" was weakened, "the race is less robust."[131] Similarly, for Muirhead, any "decline" in the family would result in a similar decline in the social body "defined by the physiologists as the 'diminution of the formative activity of an organism.' "[132] Ultimately, for these thinkers, gendered assumptions about the ethical and evolutionary functions of the family overpowered their liberal political support for women's equality.

At the same time, many idealist liberals were also heavily involved in charity organizations that encouraged women to stay at home. Bosanquet in particular translated his vision of family morality into social action through his involvement in the Charity Organization Society (COS), with which he had a long-time association and which became one of the most influential late nineteenth-century philanthropic societies in Britain. The COS championed the moralizing qualities of the nuclear family and a vision of ethical domesticity that it sought to imprint onto the working class. Prompted by the mid-nineteenth-century upswing in the number of working-class women working outside the home, the COS began a campaign to encourage a sense of "family responsibility" among

[127] Bosanquet, "The English People," 113–14.
[128] Muirhead, "The Family," 123.
[129] Ritchie, *Natural Rights*, 262.
[130] Ibid., 261.
[131] Bosanquet, "Socialism and Natural Selection," 63.
[132] Muirhead, "The Family," 126.

working-class men while at the same time extolling the virtues of domestic life for women.[133] In the view of the COS, the creation of morally pure families among the working class was an organizational rather than an economic issue. "The great problem with this class," argued Helen Bosanquet, "is how to bring them to regard life as anything but a huge chaos. The confusion that reigns in their minds is reflected in their worlds."[134]

Thus, the key to bringing domestic order into the "huge chaos" of the working-class family was to teach wives the skills of organization and thrift, skills the COS argued would make it possible for them to stay at home. This could be accomplished, the COS maintained, only through the direct intervention of privately trained case workers in homes rather than through government programs.[135] Bosanquet and his colleagues promoted this case worker approach for distinctly Darwinist reasons. In other words, Bosanquet believed that as the most natural seat of evolutionary progress and as that place where the moral souls of human beings were first molded, the monogamous family unit had to be left to evolve as it would, free from state interference (although not free from the uninvited visits of the private philanthropist). Bosanquet thus argued that the case worker approach was vastly superior to "external reconstruction or regulation" because it avoided state intervention in the natural realm of the family and thus helped promote the survival of the most fit. "It is our method and our method only," he insisted, "that goes to the centre of the great fight."[136]

The long-term policy and cultural effects of the COS were many. For instance, its case worker model justified direct intervention into the lives of working-class people by middle-class philanthropic organizations throughout the late nineteenth and early twentieth centuries.[137] In addition, the COS actively reinforced the notion that middle-class women's own public roles in society should be restricted to philanthropic rather than political work and over the years produced a number of prominent anti-suffrage women activists, including Octavia Hill.[138] Finally, as an organization that enlisted the help of a large number of reformers, politicians, and academics, the COS helped shape British social policy toward the poor through its influential membership.[139] In particular, its close association with the Poor Law Guardians guaranteed that the COS and its

---

[133] Lewis, *Women In England: 1870–1950*, 12.

[134] Helen Bosanquet, *Rich and Poor* (quoted in Lewis, *Women in England*, 37).

[135] Ibid.

[136] Bosanquet, "Philosophy and Casework," *Social and International Ideals*, 181.

[137] Lewis, *Women in England*, 82.

[138] Harrison, *Separate Spheres*, 84.

[139] Den Otter, *British Idealism and Social Explanation*, 180–81.

local affiliates exercised an extraordinary amount of power in deciding which individuals—and, more importantly, which *families*—were worthy of financial relief.[140] Paradoxically, while they presupposed that private caseworkers rather than the state ought to be pressing working-class families in a moral direction, idealist liberal members of the COS were successfully able to powerfully influence the state by convincing it to pick and choose among its citizens based upon a model of nuclear family cohesion.

CONCLUSION

Eventually, the idealist liberals came full circle in their desire to create a liberal social theory that, in Sandra Den Otter's words, "persuasively enhanced communitarian ends."[141] What began as an attempt to draw upon idealist insights and address the problems of liberalism resulted in a liberal rejection of the Hegelian state and a social theory riddled with what Hegel himself would have called "unbridgeable distinctions" between the individual, the state, and society. A number of thinkers sought to address these contradictions both through an organic analogy inherited from Hegel himself and from the new science of Darwinism. Embracing organicism, however, gave rise to its own set of philosophical and political contradictions. Philosophically, the decision by Bosanquet, Ritchie, and their colleagues to naturalize society led them to emphasize the family as the primary moral cell within the social organism. Consequently, these thinkers arrived at a theory of family morality that overflowed its banks, filling up the nation and the state with an ethical unity that looked both pre-liberal and pre-idealist. The result was an ambiguous political ideology that nominally espoused equality for men and women, supported a philanthropic movement that consistently violated the private lives of working-class families, and pushed the emerging welfare state in Britain to recognize families, rather than individuals, as the fundamental bearers of rights.

As chapter 2 elaborates, Oxford scholars Murray and Zimmern eventually incorporated many of these same ambiguities into their liberalisms. One sees in their political theories a Greenian affinity for the metaphysical, for a quasi-Hegelian, dialectical-like Spirit capable of reconciling individual freedom with the social and communal whole. At the same time, Murray's and Zimmern's liberalisms contained a number of the

[140] Ibid.
[141] Sandra Den Otter, "Thinking in Communities: Late Nineteenth-Century Liberals, Idealists and the Retrieval of Community," *The Age of Transition: British Politics 1880–1914*, ed. E.H.H. Green (Edinburgh: Edinburgh University Press, 1997), 68.

same competing philosophical and political claims that drove many of their idealistically inclined liberal forebears toward their conservative reliance on the organic and the familial, most importantly, a liberal discomfort with state power. Likewise, the most notable aspects of their internationalism—their fear of a world state, their belief in the concept of international Spirit, Murray's commitment to an organic world community, Zimmern's conflation of national morality with families—mimic the political and theoretical imaginings of an earlier generation of Oxford intellectuals.

But the linkages between this earlier generation of explicitly Hegelian thinkers and Murray and Zimmern is not an easy chain to follow, particularly since both men went to a good deal of trouble to distance themselves from what had become by the early twentieth century a school of thought widely associated with Prussianism. Chapter 2 reveals these connections. In the process, it demonstrates that the difficulties Green and his colleagues faced in their attempt to theorize community without rendering their own liberal beliefs "abstract" did not disappear with the new century.[142] Rather, they were transfigured by Zimmern and Murray into questions of international politics and international ethics.

[142] Ritchie, *Studies in Political and Social Ethics*, 37.

CHAPTER TWO

An "Oddly Transposed" Liberalism

IN A 1940 OBITUARY FOR HIS close friend and fellow liberal H.A.L. Fisher, Gilbert Murray recalled their days as young scholars at New College in the mid-1880s. "All of us," he noted, "were then deeply under the German spell."[1] Fisher had similar memories, noting in his *Unfinished Autobiography* that "Hegel, as interpreted by T. H. Green and Caird, was the reigning philosopher of my undergraduate days."[2] And yet Murray's own biographers later took great pains to remember him as impervious to the influence of German philosophy, whose liberalism was "more in sympathy with Mill and Millian Liberals than with any body of mystics or transcendentalists."[3] Murray himself made a similar gesture in Fisher's obituary, arguing that, unlike the rest of the New College fellows, Fisher had always understood the treachery of the Germans.

This posthumous reading of late nineteenth-century liberalism at Oxford reflects two basic trends in the evolution of liberal thought in Britain. First, while Green's Hegelian-inspired liberalism continued to cast a long shadow at Oxford after his death in 1882—particularly among scholars of ancient Greece and Rome—the liberal press in Britain and a growing number of liberal intellectuals (at Oxford and elsewhere) were becoming increasingly uneasy with the anti-democratic politics of a newly unified Germany, a feeling that spilled over into a general sense of discomfort with the entire legacy of Anglo-German philosophical exchange. As a result, compared to the group of thinkers who had studied with Green a decade before, many Oxford scholars coming of age in the 1880s and '90s were much more hesitant to explicitly embrace Hegelian philosophy.

Second, the anxious desire of early twentieth-century liberals to distance themselves from the "mystics and transcendentalists" of the nineteenth speaks to the even more vehement condemnation of German idealism that took place in Britain and America during and after the Great

[1] Gilbert Murray, *Proceedings of the British Academy*, vol. 26 (London: Humphrey Milford Amen House, 1940), 4.

[2] H.A.L. Fisher, *An Unfinished Autobiography* (Oxford: Oxford University Press, 1940), 50. Fisher attended New College during the 1880s.

[3] J.A.K. Thomson, *Proceedings of the British Academy*, vol. XLIII (London: Oxford University Press, 1957), 257. See also Francis West's biography, *Gilbert Murray: A Life* (New York: St Martin's Press, 1984).

War. According to influential thinkers such as Charles Dewey, Leonard Hobhouse, and George Santayana, German militarism drew its ideological justification directly from Hegel's theory of the state.[4] In this context, the actions of Murray's biographers and Murray's own ruminations on his intellectual origins make considerable sense. In other words, linking Murray's liberalism solely to Mill established his intellectual pedigree as essentially British, thus freeing him from what, by that time, had become the legacy-wrecking accusation of Prussianism.

In the end, all but a handful of the most committed, idealist liberals in Britain rejected their past intellectual connections with German theory or wrote them off as youthful dalliances. As a result, many thinkers have, over the years, failed to see the continuing influence on British politics between the wars of the Hegelian liberalism developed at Oxford in the 1870s. There has been excellent work done on the previously overlooked impact of certain strands of nineteenth- and early twentieth-century "new liberalism" on British industrial relations after 1914.[5] But the impact of an Oxford school that explicitly sought to expand liberalism in a more collectivist direction through a reliance on a particular interpretation of Hegelian theory was assumed to have died with Bosanquet in 1923.

In contrast, this chapter argues that the political philosophies of Gilbert Murray and Alfred Zimmern confound the distinction between "idealists" and "new liberals" found in most historical works on this transitional period. It argues that many of the "oddly transposed" Hegelian-inspired principles that so characterized the political thought of nineteenth-century Oxford scholars like Green and Bosanquet continued to operate within Murray's and Zimmern's social theories, especially their idealistic rejection of abstract individualism, their belief in a notion of liberal freedom conditioned by duty, their emphasis on spirituality as a necessary ingredient in the workings of liberal society, and their focus on the social order. Additionally, in their simultaneous desires to make liberalism more conducive to community and to maintain a healthy cynicism toward the state, the political philosophies of Murray and Zimmern embodied one of the key intellectual puzzles that drove their predecessors toward conservatism. As a result, their political writings often suffered from a kind of acute schizophrenia with regard to state power. Both men, in the Oxford tradition, ultimately resolved these tensions through a theory of community that tended toward a rather rosy portrayal of hierarchy and the nuclear family and that frequently sounded more Burkean than

---

[4] See D. C. Band, "The Critical Reception of English Neo-Hegelianism in Britain and America, 1914–1960," *The Australian Journal of Politics and History* 23(2) (1980): 228.

[5] See for instance Michael Freeden's work on new liberalism after the war in *Liberalism Divided* (Oxford: The Clarendon Press, 1986) and "The New Liberalism and its Aftermath," *Victorian Liberalism*, ed. Richard Bellamy (London: Routledge, 1990).

liberal in its reverence for tradition.[6] Unsurprisingly, Murray's and Zimmern's writings often appear to have more in common with those of Bosanquet and Ritchie at their most conservative than they do with those of their more progressive "new liberal" contemporaries such as Hobson, Hobhouse, and G. Lowes Dickinson.

The goal of this chapter is both to elaborate the historical connections that establish these thinkers as inheritors of a particular form of nineteenth-century idealist liberalism and to examine the overlapping (and often conflicting) visions of state and society that braided their way through the political philosophies of both men. The first section closely examines Murray's and Zimmern's own intellectual histories, paying particular attention to the changing role of German philosophy at Oxford during the 1880s and '90s when both men were undergraduates and fellows. It next focuses on the classical scholarship of these authors and argues that one can most clearly see their idealist impulses at work within their distinctly Hegelian interpretations of ancient societies. The next section examines the configuration of Greek, liberal, and idealist motifs found in Murray's and Zimmern's approaches to liberalism and suggests that many of their least theoretically coherent moments have much to say about each man's conflicted attitude toward state power. Ultimately, it was this conflict itself that gave rise to Murray's and Zimmern's similarly conservative understanding of community and the social order.

The Decline of Oxford Hegelianism

Coming of age as liberals at Oxford in the 1880s and '90s meant that Murray and Zimmern would have been exposed to two distinct and sometimes contradictory influences. On the one hand, both men experienced the legacy of Greenian idealism through their scholarship and their participation in local liberal politics and social reformism. Indeed, by the time Murray and Zimmern had begun their involvement in the Worker's Education Association (WEA) and the Oxford Union, the seamless connection that Green and his colleagues had helped establish among philosophy, liberalism, and activism was all but taken for granted by a generation of Oxford liberals. As undergraduates Murray and Zimmern, like Green's students who immediately preceded them, expected that what they learned from the *Literae Humaniores* could be applied to the real world. On the other hand, changes in Britain's relationship to Germany during this period led many liberals at Oxford and in the country at large to

---

[6] Bodl. MS Alfred Zimmern (136) fol. 166. Attempts to contact copyright holder of Zimmern papers were unsuccessful.

question the legitimacy of a previous generation's commitment to Hegelianism. Thus, as undergraduates and fellows, Murray and Zimmern witnessed a general extrusion of the explicitly Hegelian elements from the social theory of many Oxford liberals.

The early lives of Gilbert Murray and of Alfred Zimmern bare some resemblances that go a long way toward explaining the similarities of their political theories. Both men came from non-English backgrounds, both won awards to attend Oxford, both took honors in the *Literae Humaniores*, both became fellows at New College and eventually Classical scholars, and both identified themselves as committed political liberals throughout their university careers. In truth, while the presence of liberal students and teachers had increased at Oxford throughout the nineteenth century, undergraduate life at the end of 1800s was still dominated by the sons of nobly born and wealthy conservatives who were, in general, more interested in social than in intellectual life. Because of this, intellectual students from less affluent or less British backgrounds, like Murray and Zimmern, often staked out their identity as liberals early on in opposition to this confluence of "wealth, snobbery, and sport."[7]

Gilbert Murray was born in Melbourne, Australia, in 1866 and moved to England in 1877. On his mother's side, Murray was Welsh; on his father's, Murray hailed from a long line of Irish political rebels, a lineage of which he was intensely proud and that shaped his later attitudes toward Irish Home Rule.[8] He attended Merchants and Baker School in London and in 1884 won a scholarship to St. John's College at Oxford. By all accounts, Murray was a brilliant student—Jowett once referred to him as the "most distinguished undergraduate of his time"—who excelled in Greek and Latin translation, so much so that when New College offered him a fellowship at the end of his undergraduate career they proposed waiving the examination requirement.[9] Murray took the examination anyway and became a fellow at New College, where he remained until 1889 when he was elected to the Chair of Greek at the University of Glasgow.[10] While at Oxford and Glasgow, Murray was exposed to a variety of idealist influences. He studied with Jowett and other leading classical scholars with Hegelian inclinations, including Henry Nettleship. Among those whom Murray later described as having most influenced him during his days as an undergraduate was Charles Gore, the bishop of Oxford and former Balliol student, whose unorthodox theology was

[7] Stefan Collini, *Liberalism and Sociology* (Cambridge: Cambridge University Press, 1979), 57.

[8] Duncan Wilson, *Gilbert Murray OM*, (Oxford: Oxford University Press, 1987), 1.

[9] Bodl. MS. Gilbert Murray (1–2) fol. 1; Wilson, *Gilbert Murray OM*, 17.

[10] West, *Gilbert Murray*, 59.

both idealist and classical in its focus.[11] During his twenty years in Glasgow, Murray also established close friendships with a number of idealist thinkers, including A. C. Bradley (brother of Oxford idealist thinker F. H. Bradley) and Edward Caird, with whom he would remain friends after both men returned to Oxford.

Alfred Zimmern was born in 1879 in Surbiton. His father was a German Jewish businessman from Frankfurt who moved with Zimmern's mother to England following the annexation of Frankfurt by the Prussians in 1866.[12] Zimmern grew up comfortably, won a scholarship to Winchester School and then New College. He became a lecturer in ancient history and was a fellow and tutor at New College from 1904 until 1909.[13] As an undergraduate he studied with Murray's good friend, H.A.L. Fisher and, like Murray, excelled in Greek translation and won several awards.[14] Even though his career at Oxford began after Murray had already left for Glasgow, he and Murray became friends and corresponded frequently about both liberal politics and classical studies. Zimmern continued to teach at New College until 1909, when he retired his position, much to the dismay of his students and colleagues, and went to Greece to research his most famous work of classical history, *The Greek Commonwealth*.[15]

Zimmern's academic career was not as long as Murray's, but it was significantly more nomadic and diverse. While Murray involved himself extensively in countless political causes and academic societies throughout his life, from 1909 until the day he died in 1957, he remained associated with Classics at New College. In contrast, Zimmern, after he left Oxford, traveled to Greece and then taught sociology at the London School of Economics.[16] During the war he became involved full time with the intelligence division of the Foreign Office and participated in drafting the then-secret British plans for a post-war League of Nations. In 1919 he was appointed to the first independent professorship of international relations in the world at the University College of Wales, Aberystwyth. Scandal propelled him from Wales to Cornell University where he spent two years in 1922 and 1923.[17] From there, Zimmern worked

---

[11] Wilson, *Gilbert Murray OM*, 22; James Patrick, *The Magdalen Metaphysicals: Idealism and Orthodoxy at Oxford, 1901–1945* (Macon, GA: Mercer, 1985), 20, n. 60.

[12] Toynbee, *Acquaintances*, 50.

[13] Ernst Günther Schmidt, "Ulrich Von Wilamowitz-Moellendorff to Sir Alfred Zimmern on the Reality of Classical Athens," *Philologus* 2. (1989): 305.

[14] Bodl. MS Alfred Zimmern (5): fols. 11–12, 17–18.

[15] Schmidt, "Ulrich Von Wilamowitz-Moellendorff," 305.

[16] D. J. Markwell, "Sir Alfred Zimmern Revisited: Fifty Years On," *Review of International Studies* 12 (1986): 280.

[17] Markwell, "Sir Alfred Zimmern Revisited," 181.

professionally with the League of Nations and eventually returned to Oxford in 1931 as that university's first professor of international relations.[18] He was knighted in 1936 and served in the Foreign Office again during World War Two. He was a guest professor at Trinity College, Connecticut, from 1947 to 1949 and died in Connecticut, six months after Murray.

As undergraduates, Zimmern and Murray were active liberal debaters at the Oxford Union and were involved in liberal reform projects both on campus and in the Oxfordshire community. While at St. John's, Murray was an enthusiastic member of the Oxford Home Rule League, and later lobbied in support of local abstinence laws.[19] After his return to Oxford from Glasgow, he taught and consulted for the Oxford WEA.[20] As both a student and a fellow at Oxford, Zimmern threw himself almost full time into the WEA, becoming one of its most visible leaders and helping to found the Summer School in 1909.[21] In addition, throughout their careers Murray and Zimmern were also involved with a variety of new liberal socially oriented philosophical societies. Both, for instance, were members of the Oxford Aristotelian Society, founded by classics scholar and former Green student Ingram Bywater in 1885, and both published in the Society's two journals, *Proceedings of the Aristotelian Society* and *Mind*.[22] They also participated in more explicitly political discussion groups such as the Rainbow Circle.[23]

In essence, while at Oxford, Murray and Zimmern participated in a tradition of liberal activism whose original impetus had come from T. H. Green and the group of scholars he inspired. This was, however, hardly a static tradition. Changing attitudes toward Germany in the country at large and increased radicalism among an emerging group of progressive new liberals both in and out of Oxford affected British liberalism in ways that permanently changed the philosophical face of the Oxford school.

[18] Zimmern, "The Study of International Relations, An Inaugural Lecture, Delivered Before the University of Oxford, 20, Feb., 1931" (Oxford: The Clarendon Press, 1931).

[19] Wilson, *Gilbert Murray OM*, 21.

[20] Ibid., 231. In addition, during the First World War, Murray attempted to expand the organization to create educational courses for prisoners of war.

[21] See the short biography of Zimmern at the beginning of Quincy Wright, *Neutrality and Collective Security* (Chicago: University of Chicago Press, 1936); Toynbee, *Acquaintances*, 49. For a more extensive history of the WEA and adult education at Oxford in general, see Lawrence Goldman *Dons and Workers: Oxford and Adult Education Since 1850* (Oxford: Oxford University Press, 1995) Zimmern's involvement with the summer school is discussed on pp.142–45.

[22] Patrick, *The Magdalen Metaphysicals*, 2.

[23] Michael Freeden, ed., *Minutes of the Rainbow Circle, 1894–1924* (London: Offices of the Royal Historical Society, University College London, 1989), 1. Members of the Rainbow Circle sought to create a scholarly space wherein liberal intellectuals could discuss "social

According to most historical accounts, the diminution of Hegelian idealism in Britain occurred primarily during the First World War.[24] And yet looking at the political landscape in Britain during the 1880s and '90s, one can already see a decline in the sympathies of English liberals for German metaphysical thought, as evidenced by both the rise in realism at Oxford and pragmatism at Cambridge as well as the early critiques by progressive new liberals like J. A. Hobson and L. T. Hobhouse. While one sees realist and pragmatist circles mounting some criticism of Green himself, Green was still held in high regard by most of those second-generation new liberals who would eventually come to reject idealism. Hobson, for instance, always maintained that he was first inspired to think about an ethical politics in the "atmosphere of an Oxford in which Jowett, T. H. Green, and Mark Pattison were leading figures."[25] In sum, many late nineteenth- and early twentieth-century liberals (particularly the intellectual and political elite trained at Oxford) continued to draw upon the legacy of Green's commitment to social reformism, but they did so in a way that mirrored the increasing discomfort of British liberals with German politics and philosophy.

In contrast to the developing hostility of liberals toward Germany during the last two decades of the century, British liberal opinion in the 1860s and '70s was decidedly sympathetic to the cause of German unification, a feeling nurtured by the extensive philosophical, cultural, and economic exchanges that took place between the two countries during the first half of the 1800s.[26] This began to change, however, after unification in 1879 as more liberals began voicing their opposition to Bismarck's autocratic policies, a trend that continued throughout the 1880s when the liberal press accused Bismark of trying to discredit Gladstone.[27] At the same time, official relations between the two countries deteriorated over

---

questions" of current interest in a manner that fused a liberal commitment to free market economics with a more idealist vision of community.

[24] D. C. Band's exclusive focus on the war years, for instance, implies that the growth of anti-Hegelian writings in both Britain and America during the teens and twenties was entirely the result of wart-time hostilities with Germany. [D .C. Band, "The Critical Reception of English New-Hegelianism in Britain and America," *The Australian Journal of Politics and History* 23(2) (1980): 1227]. Likewise, while some scholars, such as John Morrow, concede that, although there was a "certain amount of pre-war criticism," of idealist theory in Britain, this criticism pales in comparison to the "increased tempo of wartime debate." [John Morrow, "British Idealism, German Philosophy, and the First World War," *Australian Journal of Politics and History* 28(3) (1982): 387].

[25] J. A. Hobson, *Confessions of an Economic Heretic* (London: Allen and Unwin, 1938), 26.

[26] Kennedy, *The Rise of Anglo-German Antagonism: 1860–1914*, 92.

[27] Ibid., 93.

colonial claims and naval supremacy, such that by the end of the century, anti-German sentiment in Britain was running high in both the popular press and among the liberal elite.[28]

World War One exacerbated existing anti-German feelings in Britain, provoking a widespread rejection of Germany's idealist philosophical heritage among both academics and the general public. Politicians, scholars, and public figures (both liberal and conservative) laid the blame for Germany's actions squarely at the foot of an incomprehensible state-oriented metaphysics with authoritarian implications. According to Lord Bryce, this "deadly theory" was "at the bottom of German aggression."[29] In addition, by 1917, many British intellectuals, including Zimmern, associated Hegelian theory with Marxist-Leninism and thus assumed that it posed a distinct threat to "our liberal faith."[30]

In an effort to distance themselves from the taint of both Prussianism and Bolshevism, many liberals sharpened their preexisting critiques of Hegelian idealism or revised formerly sympathetic accounts. For instance, liberal sociologist C. Delisle Burns (whose pre-war philosophical works had praised Hegel for correcting the "disintegrating individualism of the Enlightenment") argued in 1915 that "of all the nonsense that ever pretended to be a description of fact; the Hegelian state is the worst."[31] In his 1915 book, *Nationality and the War*, Arnold J. Toynbee leveled a portion of his critique at the "philosophical tradition of Modern Germany," arguing that it commanded the individual to "merge himself in the society to which he belongs: the State—that is the political Absolute."[32] Additionally, during the war a number of "new liberals" actively sought to recast their own philosophical origins as not only anti-German but unquestionably British. In 1916, for instance, Hobson went out of his way to distance his vision of the state-society relationship from any kind of German model, stressing instead his theory's adherence to a homegrown, British tradition that preserved "private liberties and ends."[33]

Finally, during the war British liberals not only responded to what they saw as the implicitly statist nature of German culture and philosophy but also began to question the wartime actions of the British state. The hotly contested issue of military conscription and the imprisonment of

[28] Bernadotte Everly Schmitt, *England and Germany, 1740–1914* (Princeton: Princeton University Press, 1918), 138.

[29] Den Otter, *British Idealism and Social Explanation*, 13.

[30] Zimmern, *Nationality and Government*, xv.

[31] Cecil Burns, *The Growth of Modern Philosophy* (London: Sampson Low, 1909) 175; Cecil Burns, "When Peace Breaks Out," *International Journal of Ethics* 26 (1915–16): 90.

[32] Toynbee, *Nationality and the War* (London: J. M. Dent and Sons, 1915), 499.

[33] Hobson, "The War and British Liberties: Claims of the State upon the Individual," *Nation and The Anthenaeum*, Oct. 6, 1916. [Quoted in Freeden, *Liberalism Divided*, 43].

many conscientious objectors (including Murray's cousin and good friend Bertrand Russell) pushed a number of British liberals toward a more acute awareness of state coercion and led to a general reclaiming of liberalism's anti-state heritage.[34] For some thinkers, such as Hobhouse, this turn away from the state involved a pointed attack on the idealist underpinnings of the Oxford liberals. Thus, Hobhouse had praised Green and his followers for "setting liberalism free from the shackles of an individualistic conception of liberty" before the war; by 1918 he openly condemned these thinkers' "confusion of the individual with the universal."[35] In Hobhouse's mind, this confusion inevitably led toward state authoritarianism.

Unsurprisingly, in the years following German unification until World War One, one begins to see a declining interest in the Germans (and, explicitly, in Hegel) among a new generation of Oxford undergraduates, evidence that, in Freeden's words, idealism was "never properly digested" by liberal students at Oxford in the 1880s and '90s.[36] This lack of interest in German philosophy stands in stark contrast to the political writings of scholars like Ritchie, Bosanquet, and Muirhead, who had studied with Green just ten years earlier. This generation's enthusiasm for Hegelian theory never flagged, not even with the onset of the Great War.[37] Clearly, though, these thinkers paid the price for their continuing commitment to Hegel in the years leading up to the war, both professionally and historically. Bosanquet, for instance, is perhaps best known to this day not for his contribution to nineteenth-century British social theory but as British liberalism's favorite Hegelian whipping boy. Likewise, Ritchie seems to have suffered professional discrimination, and his letters to Murray throughout the 1890s reveal a constant, almost pathetic, insecurity about job prospects.[38]

In contrast to Bosanquet's and Ritchie's experiences at Oxford, if one is to believe Fisher's and Murray's recollections of their undergraduate days, Green's Hegelianism was something they had already come to feel

[34] Freeden, *Liberalism Divided*, 12.

[35] L. T. Hobhouse, *Liberalism* (London: Williams and Norgate, 1911), 219; L. T. Hobhouse, *The Metaphysical Theory of the State*, 6th ed. (New York: Barnes and Noble, 1960), 66.

[36] Michael Freeden, *The New Liberalism: An Ideology of Social Reform* (Oxford: Oxford University Press, 1978), 17.

[37] See John Morrow's excellent recounting of what happened to those champions of idealism during the First World War, "British Idealism, German Philosophy, and the First World War," *Australian Journal of Politics and History* 28(3) (1982).

[38] In one letter written in 1893, Ritchie asks Murray (ten years his junior) for a testimonial. Ritchie wonders that if, when "speaking with a person of importance on my behalf" if he might "boast that you were once my pupil" because of a conversation about Plato that they had one summer. [Bodl. MS Gilbert Murray (3) fols. 80–81].

instinctively uncomfortable with, despite the institutionalization of Hegelian themes into the *Literae Humaniores*. This was no doubt exacerbated
by Green's death and the departure of many of his students, including
Bosanquet who left Oxford in the early 1880s for a career in social work.[39]
William Wallace, who succeeded Green to the Whyte Chair of Logic,
never inspired the same kind of interest in idealism as did Green. Caird
was still in Glasgow, and F. H. Bradley lived in almost complete isolation.
Even Jowett, by the time he died in 1893, had begun (perhaps sensing the
shifting political tide) to abandon his earlier commitment to Hegel.[40] In
addition, a burgeoning realist movement at Oxford, led by Thomas Case
and John Cook Wilson, challenged the idealist dictum championed by
Bosanquet and others that the real and the rational were one.[41]

That both Murray and Zimmern would have been unwilling to explicitly embrace German theory while at Oxford is understandable, not only
in light of the anti-German/anti-idealist swing of the university's political
compass but also because of the general increase in anti-foreign sentiment
expressed by Oxford men of the same era. From the 1850s onward, both
Cambridge and Oxford began accepting a small number of students from
the Commonwealth. The abolition of religious tests in the 1850s and
1870s opened the university to Jews and Catholics. In addition, after
1902, the Rhodes Bequest ensured an increasing number of German students at Oxford. While the total number of these students remained relatively small throughout the nineteenth and early twentieth centuries, their
presence provoked a considerable amount of anxiety from the predominantly privileged, Anglican, British student body, a reaction that manifested itself most vehemently in student publications.[42] According to Paul
Deslandes, throughout the second half of the nineteenth century, student
humor magazines lamented the passing of an Anglo-Christian culture at
Oxford by poking fun at the religious practices, accents, and race of the
non-British students. This included satirizing the Germans on campus.
For instance, a cartoon in a 1906 issue of *Cap and Gown* entitled "The
Teutonic Invasion. What the Rhodes Scholars Might Have Brought
About" depicts Oxford students dressed in lederhosen, the Kaiser giving
lectures on "imperial subjects," and the transformation of Worcester gar-
dens into a beer garden complete with beer flagons and sauerkraut.[43]

---

[39] Patrick, *The Magdalen Metaphysicals*, 5–7.

[40] Richter, *The Politics Of Conscience*, 71.

[41] Frederick Copleston, *A History of Philosophy*, vol. 8, part 2 (New York: Doubleday,
1962), 141.

[42] Paul Deslandes, " 'The Foreign Element': Newcomers and the Rhetoric of Race, Nation, and Empire in 'Oxbridge' Undergraduate Culture, 1850–1920," *Journal of British
Studies* 37 (1998): 56.

[43] *Cap and Gown* (1906), Bodl., G.A. Oxon. 4 to 219(16) p. 18.

Both Murray's and Zimmern's identities as Britons were tenuous when compared to those of the majority of Oxford students and Fellows at the time, and both might have either experienced outright prejudice or had reason to fear it. Murray was not only from Australia but openly identified himself with the movement for Irish Home Rule. As a result, he was lampooned as both Australian and more Irish than he actually was. In 1887 the *Oxford Magazine* described a pro-Irish speech made by Murray thus:

> Then came Murray, John's College, the darlin'!
> An Australian from over the say.
> May the Saints shower blessings upon him
> And help him to get his degray![44]

And yet Murray was also seen as a kind of hero among the Oxford liberals for his stand on Ireland, and he appears to have suffered no great professional or academic setbacks by being identified as Irish. What one finds in Murray's own remembrances (and in those letters he wrote during subsequent years at Glasgow) is not a fear of being associated with the foreign, but rather a kind of gentle insistence that his theoretical knowledge was *English* in its origin rather than arising from any Oxford affinity for the Germans.

At the same time, Murray's letters are peppered with German philosophical ideas and phrases that betray a general familiarity with the language and with idealist concepts. In 1902, for instance, in a letter to Fisher, he described his scholarly work on Greek literature as falling "halfway between" a "nice '*wissenschaftlich*' " book and an "*apparatus criticus*."[45] Murray's choice of the word "*wissenschaft*" (science) is notable here primarily because while it can refer to an academic discipline, in this context Murray's usage suggests a more Hegelian understanding of scholarship. Hegel envisioned his own work on the Greeks as scientific. He described his methodology in *Wissenschaft der Logic* (Science of Logic) as both encyclopedic and scientific, based not on the creation of a new theory but on a "remodeling" of an "ancient city," the reconstruction of Greek metaphysics and Christian ethics in light of modern conceptions of subjectivity and enlightenment.[46] Murray's letter suggests that he imagined his own work (which was densely archeological in its historical detail and equally interested in a reconstruction of Greek ethics based on the concept of "One Great City of Men and Gods") as falling within this tradition. Numerous other examples from letters exchanged with fellow

---

[44] Wilson, *Gilbert Murray OM*, 20.
[45] Bodl. MS Gilbert Murray (133) fol. 14.
[46] Wood, *Hegel's Ethical Thought*, 7.

academics like A. C. Bradley and William Archer are also filled with German philosophical, and often specifically Hegelian, phrases.[47] All of this
implies that Murray was a member of a scholarly community that took
Hegelian descriptors for granted, particularly in reference to Greek literature and thought.

Zimmern's situation at Oxford was decidedly more complex. As half-
Jewish, Zimmern was a rarity among Oxford students.[48] And as someone
whose parents were German, who spoke German at home, and whose
last name was obviously German, he would no doubt have felt the increased anti-German sentiment on campus most keenly.[49] While Zimmern's letters during his early period at Oxford never mention being the
target of any anti-Semitic or anti-German prejudice, other letters written
to his mother while studying in Berlin in 1902 reveal a rising discomfort
with German culture and politics, particularly with the regimented "spic
and span" cleanliness of the cities and the militaristic approach to education.[50] Later, Zimmern would develop an explicitly pro-British, anti-German stance to his political philosophy that grew increasingly virulent dur-

---

[47] For instance, some thirty years later, Murray referred to Fisher's *History of Europe* as
an expression of "a certain philosophy of *weltanschauung* or faith, whichever we choose to
call it" which Murray equated with "the spirit of Liberalism." [Bodl. Ms Gilbert Murray
(500)188]. In this instance, Murray also chose to describe his friend's work through a German term with clear Hegelian implications. The word *"weltanschauung"* ("world view")
first appeared in the German philosophical vocabulary in the early nineteenth century,
evoked by thinkers like Kant and Fichte to imply a moral "idea" of the world. The *Oxford
English Dictionary* today defines *"weltanschauung"* similarly as a "concept of the world
held by an individual or group." It was Hegel, however, who gave the term a spiritual conno-
tation in *Religionsphilosophe* when he argued that a subject's *"weltanschauung,"* his religion, and "philosophical knowledge" were intimately related. It was clearly such a spiritual
understanding upon which Murray based his definition of *"weltanschauung"* as "faith."

[48] When Arnold Toynbee later asked him whether or not his "Jewish background" had
had any effect on his worldview, Zimmern replied that as a boy and an undergraduate, he
had been unaware of his own difference, but this had gradually turned into what he termed
a "certain detachment" from other people, a growing perception perhaps, of his own difference that made him a more careful observer. [Toynbee, *Acquaintances*, 52]. While Zimmern
was not a practicing Jew and in fact grew up in the protestant church of his mother, others
often assumed the identity for him. Victor Ehrenberg, for instance, described Zimmern in
1939 as "a typical lively Jew of great charm." [Günther Schmidt , "Ulrich Von Wilamo-
witz," 306]. Zimmern appears to have been very conflicted about his identity. His works
are filled with what at times appears to be a rather casual anti-Semitism. And, at the same
time, he maintained a long standing interest in the Zionist movement. [Bodl. MS Alfred
Zimmern (11) 95–96].

[49] While Zimmern's letters to his mother are for the most part in English, they are frequently full of German phrases and often signed "Auf Wiederschein." [See, for instance,
Bodl. MS Alfred (5) Zimmern, letters to mother].

[50] Bodl. MS. Alfred Zimmern (7) fols. 7–9.

ing the Great War. Thus, Zimmern argued in his lecture on the "British Working Man" that that the "North Sea which divides England from that mysterious region we call the Continent is one of the sharpest moral frontiers in the world." He then goes on to favorably compare the "English qualities of personal independence, adventurousness, social ambition, responsibility, self government" with the dutifulness and predictability of the Germans.[51] Zimmern's anti-Germanism would also eventually effect his developing ideas about the possibility of modeling a post-war League of Nations on the British Commonwealth. "The fact is," he wrote to F. S. Marvin in 1915, "that in my political philosophy the bond between London and Nigeria is closer than the bond between London and Düsseldorf."[52] Through these letters and essays, it seems that Zimmern was attempting to distance himself from a cultural legacy with which he felt increasingly uncomfortable and that was rapidly becoming politically unfashionable.[53]

During the early years of the twentieth century, Zimmern's dislike for German culture developed into a more explicit critique of German philosophy, a critique that often combined a rejection of Hegelian idealism with an equally vehement aversion to class politics. Indeed, Zimmern argued that socialism and Prussianism were born from the same philosophical impulse. "There is an extraordinarily close kinship," he argued, "between the mentality of Marx and Hegel: and therefore also between that of their respective offspring—Prussian Militarist Culture and German Social Democracy."[54] In an earlier essay entitled "United Britain," Zimmern combined his aversion to socialism with an odd anti-Semitism of his own, arguing that the faults of socialism lay in the "apocalyptic vision of its Jewish originators."[55] Throughout his career, Zimmern's work reflected this largely unarticulated linkage of terms (Germany, socialism, Marx,

[51] Bodl. MS Alfred Zimmern (135) 24.

[52] Zimmern to F. S. Marvin, April 9, 1915. From Julia Stapleton, *Englishness and the Study of Politics: The Social and Political Thought of Ernest Barker* (Cambridge: Cambridge University Press, 1994), 104.

[53] By 1912, Arnold Toynbee recalled Zimmern as someone with an almost preternatural fear of Germany. As an example of this, Toynbee maintained that after returning from a trip to the continent, he mentioned to Zimmern that he thought the "mounting curve of civilization" had "reached its peak in the Rhineland." According to Toynbee, Zimmern responded that he must not "judge by outward appearances" because "what matters is something that it invisible. It is the spirit of the people; and, if you judge by that, as you should, you will not find that Germany stands at the peak of human progress." Toynbee recalled that conversation years later and could not help but admire Zimmern's prescience. [Toynbee, *Acquaintances*, 52–53].

[54] Bodl. MS. Zimmern (135) fol. 18.

[55] "United Britain" (undated) Bodl. MS Alfred Zimmern (135) fol. 148.

Hegel, and Jew) as a kind of foil for his own politics and the spiritual forces of liberalism.[56]

Zimmern, like Murray, however, was clearly educated in a tradition that took German idealism—and in particular an idealist approach to the classics—for granted, as witnessed by his decision to visit Germany extensively in 1898 and to study in Berlin in 1902 and 1903. In going to Berlin, Zimmern participated in a long-standing tradition common among Oxford classicists of that era; Green, Ritchie, Muirhead, and others had all spent time at German universities.[57] Likewise, Zimmern's often sloppy and superficial dismissal of all German theory as socialist or authoritarian is uncharacteristic of his more careful scholarly work, much of which (as discussed below) contained within it obvious traces of an idealist tradition inherited from the less apologetic neo-Hegelians.

Unsurprisingly, one first sees instances of Zimmern's anti-Germanism during the early years of the twentieth century, when British liberalism itself was undergoing a number of philosophical transformations. At Cambridge, a group of thinkers led by G. E. Moore and Bertrand Russell refuted many of the idealist assumptions that Oxford scholars like Green had so carefully aligned with liberalism, ideas to which they themselves had once been attracted.[58] As with the Oxford realists, these Cambridge thinkers dismissed the idealist notion that reality and the Idea coincided, that a "concept," in Moore's words, was "something substantive, more ultimate than it."[59] This positivist turn toward the pragmatic was to shape the political thought of a future generation of Cambridge liberals, thinkers such as John Maynard Keynes and G. Lowes Dickinson. It was a political ideology that portrayed itself in liberatory terms as set free "from the bath of German idealism."[60] It also defined itself in explicit opposition to both Greenian philosophy and Oxford idealism more generally, often carefully painting the Oxford school as sympathetic to suspect

[56] Zimmern, *Nationality and Government*, xix. One sees a similar conflation of terms in Zimmern's 1939 book, *Modern Political Doctrines*.

[57] While Murray never studied in Germany, he was rather an anomaly and later reviewers of his work would note that it "lacked the sound training which study in Germany would have given him." [Hugh Lloyd-Jones, "Gilbert Murray," *American Scholar* , 51(1) (1981–82): 55]. Murray himself noted how odd it was when his friend and classmate H.A.L. Fisher decided to study in Paris rather than Berlin in the 1880s. [Bodl. MS Gilbert Murray (500) fol. 188].

[58] See David Bell's excellent article, "The Revolution of Moore and Russell: A Very British Coup?" *German Philosophy Since Kant*, ed. Anthony O'Hear (Cambridge: Cambridge University Press, 1999). Bell argues against the long standing assumption that Moor and Russell's rejection of German theory was indicative of a resurgence of a native British empiricism or common sense.

[59] G. E. Moore, "The Nature of Judgment," *Mind* 8(30) (April 1899): 176–93.

[60] Bertrand Russell, *Autobiography* (London: George Allen and Unwin, 1967), 134.

foreign influence. Lowes Dickinson, for instance, once described Green's philosophy as "that of a tired Oxford Whig, not of a good, solid, English Liberalism."[61]

By the end of the nineteenth century and the beginning of the twentieth, many of the most progressive and influential new liberals hailing from Oxford had also discarded the philosophical commitments of thinkers like Bosanquet. Both J. T. Hobhouse and J. A. Hobson came to believe that an older generation of Oxford liberals too slavishly relied on Hegel. In 1904 for instance, Hobhouse derided Hegelian idealism for its "retrograde influence" on British liberalism, an influence that, he claimed, beckoned its adherents to "revert to the easy rule of authority and faith."[62] Likewise, Hobson maintained that Bosanquet's reliance on Hegelian organicism too readily absorbed the experience of the individual into the social and spiritual whole.[63] And yet at the same time that Hobson and Hobhouse were questioning the liberal credentials of the Oxford idealists, they were pushing liberal theory in an increasingly collectivist direction, a direction that had more in common with Fabian socialism than with Green and Bosanquet's uncomfortable and conflicted positions on state intervention.[64] Thus, while both Hobson and Hobhouse shared an earlier generation's commitment to the concept of a common good, they went a step beyond these thinkers' somewhat hesitant economics in their support for a redistribution of wealth.[65] Ironically, however, neither Hobhouse's nor Hobson's critiques of idealism ever amounted to a rejection of Green himself. Both men tended to reserve their ire for Bosanquet and those idealists still living. Green and Jowett, and the aura of social reformism

[61] Michael Bentley, *The Liberal Mind, 1914–1929* (Cambridge: Cambridge University Press, 1977), 163.

[62] L. T. Hobhouse, *Democracy and Reaction* (London: Fisher Unwin, 1904), 79. Hobhouse would sharpen this critique and level it explicitly at Bosanquet in his 1918 book, *The Metaphysical Theory of the State*, 6th ed. (New York: Barnes and Noble, 1960).

[63] For Hobson, the "social organism" itself did not experience any kind of independent existence. It was not, in his words, a "spiritual whole." Rather, Hobson maintained that "if you could talk with a 'cell' of the human body it would tell you it is not *we* who think and feel, but the separate cells, each of which is conscious in itself." [J. A. Hobson, *The Crisis of Liberalism: New Issues of Democracy* (London: P. S. King and Son, 1909), 77]. This does no mean, however, that Hobson was averse to using the language of the organic in his political theory. In fact, he frequently relied upon organic metaphors to elucidate his social vision, so much so that Michael Freeden maintains that of "all the liberal theorists who used the term 'social organism', Hobson gave it its fullest treatment and deepest analysis." [Freeden, *Liberalism Divided*, 102]. This is just one of many instances in which Hobson's political theory actually mirrored certain aspects of Bosanquet's analysis.

[64] See Freeden's excellent analysis of Hobson and Hobhouse's political theory in *The New Liberalism*. For a more extensive treatment of Hobhouse's collectivism, see Stefan Collini's *Liberalism and Sociology* (Cambridge: Cambridge University Press, 1979).

[65] Freeden, *The New Liberalism*, 19.

that developed around them were considered sacrosanct, and both Hob-house and Hobson continued to evoke Green's name for their own causes long after his death.[66]

What caused this disconnect between Green's own commitment to He-gelian idealism and how those anti-idealist new liberals who came of age after his death remembered him? Clearly, something at Oxford that went beyond a rejection of German theory had changed. This change is best encapsulated in two academic and political trends of that era. On the one hand, the last decades of the nineteenth century, as described by Reba Soffer, witnessed a general decline in student interest in the *Literae Humaniores*, that course of study so valued by Green. This decline came about largely as the result of challenges posed by an increasingly vocal and articulate group of modern historians. As Soffer argues, this new generation of Oxford historians questioned both the historical claims of the Classical scholars and their insistence that the *Literae Humaniores* was socially relevant.[67] As a result, Soffer maintains, the Classics curricu-lum came to be associated with developing "the character and mental habits of relatively idle gentleman" whereas modern history was now seen as that discipline most responsible for transforming "immature students into competent national leaders."[68]

On the other hand, as Michael Freeden explains, by the end of the nineteenth century, the social and political institutions established by Green and his colleagues had themselves changed significantly. They were no longer spheres wherein students put their recently acquired moral and

---

[66] Collini, *Liberalism and Sociology*, 45. At the height of the war, Hobhouse, for instance, still reserved almost all of his anti-idealist indignation for Bosanquet's interpretation of Hegel and seemed singularly unbothered by the fact that his hero, Green, had based much of his own thinking on Hegelian Spirit. [Hobhouse, *The Metaphysical Theory of the State*, 18, 22]. For more on Hobhouse's view of Green, see Peter Clarke, *Liberals and Social Dem-ocrats* (Cambridge: Cambridge University Press, 1978).

[67] This was a debate of which both Murray and Zimmern appear to have been painfully aware. For Murray, the tendency of the modern history department to teach Aristotle or other Greek works in translation threatened the existence of classical scholarship at in Brit-ain. In an essay on Greek translation that he wrote for the committee appointed by the prime minister to enquire into the position of the classics in the educational system of Great Britain between 1919 and 1921, Murray maintained "the absolute necessity of having a good Greek scholar to teach the class, or the advantage to the class itself, of having some elementary knowledge of Greek."[Bodl. MS Gilbert Murray (419) 59]. Similarly, Zimmern argued quite forcefully in a number of early lectures—almost as if he were under pressure from a history department that considered the study of ancient Greece too philosophical and abstract—that this was why "history and philosophy are grouped together in the Greats School."[Bodl. MZ Alfred Zimmern (135) 176].

[68] Reba Soffer, "Nation, Duty, Character and Confidence: History at Oxford, 1850–1914," *The Historical Journal* 30(1) (1987): 83.

political theory into action. Rather, institutions such as the Oxford Union, Toynbee Hall, and the WEA now embodied "an *emotional* atmosphere and motivation to study social problems" as opposed to providing "an intellectual justification and framework for social reform."[69] In other words, according to Freeden, the *content* of the Oxford *Literae Humaniores* (with its emphasis on idealist interpretations of Aristotle and Plato and its insistence that these interpretations were relevant to the modern world) was no longer as important to liberal student activists as the general environment of social reform that had grown up around it.

And yet in seeming contrast to both of these trends, Murray and Zimmern each took a stance on the social necessity of the *Literae Humaniores* that would remain consistent throughout their careers. Remarkably similar in their attitudes, both men ultimately developed an approach to the Greats curriculum more in harmony with the social philosophy of Jowett and Green than with the changing politics of turn-of-the-century Oxford. Both believed that only the course of study involved in the *Literae Humaniores* could provide Oxford students with the philosophical tools they needed to fathom the modern world in an ethical and ultimately spiritual way. Murray, for instance—who was largely responsible for organizing the yearly curriculum for the classics program through the 1920s and '30s—instructed his students in an introductory lecture to the program in 1931 that "when you read Aristotle's logic or ethics, you do not stop at making out criticizing Aristotle's theory; you also form, by the reading of modern philosophy and by discussion with your tutor and your contemporaries, your own logic and your own theory of conduct and politics."[70] Murray believed that through reading the classics in conjunction with modern thinkers, students developed autonomous means of interpreting moral and political life.

Similarly, for Zimmern, the *Literae Humaniores* offered students "a new kind of knowledge about man and the world."[71] At its heart, this was a spiritual, as opposed to instrumental or material, knowledge, and Zimmern maintained that as a pedagogical approach, the Greats curriculum provided a stark contrast to the amoral, anti-intellectual qualities of scientific inquiry. Thus, Zimmern noted in a 1905 lecture that the *Literae Humaniores* had more in common with Plato's notion of the "Eternal" than with "what Spencer would have us study; science as a Pandora bearing gifts for man, the Goddess of railroads, of malaria bacilli, of Channel

---

[69] Freeden, *The New Liberalism*, 17.

[70] Lecture, "Literature and History (probably 1931), Bodl. MS Gilbert Murray (418) fol. 179.

[71] Lecture, "Literae Humaniores" (undated: probably 1900–1905), Bodl. MS Alfred Zimmern (135) 180].

Tunnels, of sanitation."[72] Rather than passing on mere information, the study of classics taught students to be critical, moral thinkers. "How to use the intellect," Zimmern argued in this same lecture "is what we still have to learn from the Greeks and from the Greeks alone."[73]

Murray's and Zimmern's particular approaches to liberalism were constantly informed by a Classics curriculum emphasizing idealist (and for both men, this implied *spiritual*) interpretations of social and philosophical questions. In the final analysis, these political philosophies closely mirrored the conservative tendencies of a previous generation of Oxford liberals. Both Zimmern and Murray avoided the fates of Ritchie and Bosanquet, however, by quietly (and probably largely unconsciously) folding idealist concepts into their liberalism through their classical scholarship. In a very basic sense, the transcendent and dialectical power of Hegel's Spirit, as interpreted by the idealist liberals at Oxford, was still present in the work of these two scholars; it has simply been replaced by what Murray termed "the profound and permanent" message of Greece.[74]

The Spiritual Lessons of Greece

By the end of the nineteenth century, the study of ancient and classical Greece in the British academy was largely associated with idealist, Hegelian interpretations of classical texts. In the tradition of Jowett, Green, Caird, and others (a tradition by now institutionalized within the Oxford *Literae Humaniores*), this approach tended to imagine the study of classics in relation to the modern. Thus, the classical scholarship of many idealist liberals often reflected their beliefs about modern politics and society. Jowett, Green, Caird, and their coleagues read classical Greek texts in terms that championed community interests over individual desire and stressed the reconciliation of the individual with the social whole.[75] Many of these same theorists also viewed Hellenism itself as more than a static vision of community rooted in one particular ancient society. Rather, Hellenism was transcendent, always emerging, an efflorescing spirit discovered anew by each generation.[76] Murray's and Zimmern's classicism exhibited both of these qualities. Both took classical Greek, particularly

---

[72] Lecture "The Greeks and their Civilization" (June 20th 1905), Bodl. MS Alfred Zimmern (135) 65].

[73] Ibid., 99.

[74] Wilson, *Gilbert Murray OM*, 78.

[75] Frank Turner, "The Triumph of Idealism in Victorian Classical Studies," *Contesting Cultural Authority: Essays in Victorian Intellectual Life* (Cambridge: Cambridge University Press, 1993), 325.

[76] Turner, *The Greek Heritage in Victorian Britain*, 17.

Athenian, culture as a model of the kind of civic values lacking in contemporary society, and both imagined Greece in spiritual and eternal terms as human striving toward, in Murray's words, "free intellectual movement."[77]

For Murray and Zimmern, Periclean Athens illuminated the possibility for a greater, unfolding human perfection. Their Classical scholarship thus reflected an intellectual movement away from the work of earlier Classical scholars such as Grote who described life in the Athenian polis as irrational, and mired in superstition, religion, and mob mentality. For these thinkers, the trials of Socrates epitomized the triumph of Athenian superstition over rationalism and empiricism.[78] In contrast, the idealist-oriented Classicists of the late nineteenth century were decidedly more Hegelian in their attitude toward both Athens and Socrates. Thus, Hegel and many Oxford idealists read Socrates as a transitional figure whose appeals to individual reason and personal reflection were part of the more general "process" of "the turning of the spirit upon itself," away from the unreflective customs of ancient society toward a higher morality based on individual freedom and the immanent presence of the universal.[79] Socrates himself, however, did not embody this new morality in its entirety precisely because he repudiated some of the institutions that Hegel argued were intimately related to the development of the ideal state—namely, the family and religion. Hegel's attitude toward Socrates is thus somewhat ambiguous. He appreciates him as that individual who "took the first step toward finding the means of combining the concrete with the universal" but also argues that his rejection of the Athenian state rendered this first step "subjective and one-sided."[80]

Murray held a similar view of both Athenian culture and Socrates. In what Frank Turner describes as a reassertion of a "Hegelian contention," Murray's work on Greek literature described Socrates' death as a "true tragedy" as opposed to an outrage or a violation.[81] In so stating, Murray indicated his support for Socrates and the form of rationality he embodied, while simultaneously acknowledging the disruption he elicited from Athenian society. For Murray, Anytus was a truly sympathetic figure whose anger toward Socrates was, in some ways, justified given the expectations of Athenian culture. "Both men were noble," Murray argued,

---

[77] Murray, *The Five Stages of Greek Religion* (New York: Columbia Univeristy Press, 1925), 142.

[78] Turner, *The Greek Heritage in Victorian Britain*, 306.

[79] G.W.F. Hegel, *Lectures on the Philosophy of World History*, trans. H. B. Nisbet (Cambridge: Cambridge University Press, 1975 [1889]), 62.

[80] Ibid., 36ff.

[81] Turner, *The Greek Heritage in Victorian Britain*, 305; Murray, *A History of Ancient Greek Literature* (New York: Appleton, 1897), 177.

"both ready to die for their beliefs."[82] This idealist sympathy for the goals of community life is reflected throughout Murray's writings, particularly in his interpretation of Greek religion. Murray rejected the older, Grotian conclusion that if one accepted the legitimacy of Socrates' turn toward the individual and the rational, one must necessarily reject Athenian religion as mere superstition. For Murray, in contrast, the triumph of the Olympian Gods over older forms of worship in the fifth century implied, "for the higher minds of later Greece," not a rejection of individual rationality but, in much more Hegelian terms, a simultaneous awareness of one's individuality and of the greater truth that "is still to be pursued."[83] Murray claimed that the religious life of fifth-century Athens was indicative of a society in transition, a society whose spiritual and social practices gestured toward the possibility that the "inner light" of the individual and "higher ideals" of the polis could be reconciled.[84]

For Zimmern, the fifth-century Athenians had come closer than any subsequent society to reconciling individual autonomy and communal life. As he argued in his most famous work of classical scholarship, *The Greek Commonwealth*, in the Athenian polis, "Politics and Morality, the deepest and strongest forces of national and of individual life, had moved forward hand in hand toward a common ideal, the perfect citizen in the perfect state."[85] The genius of the polis, Zimmern argued, lay in its ability to instantiate this "common good" by eliciting a deep patriotism from its citizens while ensuring that individuals continued to use their reason independently. Zimmern also maintained that the Athenian household played an essential role in the life of the polis by providing its citizens with the nurturing environment wherein they first felt the nascent surge of patriotic love in the form of "one human being's natural relation to another." Once engaged in the public life of the community, however, these same citizens differentiated between these "deep seated moralities" and the "institutions which they or their lawgivers had recently devised."[86] In a manner strikingly reminiscent of Hegel's *Sittlichkeit*, Zimmern maintained that this structural understanding of distinct but interrelated spheres allowed Athenian citizens to distinguish between a primordial love for family and a rational, civic love for the community.

---

[82] Murray, *A History of Ancient Greek Literature*, 177.

[83] Murray, *The Five Stages of Greek Religion*, 100.

[84] Ibid., 98–101. For Murray, the emergence of the Olympian gods in Greek mythology represented a move away from superstition and toward a more universal awareness of human individuality. With the fall of Athens, according to Murray, one sees the disruption of this balance.

[85] Zimmern, *The Greek Commonwealth: Politics and Economics in Fifth-Century Athens*, 7th ed. (Oxford: Oxford University Press, 1961), 70, 482.

[86] Ibid., 72.

Murray and Zimmern also held similar views of Hellenism. Both men believed that ancient Greek society transcended itself, that the cultural, philosophical, and political tradition of Athenian life lived on as a kind of eternal world historical force. For neither man, however, did "eternal" imply stasis. Rather, the spirit of Hellenism was thoroughly mobile, constantly reasserting itself into the world each time a new generation discerned it through art, culture, or politics. At its heart, Murray insisted, the eternal qualities of Hellenism lay "more in a process than in a result, and [could] only be reached and enjoyed by somehow going through the process again."[87] Thus, he argued, all forms of progressive politics that challenged fixed prejudices were manifestations of a Hellenistic spirit. In stunning disregard for the centrality of the slave economy to Athenian life, Murray argued that neither the "slave driver" nor the "bloodthirsty hater of all outside his town or party" constituted Greek spirit. Rather, it was

> The movement which leads from all these to the Stoic or fifth century "sophist" who condemns and denies slavery, who has abolished all cruel superstitions and preaches some religion based on philosophy and humanity, who claims for women the same spiritual rights as for man, who looks on all human creatures as his brethren, and the world as "one great City of Gods and Men."[88]

In other words, the essence of Hellenism lay in its yearning toward "freedom and justice," two concepts, Murray argued, that were "actually realized to a remarkable degree in the best Greek communities."[89]

Zimmern's own appreciation of those "precious and permanent elements" in Greek culture centered on what he described as the "attitude of mind in which the Greek citizen approached political problems."[90] Again, for Zimmern this "attitude of mind" reconciled individualist and collectivist approaches to life in political society. The Athenian citizen was thus "both a Conservative and a Radical." He was conservative because "he reverenced tradition and recognized the power and value of custom."[91] At the same time, the Greek citizen was radical in his readiness "to apply his reason to public affairs without fear and prejudice." The brilliance of classical Greek thought, according to Zimmern, lay precisely in this ability to combine both communal and individualist instincts and thus to "see man as he is."[92] The Greeks were also unique, he argued, in

[87] Murray, "The Value of Greece to the Future of the World," *The Legacy of Greece*, ed. R.W. Livingston (Oxford: Oxford University Press, 1921), 6.

[88] Ibid., 15.

[89] Ibid., 21.

[90] Zimmern, "Political Thought," *The Legacy of Greece*, 325, 334.

[91] Ibid., 335, 336.

[92] Ibid., 338.

their ability to perceive their society "as a whole before the parts . . . setting the common before the sectional interests."

In sum, on a number of key points, Murray's and Zimmern's classical scholarship echoed the political concerns of the Oxford school. In a notably idealist manner, their work emphasized the reconciliation of individual reason and communal norms, praised what it saw as an anti-materialist Greek ethics, took a fairly conservative attitude toward social custom and institutions, and insisted that Hellenism lived on as progressive world spirit. In addition, their belief that the Athenian polis most closely approximated the perfect political community firmly placed Murray and Zimmern in the tradition established by Jowett, Green, and their immediate followers[93] This sympathy with the civic humanism of Athenian culture differentiated Murray and Zimmern from new liberals like Hobhouse who argued specifically against using an abstracted example of a slave economy as a model for modern conceptions of morality and politics.[94] While Murray's and Zimmern's interpretations of Athens tended to be more historically rooted and critical than their idealist predecessors' (Zimmern, for instance, spent a considerable amount of time discussing the political and economic implications of slavery), they remained committed, largely uncritical, fans of the polis throughout their careers.[95]

More importantly, Murray and Zimmern carried on in the tradition of their nineteenth-century Oxford counterparts by reading their liberalism through the classics. For both men, liberalism and Hellenism were virtually indistinguishable, a sentiment perhaps best expressed by Murray during the First World War. "I feel," said Murray, "that Greek and Peace and Liberalism and Idealism in general were all one, and all being threatened by the same enemy."[96] And yet despite Murray's trepidations, his own brand of liberalism weathered the war intact. In fact, both Murray's and Zimmern's Hellenistic liberalism remained remarkably consistent throughout the course of the war and in its aftermath. During the 1920s,

[93] Significantly, these thinkers often drew upon the same textual references to articulate their vision of Athens. For instance, both Bosanquet and Zimmern chose to interpret Athenian culture through a heavy reliance on Thucydides' account of Pedicles' funeral speech and his description of a citizenry whose "ideal of enjoyment," according to Zimmern, "was to do their duty to Athens." [Bodl. MS Zimmern (136) fol. 99; early lecture, "Thucydides the Imperialist"]. See Bosanquet's Introduction to *A Companion to Plato's Republic* (New York: Macmillan, 1895), 31–33.

[94] Hobhouse, *The Metaphysical Theory of the State*, 72.

[95] See Zimmern on slavery in both *The Greek Commonwealth* and "Was Greek Civilization based on Slave Labour." Zimmern argues that Athenian culture did rely on slaves but that the majority of them were what he termed "apprentices" who were "almost on equal terms with their masters." ["Was Greek Civilization," 162]. For more on Murray and Hellenism see *The Five Stages of Greek Religion*, 140–43].

[96] West, *Gilbert Murray: A Life*, 156.

when many liberals were drawn to the more straightforward and critical approach of Labour to political and economic reform, Murray and Zimmern continued to hold fast to a spiritual liberalism rooted in the idea that—according to Toynbee's description of Zimmern's political theory—Greece must have "practical significance" for the modern world.[97] In fact, by 1931 Zimmern was still characterizing the project of internationalism as a choice between "Hellinization" or a "return to the dark ages."[98]

Hellenism, Statehood, and the Liberal Social Order

Throughout their careers, both Murray and Zimmern held fast to the conviction that classical Greek scholars, not Locke or Mill, had invented liberalism, or at least had invented the notion of "freedom," which they termed most appropriately liberal. The word "*Liberalis*," Murray argued in 1938, was "a Roman idea, derived from the Greek."[99] Liberality, or freedom, in this supposedly Greek sense, insisted that individual fulfillment required more than self-interest. Rather, human beings were only free when they were both invested in the spiritual life of the community and working for the good of others, when they participated in the public religion of the polis and actively lived out their duties toward their fellow citizens. The relationship of the modern state to this more spiritually conceived notion of freedom and community, however, drove both thinkers to deeply conflicted approaches toward state power. And yet from these interstices in their political philosophies—those largely untheorized gaps between liberal and idealist understandings of statehood—did Murray's and Zimmern's trademark approach to liberal politics emerge, a politics that, in the final analysis, did not look very liberal at all.

Two basic philosophical trends, which they attributed to the Greeks, helped distinguish Murray's and Zimmern's politics from the liberal orthodoxy of the Manchester school and from the more distinctly individualist (and simultaneously more socialist) new liberalism of the Edwardian era. First, both men consistently linked liberalism with a notion of universal spirituality that stood in contrast to the materialism of the modern world. Second, both men stressed the importance of communal values and social institutions in the process of actualizing this liberal spirit.

Their belief that liberalism was more than a political theory but rather a spiritual and moral force at work in the world, played a central role in both Murray's and Zimmern's political philosophies throughout the

[97] Toynbee, *Acquaintances*, 49.
[98] Zimmern, *The Study of International Relations*, 19.
[99] Murray, *Liberality and Civilization* (New York: Macmillan, 1938), 18.

course of their careers. In an early speech, "Liberalism Old and New," given at the Russell Club at Oxford in 1888, Murray argued that this spirit of self-sacrifice, a "spirit unique in the whole of history" best characterized the approach of "Liberal England" to the rest of the world.[100] Liberalism was, according to Zimmern, a "political religion" for whom "spiritual forces are the centre of life; and the supreme aim is the application of moral and spiritual principles both to politics and to industry."[101] During the war, both men often contrasted the spiritual properties of British liberalism with the chaotic, materialist dispositions of Bolshevism and Prussianism. For Murray, liberalism in Britain embodied a form of rational human existence distinct from the "the spirit that I have called Satanism, the spirit of unmixed hatred towards the existing World Order, the spirit which rejoices in any widespread disaster."[102] For Zimmern, spiritualism provided solace to a liberal faith in crisis. As he observed in 1916, "No thinking man can live through such a time as this and preserve his faith unless he is sustained by the belief that the clash of States which is darkening our generation is not a mere blind collision of forces, but has spiritual bearings which affect each individual living soul born or to be born in the world."[103] Twenty years later, as yet another war lurked ominously on the horizon, Murray once again laid his hopes for the future on the continuing existence of "Liberality as a living spirit."[104]

A number of strikingly *illiberal* (or pre-liberal) features characterized this living spirit for both Murray and Zimmern: community concern, anti-materialism, self-sacrifice, and duty. For Zimmern, the spirit that was liberalism entailed a "particular and highly specialized form of unselfishness," an ability to think beyond one's individual concerns toward the good of all.[105] In this sense, both Murray and Zimmern were vocal in their dissention from orthodox liberalism's exclusive focus on the individual and individual rights. True liberalism, according to Murray, was "only individualist in the sense of insisting, in the last resort, each man must

---

[100] Bodl. MS Gilbert Murray (489) fol. 12. Murray's tendency to ignore both the violence of British imperialism and the complicity of the Liberal government in that violence was a trend that would resurface again and again in his political works, even after he became disillusioned with many of the "liberal imperialists" during the Boer War. Indeed, both Murray and Zimmern's notions of the empire as a moral, spiritually inspired entity would sharply differentiate their notions of international order from more explicitly anti-imperial new liberals like Hobson.

[101] Zimmern, *Nationality and Government*, xix.

[102] Murray, *Satanism and The World Order* (London: George Allen and Unwin, 1920), 33.

[103] Zimmern, "Progress in Government," 187.

[104] Murray, *Liberality and Civilization*, 83.

[105] Zimmern, "The Things of Martha and the Things of Mary," *America and Europe and Other Essays* (New York: Oxford University Press, 1929), 16.

maintain his personal freedom, must obey his own conscience and not be content to be merely an item in the multitude."[106] In normal life (not, that is, "in the last resort") true freedom could be found in what Murray insisted were the liberal values of cooperation, charity, and self sacrifice.

At the same time, their liberalism implied a particular understanding of freedom, a notion that wed traditionally negative, liberal concerns such as freedom of speech, freedom of movement, and freedom of trade with a more idealistically inclined, positive understanding of freedom as the fulfillment of one's duty. According to both Murray and Zimmern, the reconciliation of these two types of freedom was only possible for individuals who inhabited a society that closely approximated the polis, a community united by a common moral and political vision and close social bonds. For Zimmern, "fellowship and freedom" were not incompatible terms: "They are complementary; and each can only be at its best when sustained by the other."[107] Murray concurred when he argued in 1934 that "freedom is not only compatible with a good life; it is the necessary condition of good life."[108] The "good life" itself he defined in the classic Aristotelian sense as a life "lived well," that is, a life lived within a polis that had developed "all the complicated arts and laws, moral and social and economic, which go to the making of a good and progressive society."[109]

For Murray, the term that best described the actualized liberal spirit of freedom through community—the lived essence of *liberalis*—was the Greek conception of the "One Great City of Men and Gods."[110] One of the most consistent motifs in Murray's writings, the City of Men and Gods implied a social world perfectly in tune with spirit, a world in which individuals lived out their lives in complete freedom, working toward the fulfillment of both their own potential and the potential of the community, all the while guided by a higher reason, imminent in Men and eminent in Gods. To create a true moral order, one must leaven freedom with the divine, with "something higher in the world than men as now known to them; there must be those ideals and inspirations, that 'something not ourselves making for righteousness,' for which the ancients used their inadequate word. . . . 'Gods.' "[111] The word Murray used, of course, was liberalism.

---

[106] Murray, *Liberality and Civilization*, 16.

[107] Zimmern, *Nationality and Government*, 14.

[108] Murray, "The Cult of Violence ," *From the League to the U.N.* (Westport: Greenwood Press, 1988 [1934]), 60.

[109] Murray, *Liberality and Civilization*, 20.

[110] Murray, "The Cult of Violence," 60.

[111] Murray, *Liberality and Civilization*, 44.

In a modern context, the issue of where exactly to situate this City of Men and Gods in the world was a source of considerable tension within both men's political theories. Were the integuments of this city coextensive with the modern state, with all of its scientific, rational, and coercive tools? Or did they reside somewhere else—in a social world distinct from the state itself? What one sees in Murray's and Zimmern's writings is more than a reluctance to imbue the modern state with the moral qualities they associated with the polis; one also sees a liberal fear of the state itself and, in particular, an ambivalence regarding the role of the state in regulating the economy. Thus, Murray and Zimmern both clearly wrestled with many of the same opposing theoretical forces that an earlier generation of Oxford liberals had struggled to weave together: how does one combine an idealist appreciation for community values with a liberal unease with state power? How does one call into question orthodox liberalisms' commitment to an economic "harmony of interests" and still maintain that the Aristotelian principle of the "good life" can be realized through a relatively unregulated system of free trade? Like their intellectual progenitors, Murray's and Zimmern's writings on the subject are some of their weakest, and at the same time, most illuminating.

As critics of orthodox liberalism, both men were openly skeptical of its assertion that social good—indeed, society itself—would come about naturally as a product of individual self-interest. They each dismissed the "harmony of interests" doctrine as convenient (in Murray's words, a "dash of humbug") inherited from an earlier era, a nineteenth-century, industrial fantasy rooted in a base materialism no longer appropriate for the world.[112] "We all know that this reasoning so crudely and confidently set forth in the speeches and writing of Cobden proved to be quite unfounded. It was based on a false theory of human nature and society," argued Zimmern.[113] Apostles of the Manchester school, Zimmern continued, radically misinterpreted human nature by confusing "economic man" with "man." "Economics is not the sole of life," posited Zimmern during the Great War. Indeed, to interpret human history as economically driven was to "deny its spiritual meaning," that is, to deny the spirit of community that connected members of the modern polis to one another.[114] Likewise, Zimmern maintained, orthodox liberals wrongly assumed that the self-interested activity of economically minded individuals would bring society itself—"this republic, this realm of law"—into existence. Rather, Zimmern maintained that Smith's theory of enlightened

---

[112] Ibid., 33.

[113] Alfred Zimmern, "The Problem of Collective Security," *Neutrality and Collective Security*, ed. Quincy Wright (Chicago: 1936), 40.

[114] Zimmern, "Progress in Industry," *Progress and History*, 190.

self-interest required the *preexistence* of a stable, functioning society "within which economic activity could be carried on and thus be effectively safe-guarded against abuses within or interference form outside."[115] Social cohesion thus predated economic activity rather than emerging from it.

Murray and Zimmern also dismissed nineteenth-century economic liberalism's conviction that the state had no potential role to play in creating the conditions necessary for a moral community. They were well aware that to foster the kind of liberal sensibilities that they valued—community thinking, self sacrifice, intellectual engagement—want within society had to be eradicated. True liberalism was only possible, argued Murray, when an individual was "free from the pressure of daily hunger and thirst. . . . Free to do the things he really wants to do instead of merely what he must do in order to keep alive," and the state was obligated to bring about this general economic uplifting toward the "good life."[116] Nineteenth-century free-traders were wrong to assume that a completely unregulated economy would result in greater social good. When "the political sovereign during the interlude of liberal supremacy tacitly abdicated his control over the economic function," Zimmern maintained in 1934, the "generalizations" of the "Cambridge exponents" were allowed to steer the economy, resulting in massive economic disparity and widespread poverty.[117]

But while both Murray and Zimmern clearly believed that the state had some role to play in the developing industrial economy, they were less clear about *who* that state was and *what* its intervention might look like. In fact, a rather elliptical quality characterizes their political writings on the state. The idea of state drops in and out of their concern about the social good and looks remarkably different in different contexts: at one moment an extension of community, intimately involved in the upkeep of the "good life"; in the next, an aggressive power prone to authoritarian ranting, standing outside of the polis, menacing its frightened inhabitants.

Murray, for instance, was clearly uncomfortable using the word "state" much at all. In most of his political writings, Murray substituted words like polis, society, and common good, when discussing British domestic and economic issues. He clearly associated the word "state" with international sovereignty issues on the one hand and domestic coercion on the other. States primarily appear in Murray's writings as external, oppressive agents, frequently anthropomorphized into cunning, volatile bullies who command the "slavish" obedience of the Germans and the Japanese

---

[115] Zimmern, "The Problem of Collective Security," 40.

[116] Murray, "Liberality and Civilization," 25.

[117] Zimmern, *Quo Vadimus? A Public Lecture Delivered on 5 February 1934* (Oxford: Oxford University Press, 1934), 24–25.

(never the British) and who have a tendency toward irrational violence.[118] In a domestic context, Murray frequently referred to the state as government alone, a bureaucratic collection of institutions prone to changing its mind independent of the needs of the community.[119] His hesitant writings on the subject clearly reveal that for Murray "the state" never equaled "the public." In other words, the state itself, in liberal terms, provides security for—and sometimes stands in opposition to—the common good, the polis, the Great City of Men and Gods. The two are never homologous in Murray's writings. Rather, they repel each other like two negatively charged magnets, coming close but never quite cohering, and Murray makes little effort to make them speak to one another or to reconcile his own understanding of the differences between the two. The rush of his prose as he paints for us a picture of life in the polis reads almost like a willful act of avoidance, as if Murray felt focusing on *social* welfare would allow him to ignore the state—with its prickly issues of material power—altogether.

Zimmern's writings tend to spend more time thinking through (not always coherently) the qualities and characteristics of statehood. States, for Zimmern, were communities of individuals united by law, brought into existence for reasons of security, and continuing to exist "for purposes of beneficence," an idea he borrowed from Aristotle.[120] In much of Zimmern's work, the state was closely aligned with the good of the whole, more clearly in a position, as the "political sovereign," to confront capital and keep the previously unfettered selfishness of British industry in check in the name of "beneficence," or what Zimmern referred to as "community housekeeping."[121] But the term "housekeeping" itself, which appears with great regularity in Zimmern's writings, works two ways in his political philosophy. At times, is appears to mean a kind of general extension of state good to community good: the state engages in the kinds of policy work that make communal living possible. At other times, however, "housekeeping" seems to imply a kind of radical disjuncture between the agent who keeps house and the more intimate notion of home. What Zimmern calls "state housekeeping" in this context looks very different from more natural, authentic, and ultimately spiritual operations of the social.[122] In his 1929 essay "The Things of Martha and the Things of Mary," for instance, Zimmern makes a clear distinction between the spiri-

---

[118] Murray, "The Cult of Violence," 60.

[119] This characterization tends to surface most frequently throughout Murray's voluminous works on League policy in Britain wherein he chides the British state for its refusal to enact the people's will.

[120] Bodl. MS Alfred Zimmern (136) fol. 12 ("The Seven Deadly Sins of Tariff Reform").

[121] Zimmern, "Progress in Industry," 192.

[122] Zimmern, "The Things of Martha and the Things of Mary," 25.

tual life of the community (the world of Mary as she sits dreamily at the savior's feet) and the technical, rational world of state policy making (Martha's flurry of activity as she makes her guest comfortable). Martha's world may be necessary, according to Zimmern, but the things of Mary are spiritually superior.

Thus, the idea of the state in Zimmern's political philosophy, as in Murray's, is conflicted. At times, the state seems a moral extension of the polis, a people's sovereign whose job it is to regulate the economy in the name of the "good life." At other times, Zimmern clearly views the state in rational, technical terms as a kind of overblown housekeeper who merely makes life comfortable for society's more authentic inhabitants. Indeed, Zimmern's works reveal a simultaneous inclination to see the state as not only technically distant from the social whole but potentially dangerous, driven by an ineluctable desire to centralize its power. In this way, Zimmern cast a wary eye toward the increasingly bureaucratic and centralized British state, a state that took the scientific principles of the industrial revolution as its core ideology. In one early essay, probably written between 1900 and 1905, Zimmern argued that the "application of scientific" invention by the state (namely, public education) had had a destructive effect on the "spiritual and material" conditions of community life. It severed the old feudal ties and replaced them with state power. More importantly, for Zimmern, it undercut the socializing potential of the family. "Never before," he maintained, "has the State stepped in to relieve parents from the task of preparing their offspring for the battle of life."[123]

Two concerns drove Zimmern to focus on the family in this instance. First, Zimmern was developing a symbolic connection between the family and the more truly intimate realm of the social, the realm of Mary. This connection would become increasingly important to Zimmern as he developed his theory of internationalism. The state, in Zimmern's example, unsettled life in community by disrupting this intimacy, by breaking the bond between parent and child. Second, his concern with state intervention in the "battle of life" suggests that, like Bosanquet, Ritchie, and other idealist liberals, Zimmern was wary of the state's role in raising unfit individuals above their natural station. In this sense, Zimmern seemed to feel quite strongly that there was something necessarily artificial about a state taking on the educative role of the family, not because life was better in traditional society but because life was *supposed* to be competitive, a battle, in which only the fit survive. This somewhat jarring interpolation of the language of Social Darwinism into the gentle prose Zimmern reserved primarily to discuss life in community was not, in fact, that unusual. Rather, Zimmern often variegated his writings with conflicted

---

[123] Bodl. MS Alfred Zimmern (136) fol. 135–36.

visions of the political world and the common good, visions that ran parallel to each other in a largely unarticulated way. The idea of life as a gritty battle for success from which the state must steer clear became yet another of the many conflicting undercurrents that wound their way through Zimmern's political philosophy, existing alongside his often simultaneous calls for an enlarged welfare state.

The antinomy between these themes—between life as a "good" and life as a "battle"—suggests much about Zimmern's ambivalent attitude toward the state. At times, Zimmern's notion of statehood was remarkably liberal (in the most orthodox of senses), while at other times he infused it with a highly idealist form of social morality. Indeed, Zimmern's writings on the state—like those of the idealist liberals who came before him—reek with philosophical anxiety and are frequently examples of his worst writing, as if he felt he could fill in the gap between his own conflicted ideologies with verbiage. For instance, by 1936 Zimmern was still struggling to differentiate the state from a "social group." A social group, Zimmern argued, was governed by a variety of unspoken and unwritten rules. A state, on the other hand, was governed by the rule of law. Zimmern goes on to ask:

> Whence does a law derive the authority which causes men to regard it as overriding other rules which are equally a part of the normal functioning of their social group? Wherein resides this peculiar claim to obedience? It is due to its connection with one particular society or form of social grouping, 'the most authoritative and all-embracing of all.' That grouping is, of course, as the familiar words quoted from Aristotle will already have made clear, the political society, that which, since the end of the Middle Ages, we moderns know as 'the state.' Montesquieu, in his neat and penetrating French way, defined the state as 'a society where there are laws.' Putting his definition together with the definition of law at which we arrived through Aristotle, we may define the state as *a society with overriding rules.* Or we can express the matter more simply by calling it a *realm of law.*[124]

Zimmern's writing here is quintessentially tautological: what makes individuals in a society obey laws? The existence of state. And what is a state? A society with laws. What the state is *in itself* (a representative of the people, a reflection of social norms, a coercive body able to enforce law) remains curiously blank, sandwiched somewhere between Montesquieu and Aristotle. This example demonstrates that, in the tradition of the idealist liberals, Zimmern wanted it both ways: he wanted a political theory that could speak the language of social cohesion but still preserve some kind of liberal commitment to a state-free "battle of life," a society

[124] Zimmern, "The Problem of Collective Security," 14–15.

bound by the social links of tradition and a society framed by the much less personal (and much more state-like) rule of law.

In sum, both Murray's and Zimmern's ideas about the state and its relationship to the social whole hovered somewhere between idealism and orthodox liberalism, and thus echoed the similar conflict experienced by an earlier generation of Oxford liberals. Their writings on statehood, however, often seemed even *more* conflicted than those of their intellectual predecessors for two historical reasons. First, after 1914 the experiences of World War One pushed many liberals in England toward a more general wariness of state control, both with regard to jailing of pacifists by Asquith during the war and as a reflection of their increased anti-Germanism. During the war, the idea of state authoritarianism became wedded most firmly to Prussianism in popular discourse. And Murray's and Zimmern's works both reflect this new unease with state power. While in his early works Murray seemed willing to discuss state interference as a necessary component of the new liberalism, most of his writings after the war tend to shy away from the idea altogether.[125] Zimmern's attitude toward the state was also more decidedly idealist before 1914. In an essay on "Progress in Government" written before the war (but published in 1916), Zimmern argued in Greenian terms that the state could harbor within it certain spiritual issues.[126] By 1918, however, he was more openly critical of the state, particularly the German state, arguing that Germany's despotic state culture, with its "elaborate control and direction from above, dislikes the free play of human groupings, and discourages all spontaneous or unauthorized associations."[127]

At the same time, unlike their nineteenth-century predecessors, Murray and Zimmern were witness to the emergence of an actually functioning socialist state in 1917, one produced not through liberal reformism but through a revolution as committed to the destruction of liberal society and its economic base as to Czarist oligarchy. And it was willing to use state power to achieve these goals. Thus, through decrees depriving landowners of their property, massive political reform, cultural campaigns, and the creation of new legal codes requiring the economic and political equality of women, the Soviets demonstrated how a people's state could use its power to transform liberal society. And this made many liberals throughout Europe extremely nervous. It made Murray and Zimmern much more critical of state power on all levels than either their nineteenth-century progenitors or their own pre-war writings had been.

In addition, Murray and Zimmern were both acutely aware that they had a tremendous stake in both the preservation of liberal culture and,

[125] Bodl. MS Gilbert Murray (489) fol. 4 ("Liberalism Old And New," 1888).
[126] Zimmern, "Progress in Government," 188.
[127] Zimmern, *Nationality and Government*, 13.

ironically, the putatively pre-liberal class system that preceded it. As intellectuals, both men acknowledged that theirs was a privileged position, and used a logic based in both Greek and liberal understandings of the world to justify it. In Aristotelian terms, for instance, Murray often argued that the world needed more thinkers, more people with the leisure time to conceive of the greater things in life. One of the problems with the modern world, he grumbled in 1938, was the lack of leisure, "that fruitful and untroubled leisure from which spring the great advances of human thought."[128] The problem with socialism, according to Murray, was that it brought everyone down to the same base level of existence, where it became impossible to envision the good life for anyone. And yet Murray described that level of existence in liberal terms: it was naturally home to people who were lazy and shiftless, those whom liberal ideology has always portrayed as beyond redemption. "The Bolshevik remedy was very direct and simple," argued Murray:

> It was to disarm everybody who had any share in prosperity, and distribute firearms to those who had nothing else. Only when he was armed and the rest of the of the people unarmed could the real proletarian—the man who had no savings, no talent, no education, no notable good qualities, nothing that makes for success in life—hope to beat the man who always outstripped him.[129]

Thus, just as the state's intervention in the family and the economy on a domestic level could potentially raise the unfit to an artificially higher status, so too did socialism champion precisely those individuals who were least able to govern. The results were chaos, class warfare, and the dissolution of the "fundamental institutions of society."[130]

Beyond the Bolshevik Revolution, Murray's and Zimmern's liberalisms also felt the effects of domestic political change. The war was a time of unprecedented organization by working class movements in Britain, beginning with syndicalist activity in the early teens and ending with the successful passage of the Munitions Act in 1918, which required employers to recognize unions.[131] And, after the expansion of the franchise in

---

[128] Murray, *Liberality and Civilization*, 28.

[129] Murray, *The Problem of Foreign Policy* (Boston: Houghton Mifflin, 1921), 85.

[130] Ibid., 92.

[131] According to historian Keith Laybourn, British syndicalism was deeply influenced by American socialism of the early twentieth century, particularly by the Industrial Workers of the World and their notion of the "General Strike." [Keith Laybourn, *A History of British Trade Unionism: 1770–1990* (London: Alan Sutton, 1992), 100; James Hinton, *Labour and Socialism: A History of the British Labour Movement, 1867–1947* (Amherst: University of Massachusetts Press, 1983), 98]. While the first great General Strike of twentieth-century Britain did not occur until 1926, the years between 1910 and 1914 saw an extraordinary amount of industrial conflict and strike activity by miners, dockers, railway workers, and other laborers. [Laybourn, *A History of British Trade Unionism*, 100].

1918, the Labour Party began its rapid ascendance into British parliamentary politics, matched only by the equally meteoric decline of the Liberals, the party to which both Murray and Zimmern had been devoted since Oxford.[132] For the most part, the Labour Party steered clear of more radical calls for an overhaul of the capitalist system.[133] Despite James Hinton's assertion that Labour was "committed, on paper at least, to the common ownership of the means of production," other historians, such as Isaac Kramnick and Barry Sheerman, have argued that one of the most striking characteristics of British socialism was precisely its "relative absence of Marxist influence."[134] And yet despite this relatively mild approach to social reform, Murray and Zimmern both tended to view the Labour Party and organized working-class politics in general as a revolutionary threat to both their liberal politics and their ways of life.

For years the Liberals had been by default *the* progressive voice in British politics. As both liberal theorists and liberal activists, Murray and Zimmern were used to seeing themselves as politically progressive, as proponents of a world vision that claimed to *transcend* class and, as Murray declared in 1926, to speak to the universal interests of the "whole community."[135] They argued that the class politics of the Labour Party threatened to infect the transcendent spirit of social reformism associated with British liberalism. For both Murray and Zimmern, progressive politics were supposed to be about the "eternal things which unite, to the rock bottom level of our common humanity," not about class.[136] Indeed, Murray bristled at

[132] During the late 1910s and '20s, the Labour Party dramatically increased its membership. By the general election of 1922 it had taken over 142 seats in parliament. [Philips, *The Rise of the Labour Party*, ix].

[133] The war years also witnessed the organization of other leftist parties in Britain including the Socialist Labour Party, the British Socialist Party, and the Communist Party of Great Britain; the latter drew explicitly upon the experience of the Russian revolution in fashioning itself as an "agency for the overthrow of capitalism." [Hinton, *Labour and Socialism*, 116; Brand, *The British Labour Party*, 35].

[134] Isaac Kramnick and Barry Sheerman, *Harold Laski: A Life on the Left* (New York: Penguin Press, 1993), 157. Instead, the Labour Party and the socialist movement in general were influenced more by the "ethical socialism" of the Fabians who had a direct and somewhat disproportionate impact relative to their members on the Labour Party during the 1920s. [Kramnick and Sheerman, *Harold Laski*, 157; Brand, *The British Labour Party*, 57]. Fabian political thought—which was particularly apparent in the Labour's 1918 policy statement, *Labour and the New Social Order*—tended to favor democratic, parliamentary control of industry rather than worker ownership and placed a heavy emphasis on industrial efficiency and the development of the nation's resources for the common good. Historians have largely regarded even the General Strike of 1926 not as an attempt by the working class to overthrow the capitalist system but as a gesture of sympathy with the miners in their fight against a wage reduction. [Laybourn, *A History of British Trade Unionism*, 139; Kramnick and Sheerman, *Harold Laski*, 241].

[135] Murray, "What Liberalism Stands For," *The Contemporary Review* 128 (1925): 694.

[136] Zimmern, *Nationality and Government*, 62.

the suggestion that liberalism itself was merely the ideological manifestation of bourgeois interest and blamed such a misrepresentation on the materialist agenda of the socialists. "Such an idea could never have arisen except through the influence of what is perhaps the greatest and most infectious of all the fallacies of Karl Marx, the theory that all human action, or at any rate all collective action, is based on the pursuit of direct material interest."[137]

Thus, in reaction to what they viewed as an assault on their vision of the political good, after the war Murray and Zimmern retreated into an increasingly spiritualized and esoteric understanding of both liberalism and its relationship to the state.[138] Where their nineteenth-century progenitors had used the term "socialism" itself in a fairly sympathetic fashion (Bosanquet, for instance, had used the word to describe a simply more socially oriented economy), Murray and Zimmern could now only imagine it as "a lewd, crude and brutal form" of economic appeal, what Murray described as one of the "satanic" forces wreaking mischief in the post war world.[139] "To Socialism," Zimmern opined in 1918, "economics is the centre of life, and the conquest of wealth and power by the oppressed class the supreme aim."[140]

And yet, as much as Murray's and Zimmern's liberalisms rejected the material in favor of the spiritual, there was a deeply intramundane quality to their political theories. Their shared notion of freedom conditioned by duty required actualization in the concrete institutions of the polis, in the One Great City of Men and Gods brought to earth. But now, more than ever, this "City" could not be the state: following the war both men increasingly associated state power with Bolshevism, with socialism, with Prussianism, with authoritarianism, with class politics, with party politics, with materialism. In all ways the state had become the antithesis of the political community both Murray and Zimmern felt was necessary for the "living spirit of liberality" to manifest itself in the world. And yet despite the increasingly shrill tone of their anti-statism (not to mention their anti-Germanism, and their anti-Socialism), Murray and Zimmern did not, like many of their new liberal contemporaries, throw the idealist baby out with the liberal bathwater and turn their backs on the spiritual heritage of the *Literae Humaniores*. Rather than rejecting the metaphysical altogether, Zimmern and Murray made a strikingly similar philosophi-

---

[137] Murray, *Liberality and Civilization*, 32.

[138] Zimmern did have a brief and short lived association with the Labour party in the early 1920s.

[139] Zimmern, *League of Nations and the Rule of Law*, 200; Murray, *Satanism and The World Order*.

[140] Zimmern, *Nationality and Government*, xix.

cal move to that of an earlier generation of Oxford liberals. Just as Bosanquet and Ritchie's had once turned toward the social and the organic to
compensate for a never fully worked through theory of state power, so
did Murray and Zimmern cast their eyes about for some place else to
locate the Great City of Men and Gods, eventually settling on what Murray termed the "fundamental institutions of society."

Murray and Zimmern believed that the intimacy and order of life in
society protected the spiritual community they believed best fostered
liberal values from the always potentially authoritarian state. Accord-
ingly, they argued, both local and national (and later international) communities were uniquely able to supply individuals with the meaning,
context, and spiritual well-being necessary for them to become moral
actors in the world, to truly live out the meaning of liberal freedom.
Informal, traditional, non-state structured societies were perfect in this
regard because they situated individuals within an interrelated network
of families, classes, and institutions that led naturally to feelings of fraternal cohesion. Thus, members of well-structured nations and traditional societies, Zimmern maintained, necessarily understood themselves
first in terms of "corporate life, corporate growth, and corporate self
respect."[141] Likewise, for Murray, there was something wrong with contemporary society's assumption that "each man should be a masterless,
unattached, and independent being."[142] For both men, liberal freedom
demanded the kind of interdependence found within traditional forms of
social relationships.

Thus, in a manner similar to Green's and his followers' rejection of
orthodox liberalism's attempt to wrest the individual from their social
world, so too did Murray and Zimmern deny the polarized division between the individual and the community, between politics and society,
and between freedom and fraternity. And yet just as a similar focus on
communal values and social institutions (such as the family) had driven
thinkers like Ritchie to embrace a vision of the good based on social hierarchy rather than on liberal individualism, so too did Murray's and Zimmern's liberalisms begin to sound distinctly pre-liberal in their blatant
longing not only for social order but for the social order of the past. Murray was, of course, particularly fond of the Greek example. Thus, he argued that the Greeks had been the first to correctly articulate a notion of
human society that "was not a chaos of warring interests but a Cosmos,
an ordered whole, in which every individual had his due share both of

---

[141] Ibid., 65.
[142] Murray, *Satanism and World Order*, 40.

privilege and of service."[143] Similarly, Zimmern maintained that modern society must "be able to see politics as part of life before we can see it steadily and see it whole. We must be able to see it in relation to the general ordering of the world and to connect in once more, as in the Middle Ages, with religion and morality."[144] For both men, the possibility of transformation, of reforming the disintegrating individualism of the modern world, was based on the fundamental idea of return, on an application of Greek, medieval, and traditional virtues to contemporary politics. "It is only by a swing of the pendulum back to the medieval idea of Order," Zimmern thus argued, "by putting the life of the community in front of the good life of private individuals and groups, that a way can be found out of our perplexities."[145]

Zimmern's almost bizarre desideratum to return to the medieval body politic two hundred years after the triumph of liberalism was made even more jarring by the fact that he seemed singularly unbothered by the basic hierarchical assumptions at the very heart of this worldview, a view predicated on fixed ideas of social status and station from which individuals never progressed. Likewise, Murray appeared similarly untroubled by the implicit hierarchies of Greek society. In essence, as Murray and Zimmern became more committed to the idea of social order, they appeared to become less committed to the basic liberal idea of equality. Indeed, Murray argued in 1925 that socialism was driving the "less fit" of the country to embrace selfish "slogans" such as "the principle of universal human equality—which is a false and almost nonsensical piece of metaphysics, some approximation to which is likely to do good."[146] Like Ritchie's "abstract principle," the notion of equality ultimately lost its foundational cohesion in Murray's liberalism only to be replaced by an "approximation" whose no longer universal existence could be trumped by the need for order.[147]

At times, Zimmern's exaltation of the social order sounded even closer to a Burkean rant than any of his idealist liberal forebears would have been comfortable with, particularly in its wistful odes to British class culture. For example, Zimmern argued during the war that observers from other national communities were incapable of comprehending the relationship between classes in England without a right understanding of English traditions. "No one," he argued, "can understand England who does not know about the most English things in England." He continued,

[143] Murray, *Liberality and Civilization*, 44.
[144] Zimmern, *Progress and Industry*, 167.
[145] Zimmern, *Quo Vadimus?* 25.
[146] Murray, "What Liberalism Stands For," 694.
[147] Murray, *Satanism and World Order*, 40.

I mean such national institutions as the Cup Tie, the Royal Family (other nations have a monarchy, but the connation between our Royal Family and the
middle class is unique), the Nonconformist Conscience, the Derby, Mr. Horatio
Bottomley, bacon and eggs, Punch, the South Eastern Railway, the vested interest known as the Trade, and the universally recognized distinction between
mere man and gentleman.[148]

In overtly conservative tones, Zimmern argued that knowing Britons was
impossible without understanding the cultural institutions and traditions
that both shaped their relationships to one another, and, in the case of
the distinction between "man and gentleman," constituted their shared
understanding of life. Class conflict, he maintained, was a foreign impor-
tation, born out of a Continental tradition of establishing "social gulfs"
between workers, landowners, and the bourgeoisie. In England, by contrast, a shared sense of values had led to the establishment of a kind of
spontaneous social order based on universal conceptions of right conduct. Rigid notions of human equality were not necessary in a society
in which classes understood their relationship to one another through
tradition.[149]

It was through such cultural and social institutions and *not* the state,
Zimmern also argued on several occasions, that the economic structures
to improve the overall welfare of the community ought to be situated.
Thus, for Zimmern, the quintessence of liberal freedom lay in the resolution of individuality and fraternity through community. The health of
the community itself thus necessitated that economic activity not be
carried out in the name of individual greed. Rather, "every trade industry
is, or ought to be, serving a public need. That indeed is the only justification for their existence."[150] The only way to bring about this kind of spiritual connection between the economic realm and the public good was,
once again, through a return to a pre-liberal understanding of community,
in which each person was situated in relationship to other members of
the social whole. Only when the economic individual felt that his work
was "fulfilling a social purpose," argued Zimmern, would he experience
"something of the dignity, the independence, and the happiness which he
enjoyed in the days before the division of labor."[151] One could recreate
this corporate approach to the economy not by centralizing economic
power in the state but by diffusing "responsibility and initiative as widely

---

[148] Bodl. MS Alfred Zimmern (136) fol. 24.

[149] Ibid., 25.

[150] Zimmern, *The Reorganization of Industry: Papers by Professor A. C. Pigou, Arthur
Greenwood, Sidney Webb, A. E. Zimmern* (London: Active Printing Society Limited,
1916), 65.

[151] Ibid., 54.

as possible among the citizen body, amongst local authorities, occupational groups, voluntary associations, and private individuals."[152] But Zimmern was stunningly silent on the specifics of *how* this kind of informal, voluntary form of moral economy was to be reestablished in the absence of the state.

In the end, in this example and in others, a radical disconnect separates Zimmern's assertions that the ideal welfare state should be founded on the kind of community ties and social understandings that he associated with "the days before the division of labor" and his liberal reluctance to call into question the economic practices of capitalism that necessitated this division of labor in the first place. For Zimmern, political ideologies that questioned these practices by suggesting radical changes in property ownership were always motivated by a crass materialism. Socialism, Zimmern argued, was just the most insidious of the modern, materialistic forces set upon destroying the individual's sense of corporate duty; socialism "appealed to man as a worker and ignored him as a citizen."[153] True economic reform must be grounded neither in the state nor in the transformation of the means of production, but rather in the murky realm of social cohesion that—because of its voluntary, associational, and spontaneous nature—was, of necessity, difficult to locate and, clearly, even more difficult to theorize.

Thus, the essence of both Murray's and Zimmern's liberalisms ultimately lay in this conservative understanding of the social order, coupled with a belief in the transcendent power of liberalism, attached to a much more literally liberal aversion to state power, all of which effectively rendered both men unable to talk about political power. "Power politics," argued Zimmern, "are not co-operative but fiercely competitive."[154] In this sense, for both men, to acknowledge that politics, much less life in community, could be in part determined by power relations among people and institutions was to purposely infect the spiritual with all that was base and material, and thus denied the possibility of human cooperation altogether. To discuss power relations thus meant to undercut the power of spirit itself. "It is a serious thing" argued Murray in 1918, "for any organ of material power to be found fighting against the human soul."[155] And yet their unwillingness to discuss power politics meant that they were also incapable of explaining *why* merchants and business tycoons would

[152] Zimmern, *Quo Vadimus?* 31–32.

[153] Bodl. MS Alfred Zimmern (135) fol. 150.

[154] Zimmern, *Quo Vadimus?* 33.

[155] Gilbert Murray, "The Soul As It Is and How to Deal With It," *Essays and Addresses* (London: George Allen and Unwin, 1921), 151.

suddenly throw down their self-interested desire for material gain, would suddenly *stop* acting competitively, and henceforth cooperate with one another to channel all of their economic energies into the public good. Nothing in either Murray's or Zimmern's political lexicon would force capitalists to do such a thing. Not being able to talk about power also rendered Murray and Zimmern unable to face the fact that the very ordered societies that they look toward (ancient Greece and the medieval world) were unapologetically *pre-liberal* and *pre-capitalist*. Such societies only addressed the problem of resolving liberal freedom with federation by limiting freedom for the majority of people and making strict political and power distinctions between free born and slave, men and women, serf and lord.

Murray's and Zimmern's silence with regard to political power was quite accurately diagnosed by E. H. Carr in the 1930s when he examined the work of inter-war thinkers like Zimmern. Carr correctly argued that these thinkers' response to any crisis that involved a use or discussion of power was simply to reiterate their moral vision of the good in the face of political reality. For Carr this seemed patently utopian, completely out of touch with the workings of economic and political forces in the world. Again, however, for Carr, this utopianism sprang from liberalisms' continued attachment to the false economic theory of the harmony of interests. In this case, he viewed inter-war ideology as simply an extension of a nineteenth-century dogma that continued to argue for the social relevance of individual greed in the face of growing economic disparity. But Zimmern and Murray were patently *not* liberal individualists in this sense. Rather, their liberalism was a much more complex alchemy of liberalism and idealism.

Indeed, Murray's and Zimmern's constant reiteration of a spiritually informed moral order was, in many ways, one of the most idealist, even Hegelian qualities of their thinking. The real in this case *was* the rational. Spirit was not imagination, nor was it utopian. It was the living ideal, manifesting itself through individuals and communities. Social order was not something one necessarily created but a reality that one unearthed, a shared heritage rediscovered in the legacy of Greece or the medieval cosmos. At the same time, Murray's and Zimmern's insistence on the living spirit of liberalism in the world was, in the tradition of the nineteenth-century idealist liberals, patently *anti-idealist* in its refusal to link state power with spiritual order. While Hegel's dialectic required the negation of Spirit as a loving family community in the face of Spirit as state authority so that the two might be reconciled on a higher level, for Murray and Zimmern the specter of state power *had* to remain distinct from the spiritual for liberal freedom to thrive. Murray and Zimmern developed their peculiarly conservative understanding of the social order and their squeamishness with regard to political power from this disconnect—between their idealist impulses for spirit and their liberal fear of the state—and not from any orthodox belief in the harmony of interests.

CONCLUSION

In the end, Murray's and Zimmern's liberalisms held much in common with those of Green and his associates, despite the absence of any explicit debt to either their idealism or their "oddly transposed" Hegelianism. Unlike Hobson, Hobhouse, and other Edwardian new liberals, Murray and Zimmern never evacuated the metaphysical from their liberalisms, never rejected the existence of a quasi-dialectical spirit moved to reconcile individual autonomy with life in community. They simply attributed this spiritual emphasis to Greece. Like their predecessors, Murray and Zimmern were driven by a desire to reform liberalism, to transform it from a political ideology rooted in a misplaced faith in the "harmony of interests" to a theory of community. Fundamentally, then, contemporary political theorists would recognize as liberal very little in Murray's and Zimmern's liberalism, aside from both men's discomfort with state power. And yet it was this conflict, between liberal anti-statism and the more idealist and communitarian impulses in their political theories, that drove both Murray's and Zimmern's approach to the movement of "liberal spirit" in the world and cast a long shadow over the study and practice of internationalism.

Not surprisingly, the umbilicus of their internationalisms was Oxford—specifically, the spiritual and communal values both Murray and Zimmern believed embodied in the *Literae Humaniores*. In 1931, at his inaugural speech as the Montague Burton Professor of International Relations at New College, Zimmern posed the following question to his audience: "What is the connection between the discipline of *Literae Humaniores* and the understanding of the contemporary world? What room is there, in the interpretation of its multitudinous phenomena, for the special quality of mind . . . which we are accustomed to associate with this place?" Zimmern answered his own question.

> It was the philosophy of a vulgar age which imagined that the foundations of a durable internationalism could be laid in the realm of commerce, as though the weights and measures of the spirit were identical in every land and there was no variety to be encountered in that coinage of the mind in which international relations are perforce carried on between men and nations; it is not for the merchant or the money-changer but for the skilled numismatist to appraise the

quality and adjust the values of the pieces that come to his hands, minted one and all out of the precious metal of our common humanity.[156]

For Zimmern, then, the philosophy of an enlightened Oxford, not that of a "vulgar age," took the spiritual qualities of the world seriously. Like its domestic inspiration, the internationalism of which Zimmern spoke was putatively based not on the mechanical operations of free trade but on the "spirit" and "coinage of mind" unearthed by skilled intellectuals. As Oxford men had once used the WEA to expose the working class to those "eternal things which unite," Oxford men would now expose the world to those same universals, universals forged "out of the precious metal of our common humanity." Chapter 3 further explores both men's understandings of the relationship between this spirit and global liberalism.

[156] Zimmern, *The Study of International Relations*, 20.

CHAPTER THREE

Mind, Spirit, and Liberalism in the World

UNTIL FAIRLY RECENTLY, disciplinary historians have regarded all British and American inter-war internationalists as cut from the same political cloth. In the words of Scott Burchill, "Founded in a climate of reaction against the barbarity of the First World War, the discipline was established with the conviction that war must never happen again; the Great War, as it was initially called, was to be 'the war to end all wars.' "[1] Burchill's words are fairly typical in this regard, and, indeed, the war did have a profound effect on the internationalisms of many inter-war thinkers, including Murray and Zimmern. Both men claimed that one of the central features of their work was the eradication of what Zimmern referred to as "the disease called war fever" and, despite Zimmern's involvement with the Round Table Society and Murray's very brief writings on the Boer War, neither man seems to have thought systematically about international politics before 1914.[2] The war changed that. Each would spend the rest of his career not only writing about internationalism but literally living it through their involvement in the League of Nations and other international organizations.

The violence of the war was never the sole catalyst propelling Murray's and Zimmern's moves toward internationalism. Both men were haunted with equal ferocity by those long-term changes in the world economic and political order that followed in its wake, in particular the collapse of British economic hegemony, an ever widening chasm between international economic and political organization, the unsettling success of the Bolsheviks, and the quickened pace of nationalist and anti-colonial movements within the British Empire. In general, the conceptual scope of Murray's and Zimmern's internationalisms were framed largely in response to these global changes, to what they sincerely believed to be the rapid unraveling of order and stability on a global scale.

As different as these political phenomena might seem, Murray and Zimmern traced their origins to a hyper-accentuated version of a problem that they felt lay at the heart of all modern political crises: widespread selfishness and unchecked materialism on the part of individuals and

---

[1] Scott Burchill and Andrew Linklater, *Theories of International Relations* (London: St. Martin's Press, 1996), 6.

[2] Bodl. MS Alfred Zimmern (136) fol. 110.

states alike. Whether criticizing orthodox liberalism's telescopic focus on individual self-interest or the socialist theory of class, both men took the violence of the war and the disruption of the pre-war order as a sign that the world had been possessed by, in Murray's words, "the devil of massed and organized selfishness."[3] According to Zimmern, ideological responsibility for the war fell not on the shoulders of Prussian thinkers alone. "Treitschke and Nietzsche may have furnished Prussian ambitions with congenial ammunition," he argued, "but Bentham with his purely selfish interpretations of human nature and Marx with his doctrine of class struggle—the high priest of Individualism and the high priest of Socialism—cannot be acquitted of a similar charge."[4] In Zimmern's mind, the worldwide move toward universal selfishness, toward the blinding glare of materialism, had led to the Great War in the first place and continued to trouble global politics in its aftermath. According to both men, counteracting this disintegrating tendency meant injecting international relations with a healthy dose of spirituality. In Zimmern's words, internationalists must strive to ensure "that our world may be really interdependent in its spiritual relations just in the same way it is in its material and economic relations."[5]

Thus, unlike the younger so-called lost generation of the 1920s and '30s—for whom World War One prompted a general rejection of their faith in God, progress, and modernity—Murray and Zimmern responded to the war and its aftermath by expanding their pre-war faith into the global arena. Their approaches to international politics, both philosophical and political, differed little from their approaches to domestic politics. In both cases, selfishness caused conflict; in both cases, a return to a spiritualized form of liberal morality would lead to renewed order. The war compelled them to rearticulate this morality in light of global events. On an international level, then, Murray's and Zimmern's liberalisms still strained to hold together what looked like diametrically opposed concepts—only now these concepts were rooted in more than a general desire to bridge the ethical gap between freedom and fraternity. Now they also claimed to resolve the lingering dichotomies of the post-war world: free trade and socialism, imperial expansion and anti-colonialism, nationalism and international organization.

---

[3] Murray, *The Ordeal of This Generation: The War, the League and the Future* (London: George Allen and Unwin, 1929), 190.

[4] Zimmern, "Introduction," *The War and Democracy* (London: Macmillan, 1914, 1915), 11.

[5] Zimmern, "The New International Outlook: Two Lectures at the Fenton Foundation of the University of Buffalo, Delivered in November, 1926," *University of Buffalo Studies* 5(1) (1926): 22.

In this manner, Murray's and Zimmern's internationalisms also mimicked the germinal conflict at the heart of their political philosophies more generally, the conflict between spirituality and statehood. In essence, both grounded their theories of international relations in the unfolding of Spirit in the world, what Murray termed "Liberal spirit" and Zimmern referred to as the "international mind." Although distinct, both notions sought to resolve the thorny but supposedly unnecessary opposition between individuals and states, and between states and the global community by moving international actors to take the good of the international whole as their moral compass in world affairs. Murray and Zimmern, however, were both reluctant to actualize their visions of a global moral order through potentially coercive institutions like a world state or a global police force that answered to the League of Nations. To do so would, once again, simultaneously infect the spirit of international cooperation with materialism and challenge their liberal opposition to state power, or in this case, to the disturbing prospect of world-state power.

This chapter is concerned with the first half of Murray and Zimmern's unstable dialectic, with the notion of international Spirit that occupied such a large portion of both men's voluminous works on international relations. While Murray's Liberal spirit and Zimmern's international mind were somewhat fungible concepts, they differed in their emphases. For Murray, the force of the divine that worked through the notion of Liberal spirit offered to reconcile the individual with the global community (what he once again termed the One Great City of Men and Gods) through a fairly static interpretation of the Logos, or the immutable truth of global order. By contrast, Zimmern's conception of international mind was more dialectically mobile in its claim to both valorize and transcend difference on an international level, to reconcile national interests with a universal vision of global society without sacrificing the uniqueness of the local and the potentially conflicting relations of states and other international actors.

By infusing the international with spirit, Murray and Zimmern were both following in the tradition of the Oxford idealist liberals and radically departing from them. As noted in chapter 1, first-generation idealist liberals like Bosanquet, Green, Ritchie, Muirhead, and Caird had turned to Hegel's Spirit to enrich the philosophical tradition of liberalism, resulting in a theory that emphasized both the Spiritual Principle and the centrality of social interaction to human organization. British liberalism, they insisted, must be modified to encompass both the spiritual unity of the community and the moral imperative of citizens to recognize their duty to one another. Hence, they argued, the creation of a society that could resolve the conflict between individual fulfillment and community well-being—in Caird's words, the "realization of the highest"—required citizens who lived life both publicly and privately, who actively involved themselves in civic causes while nurturing their spiritual souls in churches, neighborhoods, and families.[6] In like manner, Murray and Zimmern imagined that individuals and states must also develop a kind of international civic sensibility that prompted them to participate in both national and international causes, moving back and forth between the domesticity of nation and the "*res-publica* with which it is our duty to concern ourselves" that "extends to the ends of the earth."[7] "The ordinary man," argued Zimmern, must "enlarge his vision so as to bear in mind that the *public affairs* of the twentieth century are *world affairs.*"[8]

This notion of a "*res-publica*" that "extends to the ends of the earth" was, however, a significant departure from the international relations of the nineteenth-century liberal idealists. While primarily Hegelian in their domestic theory, Green and Bosanquet were decidedly Kantian in their approach to international politics and imagined, as did Kant in "Perpetual Peace," that hostilities between states were not an inevitable condition of the world and that the key to international peace lay in the development of more democratic, republican states.[9] To varying degrees, Green agreed with Kant that peace was the natural condition of the world rather than the exception. "There is no such thing," he thus insisted "as an inevitable conflict between states."[10] Instead, Green argued (and Bosanquet agreed) that the "occasions of conflict between nations disappear" the "more perfectly" the world's states could obtain their "proper object of giving free scope to the capacities to all persons."[11] For Kant, as individual states

[6] In Caird's words, the central tenet of this form of idealized liberalism was its belief that human beings could "here and now, make our lives ideal, that the round of duties that seem commonplace and secular—these family ties, this college companionship, these professional occupations of law, or education, or commerce, these civic and political relations,—furnish the very environment that is needed for the realization of the highest." [Caird, *Lay Sermons and Addresses*, 70. See also Vincent and Plant, *Philosophy, Politics and Citizenship*, 104].

[7] Zimmern, *Learning and Leadership: A Study of the Needs and Possibilities of International Intellectual Co-operation* (Geneva: Intellectual Co-operation Section, League of Nations Press, 1927), 11. The relationship between nation and domesticity will be explored in greater detail in the final chapters.

[8] Zimmern, *Prospects of Democracy*, 26.

[9] Kant, "Perpetual Peace," *Kant's Political Writings*, 99–102. For Kant, because republican government was committed to the liberty of the individual and the rule of law, republican states would naturally extend this behavior into the international arena. [See Andrew Linklater, "Rationalism," *Theories of International Relations*, ed. Scott Burchill and Andrew Linklater (New York: St. Martin's Press, 1995), 111]. Thus, the closer to the ideal of republican statehood individual states came, the closer the world was to a peaceful "federation of free states."[Kant, "Perpetual Peace," 102].

[10] Green, *Lectures on the Principles of Political Obligation*, 170.

[11] Green, "The Right of the State Over the Individual in War," *The British Idealists*, 228, 232. Also see Bosanquet, "The Function of the State in Promoting the Unity of Mankind," *Social and International Ideals: Being Studies in Patriotism.*

approached the idea of enlightened moral statehood, the possibility of war grew more remote. The result would be the creation of an international moral community.[12]

Murray and Zimmern accepted some of the Kantian assumptions of thinkers like Green, arguing quite explicitly, for example, that "international anarchy" was not a natural state of world affairs. But perhaps because their thinking about international relations emerged from a period of significant changes in the state system itself, their approaches sought to move the Spiritual Principle beyond the state. Thus, both men disagreed with the principle that international cooperation would develop as an inevitable byproduct of each state's movement toward moral republican governance. Instead, their internationalism sought to extend the unifying possibilities of the Liberal spirit and the international mind into the "world as a whole," to locate it in the fluid interplay of states, individuals, capital, and international organizations.[13] From within this enlarged notion of global community, Murray and Zimmern argued, the economic and political disturbances of the post-war world could be analyzed and ultimately transformed.

But extending an inherited language of Spirit into the world and into the twentieth century did not come without cost. What Murray and Zimmern most often sacrificed was political coherence. Many of the ideological contradictions that nineteenth-century idealist liberals had struggled to resolve by appealing to the Spiritual Principle (e.g., the contradiction between free trade and an economically moral society, between liberal universalism and the politics of paternalism) widened significantly after the war, and Murray's and Zimmern's writings during this period suggest that their notion of liberal spirituality strained to breach the divide.

The first section of this chapter begins with an analysis of these historical contradictions and Murray's and Zimmern's reactions to them. It focuses first on the tenuous post-war economy and the decline of British economic hegemony, the relationship between this and the emergence of the Soviet Union, and, finally, the post-war proliferation of nationalist and post-colonial movements in the British Empire. The second section then critically engages Murray's notion of Liberal spirit and its relationship to the metaphor of the One Great City of Men and Gods. It closely examines Murray's idea of the international City itself and the form of Logos, or divine truth, that it was intended to generate. The section then moves on to analyze the truncated form of democracy this understanding of Liberal spirit inspired, and concludes by examining how Murray imagined a world organized around the Logos would go about solving

---

[12] Boucher, *The British Idealists*, xxxi.
[13] Zimmern, *The League of Nations and the Rule of Law*, 194.

the problems of the global economy. The third section concentrates on Zimmern's understanding of the international mind by first comparing it to several other usages of the term in wide circulation at the time. It then examines how Zimmern expanded Murray's conception of Spirit in a much more specifically dialectical direction. It also examines how Zimmern, by theorizing internationalism through the international mind, could simultaneously call for a system of world organization that was potentially universal, transcending class and racial difference, and insist on the continuation of these differences in the name of diversity. The three sections gesture toward the inevitable conflict that takes center stage in chapter 4: the conflict between the Spirit of liberalism and the potentially coercive—nominally state-like—power of the League of Nations.

Murray and Zimmern on Economic Crisis, Bolshevism, and the Empire

World War One brought with it a number of global economic and political developments that profoundly affected the nascent internationalisms of Murray and Zimmern. One of the most deeply felt of these changes was a fundamental shift in world trade patterns that permanently displaced both British industry and London financiers from their place at the center of global capitalism. Although some political economists argue that the origins of the inter-war economic crisis predate World War One, even these thinkers agree that the war brought the underlying weaknesses of the global economy into sharp and irrefutable focus.[14] The war instigated a nationalization of world economic systems as states disengaged from international exchange rates based upon the leadership of the Bank of England and the gold standard.[15] The wartime focus on arms production and a general retreat from peace-time industry by the belligerents meant that many non-European states began developing their own industries or turning toward alternative sources of supplies.[16] In general, by the

[14] See Karl Polanyi, *The Great Transformation* (Boston: Beacon Press, 1944); Barry Eichengreen, *Golden Fetters: The Gold Standard and the Great Depression, 1919–1939*, (Oxford: Oxford University Press, 1995), 199; Mary Rose, "Britain and the International Economy," *The First World War in British History*.

[15] Robert Gilpin, *The Political Economy of International Relations*, (Princeton: Princeton University Press, 1987), 127.

[16] A. G. Kenwood, *The Growth of the International Economy, 1820–1989* (London: George Allen and Unwin, 1983), 176; James Foreman-Peck, *A History of the World Economy: International Economic Relations Since 1850* (Totowa, NJ: Barnes and Noble Books, 1983), 191. Chile, for instance, developed its mining industry during this time while the general industrial development of the United States and Japan increased markedly.

end of the war and in the absence of an international gold standard, the industries upon which many European states (particularly Britain) had relied were now significantly undermined, and the tradition of free trade guided by London banks, upon which British industry had been dependent, now floundered. In sum, the war tilted economic power away from Europe, shattered Britain's international economic hegemony, and began the process of moving this hegemony toward the United States.[17]

Even as this system of London-based global capitalism was in such flux, Bolshevism was providing the world with an ongoing radical alternative to the material, political, and cultural practices of capitalism. Immediately after the revolution, for example, the Bolsheviks made a series of general decrees, the first of which stated simply that "[t]he landowners' right of ownership over the soil is abolished forthwith, without compensation."[18] Another decree officially legalized the "intervention of workers in the management of factories," thus clearing the way for the nationalization of banking and credit institutions.[19] The early years of the regime also saw massive political reform. According to Israel Getzler, the individual soviets of the Provisional Government engaged in democratizing campaigns aimed at educating the masses in the practices of "political pluralism and parliamentary procedure."[20] Communist activists also called for a radical transformation of bourgeois culture more generally. As party activist Lebedev-Polansky argued before the first All Russian Conference of Proletarian Cultural Enlightenment Organizations in 1918, "Our proletarian culture is replacing bourgeois culture. . . . The capitalist system is anarchistic and its ideology individualistic. The socialist system bases itself on collective creative labour; its ideology will be strictly monistic, integral."[21] Part of this integral ideology meant developing alternative, proletarian forms of cultural and artistic expression. It also meant challenging bourgeois social institutions at every level, including relationships between men and women and within the family. Thus, barely a year after coming into power the Bolsheviks introduced the Code on Marriage, the Family, and Guardianship, a legal code based on "women's equality and

[17] Rose, "Britain and the International Economy," 231, 249.

[18] Victor Serge, *Year One of the Russian Revolution* (London: Pluto Press, 1992), 81. In Lenin's view, the war itself represented nothing more than an "armed struggle between the 'Great' Powers for the artificial preservation of capitalism by means of colonies, monopolies, privileges and national oppression of every kind." [See Vladimir Ilyich Lenin, "Socialism and the War," *The Lenin Anthology*, ed. Robert Tucker (New York: Norton, 1975 [1914]), 186].

[19] Lenin, "Socialism and the War," 135.

[20] Israel Getzler, "Soviets as Agents of Democratization," *Revolution in Russia: Reassessments of 1917* (Cambridge: Cambridge University Press, 1992), 17.

[21] Lebedev-Polyansky, "Revolution and the Cultural Task of the Proletariat," *Bolshevik Visions*, ed. William G. Rosenberg (Ann Arbor: University of Michigan Press, 1990), 1.

the 'withering away' of the family."[22] In short, the Bolshevik victory of 1917 held out the possibility of transforming liberal, bourgeois society in its entirety.

The effects of the Bolshevik Revolution were not, however, limited to Russia but influenced working-class movements throughout Europe. The Bolsheviks exported revolutionary consciousness to European workers not only through interpersonal forms of intellectual exchange and political organizing but also through the use of radio technologies, which had improved during the war. These technologies provided the emerging Soviet Union with a transnational means of appeal to the working-class organizations of Europe.[23] At the same time, the success of this organizing campaign generated a fear of Communist propaganda among both the conservative and liberal ruling elites and convinced state leaders to bar the Soviet Union from the Paris Peace Conference. Despite its official absence, however, the specter of Communism loomed large amongst the delegates. For Herbert Hoover, "Russia was probably amongst the worst problems before the Peace Conference. . . . It was the Banquo's ghost sitting at every Council table."[24] According to Konni Zilliacus, one of the outstanding features of the conference was "the lively and constant fear exhibited by both liberals and conservatives . . . of the danger of pressure from the Left, from the working class and the Russian Revolution."[25] In sum, for the leaders of the capitalist west, the Soviet Union quickly became what George Kennan termed a "single hostile eye," leering at Europe from the Russian plain, excluded but present, distant but menacing.[26]

As chapter 2 explained in greater detail, Murray and Zimmern were vocal in their opposition to socialism. Like many inter-war liberals, they felt particularly threatened by what they saw as a Europe increasingly permeated by "the secret propaganda of Bolshevism."[27] But despite their distaste for Bolshevism, both men were equally convinced that the underlying self-interest of liberal capitalism had led the world to war in the first place. "Capitalism did not cause the war," argued Zimmern in 1917; "it was the Kaiser, not Rothschild, who pulled the trigger; but capitalism

[22] Wendy Goldman, *Women, the State and Revolution: Soviet Family Policy and Social Life, 1917–1936* (Cambridge: Cambridge University of Press, 1993), 1.

[23] Robert Fortner, *International Communication: History, Conflict, and Control of the Global Metropolis* (Belmont, CA: Wadworth, 1993), 104.

[24] John Thompson, "Introduction," *Russia, Bolshevism, and the Versailles Peace* (Princeton: Princeton University of Press, 1966).

[25] Zilliacus, *Mirror of the Past*, 224.

[26] George Kennan, *American Diplomacy, 1900–1950* (London: Secker and Warburg, 1952), 68–69.

[27] Murray, *The Problem of Foreign Policy*, 93. Zimmern also argued in his Foreign Office memo of 1918 that for the Soviets, "propaganda in foreign countries is a leading feature of their policy."[Bodl. MS Alfred Zimmern (82) fol. 39 (Foreign Office Memorandum)].

and the philosophy of self interest on which it reposes were intimately connected with the atmosphere of selfishness and domination which made the war possible."[28] For Zimmern, this atmosphere resembled a kind of pre-liberal state of nature transposed onto the international realm, where neither individuals nor states owed anything to one another, where international agreements were based not upon universal principles but upon deals worked out in secret by state leaders and diplomats.[29] Before the war, Zimmern argued, political leaders had ceded their civic sensibilities to the logic of the market. "Men had not realized," he later maintained, "that the methods and principles underlying so much of our commercial and industrial life could be transferred so completely to the field of politics so ruthlessly pressed home by military force."[30] Zimmern also worried that the evolving network of dense economic connections between individuals and states on a global scale was not being properly matched by the evolution of parallel political connections, resulting in a world trend "towards the development of international syndicates exercising large political influence."[31]

Simultaneously, however, Murray and Zimmern also believed that something not only moral but also potentially progressive and unifying could be found in the movement of the global market. Zimmern, for instance, credited the "private organization of trade and industry" with making "such enormous advances in its international quality."[32] Likewise, Murray saw an almost direct relationship between free trade and world peace, arguing shortly after World War One that because Great Britain had "kept her doors everywhere open to the trade of the world" it bore comparatively less guilt than did other nations "in preparing that international atmosphere in which made the war of 1914 possible."[33] Indeed, at the height of the Depression, Murray was still arguing that "wider freedom of trade and intercourse is seen to be in the interest of the world not only by every Liberal but by every competent economist."[34] Thus, like their intellectual predecessors, Murray and Zimmern maintained a somewhat quixotic relationship with the economic practice of free trade. On the one hand, it was inherently selfish and suspect; on the

[28] Zimmern, "Capitalism and International Relations," 64.

[29] Thus, for these scholars, nothing was more important to the post-war world than the "complete departure from the old methods of secret diplomacy." For more see the Information Section, "The League of Nations and The Press: International Press Exhibition, Cologne, May — Oct. 1928" (Geneva: League of Nations Press, 1928).

[30] Zimmern, "Introduction," *The War and Democracy*, 11.

[31] Bodl. MS Alfred Zimmern (85) fol. 40.

[32] Zimmern, "The Development of the International Mind," 6.

[33] Murray, *Problems of Foreign Policy*, 107.

[34] Murray, *Liberality and Civilization*, 78.

other, its focus on individualism was preferable to the "evil" of class politics. While the movement of capital opened up the world to the possibility of real international communication, the collapse of British economic hegemony marked the end of world order and the inception of what Murray termed "our modern anarchy."[35]

Indeed, the sense of chaos that both men continually argued was so characteristic of the post-war world was largely a reaction to Britain's lost economic and military power. Without such an anchor, the world appeared loosed from its moorings, "overwhelmed" argued Zimmern, "by events beyond our control."[36] Consequently, while these thinkers longed for a truly internationalist world, they also longed for an *ordered* world; while they gestured toward the creation of a moral global economy, they also believed that freedom of trade must be protected against the threat of socialism. Perhaps Murray put it best when he argued in 1925 that what liberals wanted was "the re-establishment of order and the continuance of trade. We do not want revolution."[37]

But Murray and Zimmern also worried about the specter of revolution on another front. For both men, liberalism was equally threatened by the rise of the anti-colonialism throughout the empire. In this sense, their attitudes toward imperialism bore the unmistakable stamp of their nineteenth-century Oxford predecessors. While most nineteenth-century idealist liberals, including Green, often objected to the practice of imperialism on free trade grounds, they also believed that imperialism, rightly carried out, could uplift backward, uncivilized societies.[38] In this spirit, a

[35] Ibid., 62.

[36] Zimmern, "The New International Outlook" 11. Zimmern used the word "events" almost ubiquitously throughout his early writings on international relations, particularly with reference to the international economy, almost as if the decentering of economic order was the result of huge natural forces that felt beyond the control of human beings. For Zimmern, the word "events" clearly conjured up images of chaos, of the sheer momentum of the massive political and economic changes engendered by the war, changes that, he argued, continued to haunt fragile efforts at international cooperation well into the inter-war era. "If there is one clear deduction to be drawn from the events of the last few years," Zimmern argued in 1927, "it is that statesmanship has not yet recovered the control which it relinquished in 1914 over the fluid and tumultuous interaction of human wills and passions which we like to describe fatalistically as 'events.' " [Zimmern, "Learning and Leadership," 11].

[37] Murray, "What Liberalism Stands For," 689.

[38] While British imperialism dates back to the sixteenth-century expansion of the Tudors into Ireland, the practice was significantly accelerated during the early and mid-nineteenth century, culminating in Queen Victoria's Colonial Conference of 1887. [Robert Huttenback, *The British Imperial Experience* (New York: Harper and Row, 1966), 160]. Most nineteenth-century liberals with any idealist or reformist agenda tended to agree with T. H. Green that individuals could be morally uplifted through their engagement with the machinations of free trade, but, in the case of the colonies, this trade was not in fact "free"

number of Green's former students founded the Round Table Society at Oxford in the mid 1880s to promote a specifically moral form of imperialism (and, in the process, supplying much of the intellectual justification for Victorian and Edwardian imperialist expansion). Key Round Table figures like Lord Milner, for instance, argued that British imperialism be practiced not as a policy of economic expansion but to set a moral example for colonials. Through this moral example, so the logic went, empire would prepare uncivilized peoples for democratic government. In Muirhead's words, the crux of the empire's "mission of civilization" was its commitment to the "spread of European ideas of truth and justice."[39]

In 1899, the Boer War initially shattered idealist liberal opinion on colonialism into two opposing camps, "liberal imperialists" like David Ritchie and Henry Jones who supported the Conservative government's offensive against the Boer Republics in South Africa, and those, for example, Bernard Bosanquet and Edward Caird, who condemned both the war and the policies of the imperial state in South Africa in general.[40] Paradoxically, however, while the war produced tremendous strife within the Liberal Party, it also served to solidify the idealist liberals' vision of what constituted a moral imperialism.[41] Whether they supported the actions of the Conservative government, the particularly brutal nature of the Boer War—and the controversy that surrounded it—forced idealist liberal thinkers to define their own approach to colonialism. John Muirhead argued in 1900 that such an approach must be based on England's moral imperative to oversee "the reconstruction of the moral, industrial, and political ideas of some four or five hundred millions of souls of every race and religion and at every stage of civilization except our own."[42] Thus, although a number of liberals during the Edwardian Era rejected imperialist expansion on its face, most Oxford liberals and the ascending Liberal Party of 1906 were decidedly pro-imperial. As David Boucher argues, even new liberals like Hobson and Hobhouse believed in a "right kind of imperialism," which sought to prepare indigenous people for self-government.[43]

For most turn-of-the-century liberals, this "right kind of imperialism" was still couched in the language of Social Darwinism, a language that divide the world into innumerable races, each of which occupied a discrete space along a continuum ranging from civilization to barbarism.

since prices and markets were fixed by the imperial state. [See Green on the "moral functions" of trade and property in "The Right of the State in Regard to Property," 226–32].

[39] Muirhead, "What Imperialism Means," 249.

[40] Boucher, *The British Idealists*, xxix.

[41] Hinton, *Labour and Socialism*, 72–73.

[42] Muirhead, "What Imperialism Means," 246.

[43] Boucher, *The British Idealists*, xxx.

Idealist liberals like Muirhead set their particular evolutionary vision against the exploitative economic practices of Manchesterism.[44] In contrast to laissez-faire accounts of the infinite, exploitative potential of the colonies (and indeed, contrary to Spencer's more brutal formulation of "survival of the fittest"), these thinkers imagined that the existence of "lower races" necessitated the benign intervention of the imperial state. In 1900, for instance, Ritchie argued forcefully that the British state had an obligation to protect these lower races from the exploits of the native despot, the slave trader, and the European adventurer alike.[45] In a similar vein, Muirhead maintained that the proper approach to subject races was one of carefully controlled enlightenment.

Murray and Zimmern inherited both this belief in the empire's moralizing mission and an evolutionary attitude toward race.[46] According to Zimmern, who was a long-time member of the Round Table's powerful London Group, "if the British Empire is destined to endure, it will be only as the guardian of the moral welfare of its peoples. Faith in this mission alone can justify the effort to further its consolidation."[47] Developmental and evolutionary references to "lower" and "backward races" punctuated both Murray's and Zimmern's wartime and inter-war writings. Likewise, in the tradition of nineteenth-century colonialists, both Murray and Zimmern tended to frame their evolutionary descriptions of colonized peoples in familial terms, using what Anne McClintock has called the "family of man" metaphor to describe both the immaturity of the colonial children and the wisdom of the imperial parent.[48] Thus, the imperial state had the right, they argued, to intervene in the lives of its colonial subjects to prepare them for the burdens of freedom. In Murray's words, "we govern backward races that they may be able to govern themselves; we do not hold them down for our own profit."[49]

At the heart of this imperialist ideology lay a firm belief in obvious and scientifically observable distinctions between the races. As Ann Stoler argues in her work on the relationship between sexuality and colonial practices, the construction of Europeans and non-Europeans into "discrete biological and social" entities made the maintenance and expansion of colonial domination possible.[50] Transgressions of these carefully

[44] Muirhead, "What Imperialism Means," 241.

[45] Ritchie, "Ethical Democracy: Evolution and Democracy."

[46] Murray, *Liberalism and the Empire*, 147.

[47] Zimmern, "The Ethics of Empire," *The Round Table* (1913): 484.

[48] McClintock, "No Longer In a Future Heaven," 91.

[49] Murray, *Satanism and World Order*, 41.

[50] Ibid., 346. In Foucaultian terms, Stoler maintains that this project of differentiation did not proceed solely from the state but permeated colonial discourse and administration down to the most minute sexual, educational, and material practices of everyday life. For Stoler, the inherently indistinct nature of race as a category meant that racial differences in

constructed boundaries of racial difference—ranging from intermarriage to political calls for civil equality or national autonomy—not only questioned the foundations of colonial governance but also threatened the racial identity of Europeans by challenging the fixed opposition between the colonizer and the colonized.[51] Thus, during this period fears of "race suicide" began to surface in both the British popular press and within academic and intellectual circles.[52] The period also saw many influential British thinkers—including Fabians like Sidney Webb, liberals like George Bernard Shaw, and socialists like Harold Laski—become interested in eugenics.[53] For both Liberal and Conservative imperialists alike, the decline in the British birthrate and the supposedly unfettered rate of reproduction among "inferior black and yellow races" was an ominous indication of Western civilization's creeping decline.[54]

Murray's and Zimmern's writings in the wake of the Great War suggest that they experienced this loss of racial identity acutely. Their prose were redolent with anxiety, heavy with the sense that Western culture was under attack. The hum of fear—of the encroaching "Oriental mind," that the "immense number of different breeds of men" were becoming less differentiated, that the war had shifted world power away from Europe and toward the "politically immature peoples" of the world—played like a constant low drone throughout their work.[55] Murray succinctly identified the problem in 1926 when he stated before a crowd of Liberal activ-

---

the colonies had to be constantly policed, re-invented and maintained through sexual discourses and policies which relied upon the notion of female contagion and the restriction of sexual contact between European and non-European men and women. [Ann Stoler, "Making Empire Respectable: The Politics of Race and Sexual Morality in Twentieth-Century Colonial Cultures," *Dangerous Liaisons*, 344].

[51] Gyan Prakash, "Postcolonial Criticism and Indian Historiography," *Dangerous Liaisons*, 498.

[52] Richard Soloway, *Demography and Degeneration: Eugenics and the Declining Birthrate in Twentieth-Century Britain* (Chapel Hill: University of North Carolina Press, 1995), 5.

[53] Soloway, *Demography and Degeneration*, 61; Kramnick and Sheerman, *Harold Laski*, 32–48.

[54] Soloway, *Demography and Degeneration*, 61. In addition, the popularity of eugenics among Britain's middle and upper classes was also related to an acute fear of a newly politicized working class. Thus, in 1905 the president of the Royal Anthropological Institute, John Beddoe, bemoaned "the diminution of the old blond lympho-sanguine stock, which has hitherto served England well in many ways, but is apparently doomed to give way to a darker and more mobile type, largely the offspring of the proletariat . . ." As Beddoe's racialization of the working classes suggests, many of Britain's ruling elite turned to racial categories to speak to their own loss of class identity as well as to their fears that Britain's imperial civilization had entered a period of inevitable deterioration.

[55] Murray, "What Liberalism Stands For," 687; Murray, *Liberalism and the Empire*, 119; Zimmern, "Liberty, Democracy, and the Movement Towards World Order," *Problems of Peace* (1936): 159.

ists "The domination of the white races is shaken. In the war we taught the coloured peoples to fight, and we taught them that white men could be defeated."[56]

In this key respect, Murray's observations on the post-war world were correct. While the British Empire emerged intact from World War One, the seeds of its eventual demise had been sown by the imperial government's own war-time strategies. The war itself thus produced a number of unintended consequences for the imperial system and the balance of power more generally. In some cases, merely the diminished military presence in the colonies made it possible for anti-colonial groups to organize.[57] More importantly, however, Britain's decision to encourage revolt within Germany and the Ottoman Empire resonated deeply with colonized peoples within its own empire. Thus, while the speeches and covert operations designed by the Foreign Office to inspire the spirit of "national self-determination" might have had the desired strategic effects in, say, Poland, they also reached equally receptive audiences in Ireland, India, and Egypt.[58]

During the war, the British government recruited combatants from a number of its colonial territories, including Ireland and India. The irony of Irish men dying in a war to protect small eastern European nations from the imperial abuses of the Germans did not go unnoticed in Ireland. In songs written to memorialize the 1916 Easter Uprising in Dublin, lyricists lamented the loss of Ireland's "wild geese" in the service of an imperial army.[59] Sinn Fein took Britain's call for national self-determination one step further by organizing an anti-colonial campaign while the British military was occupied on the continent. After the war, Britain's massive deployment in Ireland of particularly repressive troops led to a two year guerrilla conflict that eventually resulted in partition and the creation of the Irish Free State in 1921.[60] When one Conservative member of Parliament was later asked to explain the government's concession to the Irish rebels, he responded that "instead of deluding public opinion with a notion that a sufficient application of force will provide a remedy, a wiser

---

[56] Murray, "What Liberalism Stands For," 686.

[57] Low, *Eclipse of Empire*, 26. Hence, it was during the war that the Ceylon National Congress and the General Council of Buddhist Associations in Burma first began attracting significant numbers of supporters.

[58] Sharpe, "The Genie that Would Not Go Back in the Bottle," 15.

[59] "Twas England bade our wild geese go / that small nations might be free. / But their lonely graves are by Suvla's waves / On the fringe of the gray North Sea. / But had they died by Pearse's side / Or fought with Cathal Brugha, / Their names we'd keep where the Fenians sleep / 'Neath the shroud of the foggy dew."

[60] Seamus Dunn and Thomas Hennessey, "Ireland," *Europe and Ethnicity* (London: Routledge, 1996), 188.

course would be to set about taking such steps as may be the means of recovering that consent without which society in Ireland cannot exist."[61] Edward Wood's suggestion that the consent of the colonized was in any way necessary to the maintenance of Britain's imperial presence marked a radical break with pre-war colonial policy, and is suggestive of the larger, patchwork approach that Parliament would take toward the empire between the wars. Having held out the carrot of self-determination to millions of colonial subjects, the British government was now constrained to at least gesture in that direction by creating odd pockets of autonomy within the empire.

At the same time, the imperial government continued to enforce racist, repressive policies within the colonies and, in some cases, expanded these policies in response to anti-colonial agitation. As the cases of India and the Middle East suggest, the most outstanding feature of Britain's interwar colonial policy might well have been this checkered, half-hearted approach to self-government, an approach based largely on race. Thus, while Indian troops also fought for the empire during World War One, unlike the Irish they were not granted even the tempered status of a free state. While during the war the imperial government made vague promises about India's gradual independence, following the war the British began a crack down on "revolutionary crime" in India, beginning with the Defense of India Act in 1918 and the particularly repressive Rowlett Bill of 1919.[62] In response, Gandhi organized his first non-cooperation campaign, the Satyagraha Sabha, whose goal was to challenge the Rowlett Bill through direct action.[63] Likewise, the imperial government's visible commitment to self-determination during the war also created problems for it in the Middle East. In perhaps this most egregious of cases, the British decision to arm rebel forces in the Ottoman Empire, promise them independence, and then divide up the region with the other Allied powers when the war was over, backfired. Nationalist agitation in Egypt immediately after the war forced the British to officially terminate their protectorate in 1919. For similar reasons, the imperial government renounced

---

[61] Correlli Barnett, *The Collapse of British Power* (Hoboken, NJ: Humanities Press International, 1986), 157.

[62] The Rowlett Bill stipulated that not only was possession of any seditious document punishable for up to two years imprisonment but that the courts which were to hear these cases consist of only a three member panel. [Huttenback, *The British Imperial Experience*, 176].

[63] The campaign, which lasted from 1921 until 1922, was the Congress Party's fist extensive experiment with the principles of *satyagraha* (non-violent resistance) in India, a method which came to characterize nationalist strategies throughout the 1920s and '30s. [Low, *Eclipse of Empire*, 26]. Ghandi had experimented with non-violent strategies earlier in South Africa.

its formal rule over Iraq in 1922. [64] But these concessions did not include formal withdrawals of military power. In Egypt, the British actively supported King Fu'ad and maintained its military bases, while in Iraq they continued both their military presence and kept privileged commercial access to Iraq's oil.[65]

It was this somewhat lurching approach to the empire—constructed of states and colonies with varying degrees of political autonomy—that best characterizes British imperial policy between the wars. In addition to legitimizing the call for self-determination, the war had set the stage by expanding the role played "white dominions" in foreign affairs.[66] Thus, while before the war the British government had insisted that foreign policy remain within British hands, during the war they opened the formulation of foreign policy to the self-governing dominions of Canada, Australia, New Zealand, and South Africa.[67] In 1921, the dominions met again at another imperial conference, only this time their meeting focused on the creation of a voluntary commonwealth to replace the imperial system.[68] For some non-white colonies, however, inclusion in the commonwealth was not voluntary; for instance, India participated as a commonwealth nation even though it was not self-governing. In the end, the inter-war British Empire consisted of two racially constructed tiers: one occupied by the self-governing white dominions, the other by non-white, non-self-governing colonies under the direct or indirect administration of the imperial state.

In sum, the gradual splintering of the imperial edifice characterized by a post-war rise in colonial nationalism and the emergence of semi-autonomous colonial entities set the stage for the massive decolonization of the 1950s and '60s. Many British leaders and intellectuals thus emerged from the peace conference with a general sense of foreboding about the empire, which in many ways outweighed their relief that the empire was still intact. For Murray and Zimmern, colonial agitation for increased autonomy, democracy, and even statehood, posed an inherent threat not just to Britain but to the entire western order. "Not one who studies even superficially the history of average Oriental governments," Murray argued shortly after the war, "from Morocco or Bokhara to Oudh, can be surprised or sorry that they have been superseded by the better governments of the West.

---

[64] Constantine, "Britain and the Empire," *The First World War in British History*, 275.

[65] Ibid., 275.

[66] Low, *Eclipse of Empire*, 26.

[67] Huttenback, *The British Imperial Experience*, 162. In addition, India, which was not self-governing, was also invited to join this Imperial Conference in 1917. Along with the other dominions, India "participated fully with the other former combatants in the proceeding of the Peace Conference" and was rewarded with a seat in the League Assembly.

[68] James Powers, *Years of Tumult: The World Since 1918* (New York: Norton, 1932), 165.

The peoples of the East themselves have gained by Western penetration; nay, more they are conscious of their need of the West. But they have had too much of it; they resent it, and they are frightened of it."[69] This fear, according to Murray, made the entire Islamic world fundamentally unstable. Islam itself, he argued, posed a direct threat to "the World Order which we embody."[70] Zimmern also felt deeply threatened by the notion of people who had not yet reached a certain level of civilization demanding democratic governance. Democracy, he cautioned during the war, was not a "magic formula. It is open to limitation obvious enough to the student of non-adult races."[71] But perhaps Liberal Prime Minister Lloyd George expressed this sentiment of fear and resentment best in 1920 when he quipped, "There was a time when Downing Street ruled the Empire. Now the Empire rules Downing Street."[72]

Murray's and Zimmern's response to what they viewed as a kind of Platonic inversion of the imperial order was not to insist on the reestablishment of British economic hegemony or a return to an unfettered policy of colonial expansion. Rather, they argued that through a reassertion of liberal ethics—an ethics they believed were rooted in communal cohesion and spiritual transcendence—the older economic and imperial order could be moralized. In this sense, the language of sprit that so permeated their writing on both domestic and international politics served a specific purpose: it helped Murray and Zimmern develop an ideological response to what they saw as a radical *coming apart* of the economic and colonial world order by sewing together what looked like antithetical claims: free trade and the creation of a moral economy, the continued existence of colonial inequality and a new form of world politics premised on the universal equality of man. The remainder of this chapter examines the conceptual motifs that Murray and Zimmern used to weave together these conflicting ideologies through the world proliferation of Liberal spirit.

MURRAY'S LIBERAL SPIRIT AND THE ONE GREAT CITY OF MEN AND GODS

Murray's writings on international relations were tinged at all times with a nagging sense of urgency. Even immediately after the representatives at the Paris Peace Conference had successful passed the League of Nations Covenant, Murray took no time to bask in any sense of triumph. The war had severely damaged civilization, Murray believed, and the unraveling

---

[69] Murray, *The Problem of Foreign Policy*, 72.
[70] Murray, *Satanism and the World Order*, 34.
[71] Zimmern, *Nationality and Government*, 15.
[72] Quoted in Powers, *Years of Tumult*, 165.

of the world into chaotic fragments loomed large against the horizon unless the forces of darkness were vigorously opposed by the forces of light.
And indeed, this is how Murray framed his understanding of international
politics: as a constant, quasi-religious battle of good against evil. Although an odd choice of words for a committed agnostic, Murray never
hesitated in describing the ruinous forces at work in the world as Satanic.
"The spirit I have called Satanism" he argued in 1924, "rejoices in any
widespread disaster and also a disaster to the world's rulers."[73] Satanic
forces, for Murray, included all political, social, and economic phenomena that threatened the imperial order, the movement of free trade, and
the idea of Western Civilization more generally. These included nationalist and anti-colonial movements, Bolshevism, the munitions industry, and
unscrupulous free traders. And despite the differences between these phenomena, Murray seemed incapable, or unwilling, to differentiate between
them in terms of their motives. All of the "forces of uncontrolled and
irresponsible covetousness" that fell into the category of the Satanic were
motivated by a selfish desire on the part of individuals and states alike to
promote their political causes or economic agendas over the peace and
stability of the world.[74] If left to their own devices, these "selfish passions"
would take over global politics and lead to another world war.[75]

The only way to counteract the fissiparous tendencies of the modern
world, Murray argued, was through a massive effort to rekindle what he
described as "Liberality as a living spirit" or "Liberal spirit."[76] Throughout his long career, Murray would return to this theme with absolute
consistency. Indeed, even at the height of the Liberal Party's tremendous
slide into political obscurity, Murray insisted that the path to political
salvation continued to run through liberalism alone.

> Not Fascism nor Bolshevism; not Socialism nor Conservatism; not the victory
> of one class or another class; only the Liberal spirit of trying to find what is
> true, irrespective of prejudice, and the Liberal spirit of trying to do what is best
> for the whole, irrespective of passion or class interest.[77]

For Murray, the spirit of liberalism implied an understanding of freedom markedly different from traditionally negative, liberal conceptions
of the term.[78] Thus for Murray, freedom implied much more than a laun-

[73] Murray, *Satanism and the World Order*, 33.

[74] Murray, "Orbis Terrestris," *Essays and Addresses* (London: George Allen and Unwin
Ltd, 1921), 196.

[75] Murray, *Liberality and Civilization*, 37.

[76] Ibid., 83.

[77] Murray, "What Liberalism Stands For," 696.

[78] In Lockean liberalism, for instance, liberal freedom was constituted by as a constellation of "rights" which one could not be prevented from enjoying by the state. Murray did

dry list of inalienable rights. Rather, Murray also understood freedom in more positive terms as a spiritually conceived notion of the good that grew out of one's duty to one's fellow citizens and service to the community. As he explained to an audience of college students in 1934,

> I would ask you, who will have your influence in the world and will be here long after I have gone, to be champions of freedom in this sense; freedom to live according to your conscience, freedom to seek truth, and to utter what you believe you have found; freedom to serve—yes, by all means; the very essence of good life is service; to not serve in fear the man who stands over you with a bludgeon, but to serve in goodwill some whole of which you are part and to which you are bound by the links of love or duty; your comrades, your University, your nation, the great Society of Nations which has now at last taken concrete form, and beyond all, so far as you can discern the outlines of it, that Divine Order, or Cosmos, to which the ancient Stoics gave their loyalty, above the barriers of creed or nation, the One Great City of Men and Gods.[79]

This quotation also gestures toward both what Murray termed his "theory of international duty" and the constellation of intellectual problems that this theory would eventually encounter.[80] Most revealing, however, is the phrase "freedom to serve." On an international scale, Murray believed that an extension of this particular reading of liberal freedom throughout the world would lead inevitably toward that moment when individuals and heads of state would be moved by "the spirit which subordinates the nation's immediate interest to the interests of the whole community of nations."[81] Murray felt that the war had demonstrated the necessity of this approach to world politics, and that the emergence of the League after the war served as tangible evidence that the spirit of liberal service was now actively shaping the discursive framework in which international and domestic politics now took shape. Politicians considering trade legislation, for instance, would now have to consider not just the good of their own people but the good of the world community. "I think that some consciousness of the ultimate solidarity among the peoples of the world has really begun to penetrate the minds of ordinary practical politicians" Murray argued in 1920. In the future, he predicted, "it will

---

not have a problem with this conception of rights per se. Indeed, he tended to treat the existence of negative rights as yet another necessary component of a truly liberal society. "What you mean by saying that some one has a right to do something if he likes," argued Murray in a 1922 article for *International Affairs*, "is merely that no one else has a right to prevent him, or even more simply, that he ought not to be prevented, and if any people do try and prevent him you will think them wrong." [Murray, "Self-Determination of Nationalities," *International Affairs* 61 (1922): 8–9].

[79] Murray, *From the League to the U.N.*, 62.
[80] Murray, *Essays and Addresses*, 200.
[81] Murray, "A Survey of Recent World Affairs," 5.

become within a measurable time almost impossible for a decent and intelligent statesman to profess absolute indifference to the welfare or suffering of other parts of the human race."[82] "Liberal spirit," in this sense, was both the goal toward which internationalists should strive and the march of history, the unfolding force of truth in the world.

As the quote above also suggests, Murray had no trouble articulating this vision in allegorical terms; he simply drew upon an already powerful motif in his political philosophy. "On the whole," he argued, "I think it looks as if we were moving in the direction of realizing upon the earth something like the Once Great City of Gods and Men."[83] This metaphor proved useful to Murray for a variety of reasons. First, it provided him with a symbolic structure and a philosophical precedent for explaining why human beings in one part of the world should care about human beings in another. It was the Stoics, argued Murray, who had first imagined the world in these terms by "rejecting all divisions made by nation or race or class: the world was One Great City of Men and Gods."[84] The concept thus embodied that moral imperative to which Murray felt liberalism alone spoke so powerfully: the transcendence of human divisions in the name of the common good. Murray argued that liberals were more likely to "act rather less in the direct interest of the oppressed class, rather more in the interest of the whole community."[85] Conceiving of the world as One Great City let Murray expand this symbolic community beyond the boundaries of nations and states, thus extending the bonds of liberal duty around the globe.

Second, imagining the world as One Great City of Men and Gods also enabled Murray to express his equally firm conviction that liberality was, first and foremost, a spiritual phenomenon. For a truly moral world order to develop out of the fractious ruins of the war, individuals, on a global scale, must experience not just an expanded sense of altruism but an enriched spiritual life. The true test of any emerging world society, Murray was still arguing in 1948, was not only the extent to which its people understood themselves as connected to one another through duty but "what heights it reaches or is capable of reaching in the things of the intellect and the spirit."[86] Murray was adamant in his insistence that those individuals who did the work of the League, those who strove to understand international problems through the lens of global good, were already thinking on a higher plane saturated with the divine.[87] The Great

---

[82] Murray, "Orbis Terrestrius," 200.

[83] Ibid.

[84] Bodl. MS Gilbert Murray (436) fol. 130 (undated lectures).

[85] Murray, "What Liberalism Stands For," 694.

[86] Murray, From the League to the U.N., 41.

[87] Murray, Liberality and Civilization, 46.

City metaphor enabled Murray to express this vision of the good as a blending of the metaphysical and the material—Gods and Men—which, in itself, also served two related purposes.

For Murray, the inherent connection between the terrene and the celestial provided a counter-logic to nationalism by legitimating the world community as a cause worth suffering and even dying for. On a number of occasions, Murray's works called upon the world's people to make sacrifices in the name not only of the new internationalism but also of the spiritual forces behind it. Murray characterized this as "that spirit which, since the very beginnings of history, men have expected and found in the average common soldier—a will to endure hardship for the sake of duty and to use life as one who knows of things better than life."[88] Creating a peaceful world order united by institutions like the League of Nations thus carried with it no ordinary set of policy imperatives but rather demanded that states and individuals understand their own roles in such a system as spiritually, rather than materially, motivated, as performed in the name of those "things better than life" as opposed to security concerns, better trade agreements, or any of the other self-serving motives that usually lurked behind international cooperation.

On the other hand, the City of Gods and Men allowed Murray to express his idealist conviction that Liberal spirit embodied neither utopian longing nor situated self-interest but rather the actual underlying essence of existence. The proper political, economic, and social ordering of the world was not, according to Murray, something developed by a particular group of British thinkers following the war that just happened to find its way successfully to Geneva. Rather, cooperation, solidarity, sacrifice, and collective security were reflections of a correctly ordered reality, of what would be (once the world was properly aligned with the spirit of reason) a normal state of affairs. Murray's writings on education are particularly laden with an urgent desire to make the current generation cognizant of this. "Can any method be found," he asked in 1929, "for making the rising generation throughout all the states of the League acquainted with the principles and practice of the League and familiar with the thought of international co-operation as the normal method of civilization?"[89] For Murray, war, violence, revolution, and expansionism were all deviations from a correctly ordered "normal" world, indeed, from truth itself. Students needed to at least have some understanding of this essential truth for world peace to prevail. "Let the younger generation have a better chance than we had of acquiring a reasonably true picture of the world

---

[88] Murray, *The Ordeal of This Generation*, 196.
[89] Ibid., 194.

and a reasonable approximation to the spirit of human brotherhood" Murray begged his readers in 1935.[90]

The problem that Murray wrestled with throughout his career was the seemingly irrational behavior of states and individuals in the face of what should have been a "true picture of the world." This incongruence plagued Murray, and indeed it was when he wrote about the disconnect between actuality and truth, between the material workings of diplomacy and the essence of Liberal spirit, that he sounded most hopelessly utopian. But for Murray, of course, this wasn't utopian. Again, in the most classically idealist sense, the Great City of Men and Gods was *more* real (in the sense of being rational) then anything else Murray witnessed in the world around him. Some mechanism, he argued, had to allow for tapping into this wellspring of correct answers, for determining the right course of action in all world affairs, ranging from a correct demarcation of national boundaries in the Balkans to a proper understanding of the world financial crisis. And for Murray that mechanism was the unofficial, seemingly powerless, but, he argued, morally superior set of committees, conferences, and special "bodies of experts," associated with the League.

Both critics and admirers of the liberal internationalists associated with the League period tend to view this general veneration of experts as a kind of naive, Enlightenment-inspired faith in reason and scientific inquiry. Since Kant, Mueller, and Rousseau, this line of argument maintains, internationalists of the idealist persuasion have insisted that people were fundamentally rational, that war was irrational, and that international institutions could discover alternatives to war (and other international problems) through a combination of inquiry into the facts and reasoned debate and discussion. By contrast, Murray's understanding of the passage from unenlightened befuddlement to enlightened truth looked remarkably pre-Enlightenment in nature. In fact, his description of the process by which League institutions could find correct answers in the vortex of post-war world events harkened back to a kind of medieval faith in the constancy of divine order, a rearticulating of what often looked like natural law theory.

This is not true at first glance, however. Indeed, Murray's descriptions of his favorite League committee, the Committee on Intellectual Cooperation, frequently sounded quintessentially rationalist. For Murray, this committee (not coincidentally the one with which he and Zimmern were most closely associated) was "the characteristic instrument by which the League does most of its work."[91] What the committee did, Murray argued, was to "pool the best brains of all nations for the common service

---

[90] Murray, *The Schools of Europe* (London: League of Nations Union, 1935), 3–4.

[91] Murray, *The Ordeal of This Generation*, 191.

of all."[92] And yet one does not have to read too far into Murray's descriptions of the committee before it becomes clear that he expected these "brains" to engaged in matters strikingly different from what most children of the Enlightenment would have expected. For Kant, "pooling the best brains" of the world no doubt have implied a process of critical inquiry. True knowledge was only possible, Kant argued, through critique, in which different perspectives, each with a margin of validity, were compared against one another. By contrast, Murray's description of what went on (and what ought to go on) in these committees was remarkably uncritical. There was no debate. There was no conflict. There was nothing, for Murray, except a kind of placid channeling of "the word made flesh," the gradual, beatific emergence of the Logos.

Murray's consistent use of the term "Logos" differed only slightly from the ancients he so admired. For Greek philosophers, Logos denoted a divine reason or plan behind human existence. Implicit in this assumption was the idea of Logos as language, as spoken truth, which implied an intersection between the metaphysical and the material worlds. A such, Logos was immanent in the world and eminent in the realm of divine reason. Thus, for thinkers like Heraclites, Logos embodied a conceptual gathering or intersection of all that existed, a spoken reflection of the true world order. Later Christian thinkers used the word to refer to Jesus Christ as the vessel of the word of God, "the word made flesh." Murray understood Logos largely in these terms, as "*the word*," or "the thing said," which embodied divine truth in its essence. For Murray, what thinkers in the League ought to be doing was, quite literally, sitting around a table and waiting to find "the thing said." In a 1924 League of Nations Union address, for instance, Murray described the problem solving activities of the League to his audience.

> Now, one of the great discoveries made by the Greeks in their very earliest time, before the classical times, was the discovery of the immense value of what they call the *Logos*. We translate it "*the word*", it is rather "the thing said." They discovered that when men are involved in a quarrel or in, say, a great disturbance, there was a possibility that *something might be said* which would content both parties. Perhaps there was always the *thing to be said* which, if you could find it, would solve the difficulty. And there came to the Greeks and extraordinary enthusiasm for what they called the *Logos*. As you know, it developed a religious side, and is a very typical element in the early Christianity, where the *Logos* is *something or other which God is saying to us*, and by which, if we can only get it into our minds, the riddle of the world is solved. Now, in an ordinary dispute, I think that *Logos*, is what we believers in the League are

[92] Ibid., 193.

feeling for. We want people to sit round a table, of course in the right spirit: there must be no lies, not threats of force, there must be no deafness—no unwillingness to hear what the other person has to say; and that then, as you sit round a table trying to find out what is true and what is fair, you will eventually find the *thing to say* which will clear up difficulties.[93]

What is unclear from this paragraph (and from others like it in which Murray illustrates a similar process) is what exactly people are *doing* around the table. Murray argued that "as you sit around the table trying to find out what is true and what is fair, you will eventually find *the thing to say.*" What Murray could never articulate was the role of conflict or the possibility that the Logos might not be so easily discernable—that there might be disagreement at the table and that these disagreements might, in and of themselves, prove useful for reaching a solution.

Murray's discussions of the relationship between Logos and the activity of international experts epitomize his fear of a disintegrating world order, almost as if he believed that the mere mention of conflict or difference might invert the Logos and evoke some kind of chaotic power of its own, some Satanic-inspired version of the "word made flesh." Murray was thus completely unable to admit that any solution reached by experts who were truly concerned with "what is true and what is fair" might be partial, might be studded with individual interests and desires, *and yet still work reasonably well.* As a result, Murray's writings on international institutions elide the question of process and instead assume that the *way* we get to truth is simply not as important as allowing truth to get to us.

In this manner, Murray's notion of Logos remained rooted in what Hegel would have termed "speculative idealism," an idealism that had not yet theorized the process or movement by which Idea (what Hegel, in some contexts equates with the Logos) becomes Absolute Knowledge. In Murray's vision, the truth of the world (or the correct ordering of society or the "good life" itself) was inscribed on a cosmic tablet, locked behind an obfuscating wall of material greed and amoral politics. People of good will could access the Logos by simply approaching it in the "right spirit." The key was not human agency, but rather a kind of quasi-religious prostration, falling before deity of truth in the spirit of good will and assuming that this deity would provide the answers you sought. Wrong answers were easily blamed on the faulty conclusion on the participants themselves; they had not approached the problem in the right spirit, they had not offered the divine its proper oblations. And in fact, this was Murray's classic response to anyone who called the League a failure. "You can tell

[93] Murray, *The World and the League: An address delivered at the Annual Meeting of the League of Nations Union General Council by Professor Gilbert Murray, L.L.D., D.Litt., June 17th, 1924* (Geneva: League of Nations Union, 1924), 3.

me that the League has failed; my answer, of course, is that the League has failed because the Covenant was not carried out."[94] People were to blame for the League's demise—not the League itself nor the skeleton of spiritually inspired committees, panels, and bodies of experts that Murray believed constituted its real existence.

Murray's static vision of the process by which international organizations were to channel the Logos raises a number of critical issues for his political theory. On the one hand, Murray was a humanist who valued human agency and human reason. Indeed, one of the things he found most moving and exciting about Greek society was its capacity to promote free and independent thought.

> The great charm about these Greeks is that they did think and set the world thinking. It is not that they found the right solutions; many of these problems cannot be solved or at least have not been solved. But they thought, and thought very simply and clearly and boldly and without prejudice. So too in social things. Some people blame them because they had slaves. So they had, and so had all peoples in Europe and Asia and America for 2,000 years after; but the Greeks were the first people to think *about slavery*, to be troubled about it and to ask whether it was not contrary to nature. The same about the position of women. They did not solve the problem, but they raised the question and made people think.[95]

But Murray didn't seem to have the same patience for modern intellectual forums as he did for the ancients. The ancients were allowed to circle around a problem, to think it through "boldly and clearly," and maybe, in the end, to find no solution. Not so with the modern international community. Either human beings submerged themselves in the altruistic spirit of liberality and in this fashion discovered the key to reality itself, or civilization would unravel. In this way, Murray undermined his own liberal commitment to freedom of thought as an essential characteristic of liberal society. In the international realm there was no time for free intellectual movement, for debate, for critique: there was only time for truth.

And in this way Murray also undermined the most characteristically idealist aspect of his political thought. In the tradition of the Oxford idealist liberals, Murray had theorized the modern world through the lenses of a Hegelian Greece, that is, Greece read through the dialectic. What made the Greeks so unique in their political and social organization, Murray argued, was the extent to which they had combined subjective free-

[94] Murray, "The League of Nations: the First Experiment," *From the League to the U.N.*, 66.

[95] Bodl. Ms. Muuray (436), fol. 131.

dom with objective truth, thus reconciling the "inner light" of the individual and "higher ideals" of the polis.[96] But Murray parts ways with the Hegelian dialectic precisely at the point where Bosanquet and Ritchie were also unable to follow: the point where Hegel's notion of the Idea/ Logos confronts its own negatively projected self and is ultimately reborn on a higher plane. In a social context, Hegel rooted this moment of negation in the unfolding of *Sittlichkeit*, in the process whereby the subjective wills of individuals and the objective will of Spirit were dialectically reconciled and found their "concrete meeting point."[97] For Hegel, the subjectively constituted individual was born into a community of love but reached maturity in the context of civil society where he found himself in contest with others and, through these negative relations, was ultimately reconciled with Spirit at its most transcendent. Importantly, for Hegel civil society must not be directly controlled by the state but rather only structured by its authority. But for Murray, as with Bosanquet and Ritchie, the language of liberalism ultimately intervened at this point and prevented him from talking about the state's authority in coercive terms. In the context of his domestic political theory, the state manifested itself as a low background hum, existing somewhere around the edges of society but never falling within the realm of sight. And this is how he interpreted the Greeks. What made them great was the visible *absence* of authority, the *absence* of coercion of any kind. The Greeks, Murray argued, "however much they differed, were all alike in trying to solve their problem by thinking—never by a mere appeal to authority."[98]

The dearth of state authority in Murray's political theory prevented him from confronting politics as power. State authority was, according to Murray, antithetical to the process of thinking truth because it confronted that truth not with Liberal spirit but with coercion. For Hegel, state authority made civil society possible because the state provided the legal apparatus that allowed people (men) to truly live a vibrant social life filled with trade, conflict, disagreement, and psychic battles of will. Only when the loving realm of the family confronted its negation (the competitive realm of civil society) was transcendence possible. On an international level in particular, Murray's political theory never trusted that a world authority could create a similarly secure civil space capable of promoting both the harmony of shared moral values and the conflicts of life in society, a space where state delegations might argue loudly with one another or where members of the Committee on Intellectual Cooperation

[96] Murray, The Five Stages of Greek Religion, 100.

[97] Hegel, *Introduction to the Philosophy of History*, trans. Leo Rauch (Indianapolis: Hacket, 1988), 26.

[98] Bodl. Ms. Muuray (436), fol. 131.

might have an intense debate and come away not with the answer but "having raised the question." In the end, for Murray, such an intensely fluid understanding of international society was impossible because the state—or meta-state—apparatus necessary to create it was impossible to imagine. He thus reduced the "committees of experts" associated with the League (where the intellectual life of the world was supposed to take place) to a kind of Roussean assembly, where members simply proclaimed the legitimacy of the General Will rather than engage in debate.

Murray's response to both the collapse of the gold standard following the war and the economic crisis of the 1930s was characteristic in this regard. For Murray, the Liberal spirit that conditioned the Great City of Men and Gods acted as a kind of centering, unifying tonic for a world frantically pulled in any number of new directions. Using the corporeal language so characteristic of internationalist thinkers during this era, Murray described the world economy of the early 1930s as

> a patient suffering from a complicated disease due in large part, though not entirely to alcoholism; the old Liberal Free Trader said: 'Let him alone. Cut off his drink and he will recover in course of time.' The Protectionist said: 'We cannot let him alone when he is as ill as this. The poor fellow must have medical treatment . . . and the best treatment of all is plenty of good nourishing brandy.'[99]

In a somewhat perplexing and drawn out response, Murray argued that the solution to this malady lay not with either of these medicinal extremes but instead in maintaining a steady grip on the underlying morality and truth of international cooperation, the "unconscious wisdom" at the heart of the League of Nations.[100] In another essay written that same year, Murray maintained that the spirit of the League, the "spirit which subordinates the nation's immediate interests to the interests of the spirit of the world community of nations," should influence states and international relations experts alike in their diagnoses of the world economy.[101] Failure to adequately live this spirit would inevitably lead to "barbarism."[102] Murray thus argued that only a sustained belief in the power of Liberal spirit—in this case, a spirit equated with the League—would reveal global economic solutions to world leaders and diplomats. Finding the correct answers to the world's economic questions thus implied that experts of good will gather in the name of liberality, open themselves to the Logos,

---

[99] Murray, "Epilogue," *The Evolution of World Peace*, ed. F. S. Marvin (Oxford: Oxford University of Press, 1933), 202.

[100] Ibid., 208.

[101] Murray, "A Survey of Recent World Affairs," 5.

[102] Murray, "Epilogue," 202.

and then make this wisdom public. "Say that the currencies of most nations in Europe are breaking down, as they were in 1921," mused Murray, "what is to be done? Call a conference of financial experts; let them show what is wrong and recommend remedies; let their report be recorded and published."[103]

Murray also assumed not only the fundamental good but also the fundamental truth of free trade, if it was handled in a particular manner. Free trade, he argued, made internationalism possible by opening the world to the flow of civilization. Looking back on the causes of the Great War, Murray argued in 1933 that "[p]eople say there was a breakdown of the old laissez-faire system; but we should remember that there was no laissez-faire system in existence. There was only a queer jumble of laissez-faire here and violent nationalistic protection there—the same lack of anything like world order or organization."[104] Returning to his tried and true theme, Murray argued that the world needed a coherent return to the One Great City of Men and Gods, that is, an understanding of free trade guided by the liberal principles of duty and responsibility—in essence, a "bringing of a cosmos into the world economic life."[105] For Murray, free trade could function as a true cosmos once it had been infused with a higher notion of the good, a truly moralized understanding of liberal order.

Murray's coupling of Liberal spirit with a vision of the world as One Great City allowed him to elide some of the essential ideological contradictions of the post-war economy. It enabled him to speak to the potentially liberating, world-opening possibilities of international free trade while simultaneously addressing his fear of international chaos and a loss of elite control. At the same time, the spirit of liberalism was explicitly opposed to the more selfish moments of capitalism, even while it argued in favor of its moralization and expansion. The creation of an international system united by Liberal Spirit appeared to offer the workers of the world precisely the kind of "alternative to Bolshevism" that Lloyd George had called for, without actually creating any kind of super-state authority to safeguard this alternative. And, perhaps most importantly, the centrality of the Logos in any world economic debate would ensure that the terms of that debate were never challenged. The goal of League experts, according to Murray, was not to create conflict by raising potentially divisive issues such as a radical reallocation of the world's economic resources, or the creation of a world body capable of regulating global capital, but rather to wait patiently for the spirit of truth (a truth

---

[103] Murray, *The Ordeal of This Generation*, 192.
[104] Murray, "A Survey of Recent World Affairs," 4.
[105] Ibid.

Murray grounded in a moral vision of free trade) to sit down with them at the table.

And yet Murray himself sensed that, in the end, Liberal spirit alone might not be enough to compensate for the forces of self-interest on a global level. He realized that a real danger lurked in pouring the faith of internationalism into a completely powerless vessel. How does one then enact Logos? How are states and individuals made to see the light which the "best brains in the world" have found in the "thing that is to be said?" "The present disorder of the world is one of those in which the remedy is not obscure, but perfectly ascertained," Murray argued in 1921. "The only difficulty lies in applying it."[106] In this sense, Murray believed that even the Great City of Men and Gods "will have, like other cities, its bad citizens as well as its good."[107] What would have to be done to those obdurate citizens who refused to obey the laws of the City, who refused to comply with the truth once it had been made plain? If the League lacked authority, wherein lay its power to convince? In the end, it is within Murray's tortured understanding of the relationship between the League of Nations, the One Great City, and coercive authority that we begin to see many of the same fissures and hesitancies that plagued his domestic writings on the state and that, ironically, eventually led him to embrace his own brand of authoritarianism.

THE INTERNATIONAL MIND: THE DIALECTICS OF COLONIAL DIFFERENCE

Like Murray, Zimmern grounded his response to the war and its aftermath in a spiritual hunger for international cohesion. The only way to counteract the chaotic tendencies of the post-war world, he argued, was make that world itself more "interdependent in its spiritual relations."[108] For Zimmern, however, these spiritual relations amounted to more than an assertion of the inherent connectedness of all people and the universal truth of a peaceful order. While Zimmern believed in both of these ideas, his understanding of the relationship between spirit and international relations went beyond Murray's ossified notion of the Logos. It embraced a much more dialectical understanding of spirit itself. While Murray had difficulty conceiving of an international community that was simultaneously united by a shared understanding of the good and a world in which debate, even conflict, was an acceptable fact of life, Zimmern, argued that the "life of the world" was characterized not by "uniformity but

---

[106] Murray, *The Problem of Foreign Policy* (Boston: Houghton Mifflin, 1921), 123.

[107] Murray, "Orbis Terrestries," 199.

[108] Zimmern, "The New International Outlook," 22.

multiplicity: not agreement but controversy: not the idylls of brotherhood but the shocks and jars of corporate existence: in a word, not peace but *life in society.*"[109] World society was thus infinitely more fluid for Zimmern than for Murray, and the key to creating order out of its fractious elements was to promote the gradual unfolding of a spiritual sensibility that both celebrated the "shocks and jars of corporate existence" and still reconciled these competing interests on a higher, more ethical plane. Zimmern referred to this spiritual sensibility as the international mind, a term he infused with his own particular reading of liberalism that ultimately rendered his interpretation more complex, more distinctly idealist, and (ironically for a man who rejected all German philosophy as inherently Prussianist) more *Hegelian* than both Murray's understanding of Liberal spirit and the panoply of other international minds articulated by any number of authors during this period.

The term was so widely used by internationalists during the inter-war era that Hedley Bull referred to it as one of their most distinctive characteristics. Inter-war thinkers were united, Bull argued, by not only their commitment to progress but to the idea that international relations were

> capable of being transformed into a fundamentally more peaceful and just world order; that under the impact of the wakening of democracy, the growth of the 'international mind,' the development of the League of nations, the good works of men of peace or the enlightenment spread by their own teaching, it was in fact being transformed.[110]

What Bull fails to explain however (and this is fairly typical of most post–World War Two readings of the inter-war period) is that the international mind itself meant different things to different internationalists.

American idealist scholar Nicholas Murray Butler first coined the term in 1912, and described it for his audience at the Lake Mohawk Conference on International Arbitration as

> that habit of thinking of foreign relations and business and that habit of dealing with them, which regard the several nations of the civilized world as friendly and co-operating equals in aiding the progress of civilization, in developing commerce and industry, and in spreading enlightenment and culture throughout the world.[111]

---

[109] Zimmern, *The Study of International Relations*, 17 (emphasis original).

[110] Hedley Bull, "The Theory of International Politics, 1919–1969," *The Aberystwyth Papers: International Politics, 1919–1969*, ed. B. Porter (Oxford: Oxford University Press, 1917), 34.

[111] This address is included in a collection of Murray Butler essays that first appeared in 1913. See Nicholas Murray Butler, *The International Mind: An Argument for the Juridical Settlements of International Disputes* (New York: Shares Scribner's Sons, 1913), 102.

That international mind would come to cross the Atlantic sometime before the Great War is hardly surprising given Murray Butler's long-standing connections with British idealists. Idealistically inclined liberal scholars in Britain recognized Murray Butler, who would later become the president of Columbia University, as a kindred spirit, so much so that H. G. Wells once referred to him as the "Gilbert Murray of the United States."[112] Whatever its transatlantic origins, both British and American internationalists quickly adopted the concept as their own. Developing a theory of world organization based on the primacy of the international mind rapidly became a defining feature of many of these thinkers' work. As a result, when one reads the vast body of international relations literature produced both during the First World War and throughout the inter-war period, one cannot help but be struck by the almost numbing repetition of the term.[113] In many ways, its presence in the title of a book, article, or speech immediately alerted fellow disciples to the author's belief in the League of Nations system. Likewise, acceptance of the term seems to have become almost a prerequisite for participation in League-associated think-tanks like the Geneva Institute for International Relations, as well as in some official League organizations such as the International Institute for Intellectual Cooperation, whose quarterly journal was entitled *International Mind*.[114]

Although British and American internationalists were all using the same term, they clearly intended it to mean a variety of different things. His long-standing interest in Hegel aside, for instance, Murray Butler himself avoided the dialectical implications of his own use of Mind.[115] Rather, Murray Butler tended to equate the international mind with objective, scientific methodology. In this sense, his definition reflects a more traditional Enlightenment notion of reason as exclusive of and counterpoised to passion. In his opening address as chairman of the Lake Mohawk Conference on International Arbitration in May of 1912 for instance, Murray Butler argued that the international mind was present whenever enough of the world's reasonable people could "stand with patience and self control in a post of high responsibility when a strong current of public opinion goes sweeping by, careless of consequences and unrestrained in its

---

[112] Albert Marrin, *Nicholas Murray Butler* (Boston: Twayne, 1976), 14.

[113] Indeed, the term is repeated with such frequency by these authors that it is easy to see how Hedley Bull would identify it a defining feature of inter-war internationalism.

[114] Published from 1927 through 1940.

[115] This was an interest widely reputed to have been received "largely secondhand and in its American garb" through the work of William Torry Harris [Marrin, *Nicholas Murray Butler*, 65].

expression of feeling."[116] "The moment that sober reason resumes its rule," Murray Butler continued, "our cause will be secure."[117]

Others used the term to support a variety of different political agendas. Between the wars, liberal pacifists in the United States such as John Haynes Holmes contrasted the concept of international mind to an outdated European approach to diplomacy of suspicion and fear, a mindset that inevitably resulted in war. For committed League of Nations supporters (most of whom had not taken up pacifism until after the war), the international mind implied something akin to one aspect of Murray's One Great City metaphor. As Lord Bryce explained it, "what might in fact be called an International Mind" was just a "feeling of allegiance to humanity, and of the interest in the welfare of other nations as well as one's own."[118] For Hobson, by contrast, the widespread emergence of a discernable international mind meant that enough people had started thinking about developing a "larger constructive policy of internationalism" to supply the "preliminary conditions" for a move toward international government.[119]

Zimmern's own use of the term sometimes echoed Murray Butler's definition of international mind as form of applied reason. "The international mind," argued Zimmern in 1924, implied a kind of "intellectual integrity, of applying one's reason to all and not only to selected problems."[120] In this context, the international mind simply reflected a particular way of thinking—reasonably—about the world and the "increasing body of persons in all countries for whom that kind of thinking, that kind

[116] Murray Butler, *The International Mind*, 98. The racial and class undertones of this statement are clear and reappear throughout Murray Butler's work. Murray Butler himself was not only deeply fearful of "the populace" but disparaging of its ability to think rationally, and as such, suspicious of democracy in general. In a strange inversion of the monarchy and the people, Murray Butler argued in his Lake Mohawk address that "[i]t is not fashionable just now in some influential quarters to have any fixed principles. There are those who think it becoming to court the favor of the populace by inquiring of them, as did the frightened peasants of Louis XI, "Sire, what are our opinions?"[Murray Butler, *The International Mind*, 112]. Likewise, Murray Butler had a tendency to equate irrationality with femininity, arguing that the ability to stand alone with conviction in wake of a nationalist mob was the mark of a "real man."

[117] Murray Butler, *The International Mind*, 113.

[118] James Bryce, *Some Historical Reflections on War, Past and Present*, 27 [quoted from Margaret Jourdain, "Some Recent Literature Upon a League to Enforce Peace," *International Journal of Ethics* 28(1) (Oct.1917): 32].

[119] J. A. Hobson, "The International Mind," *Towards International Government* (London: Garland, 1971), 175.

[120] Zimmern, "The Development of the International Mind," *Problems of Peace: Lecture Delivered at the Geneva Institute of International Relations* (Oxford: Oxford University Press, 1926), 3.

of use of mind, has become not merely habit but a need."[121] In this regard, Zimmern's notion of international mind matched Murray's understanding of the powerful role of intellectual cooperation in the world, which is hardly surprising considering that Zimmern, like Murray, was deeply involved with the League's Committee on Intellectual Cooperation. Also not surprisingly, considering that both men had such similar political theories, in many instances Zimmern's understanding of international mind corresponded exactly to Murray's notion of the world as One Great City. Like Murray, Zimmern accepted the idealist adage that the "real is the rational," or, in Green's words, that "there is one spiritual self-conscious being of which all that is real is the activity and the expression."[122] For Zimmern the international mind was immanently real, identical to the "true progress of humanity," based "on belief in the transforming power of the mind and spirit of man when employed faithfully and unflinchingly in the cause of truth."[123] Hence, Zimmern was defiant in his assertion that the international mind and the logic of internationalism embodied in the League of Nations were not the products of some utopian musing but reflections of a deeper reality that could not be ignored.[124] The League of Nations by itself, he argued, "is nothing. Yet the people persistently regard it as Something. That impalpable, Something is not a legend or a myth. It exists."[125]

That the world did not always conform to his vision of a global res publica guided by the timeless workings of the "that impalpable Something" did not frustrate Zimmern to the same extent that it did Murray. The failure of the world to comply with the vision of the moral good implicit in the international mind simply meant that the international mind itself had not yet completely bubbled to the surface. More than Murray, Zimmern had a sense that the development of the international mind entailed both moral truth and process; the more that adherents supported the process of international cooperation, the more the spiritually conceived understanding of international mind would express itself as fundamentally real. Zimmern was still arguing in 1930, long after the creation of the League, that the birthing of the international mind continued and was still incomplete. "We have got to create machinery which will gradually bring the corporate sentiment into existence," he insisted, "and that is what we are doing through developing this very

[121] Ibid., 5.

[122] Green, *The Works of Thomas Hill Green*, vol. III, 146.

[123] Zimmern, ed., "Introduction," *The New Germany: Three Lectures by Ernst Jackh* (Oxford: Oxford University Press, 1927), 8.

[124] Zimmern, "Progress in Government," 187.

[125] Zimmern, *The League of Nations and the Rule of Law*, 9, 284.

elaborate system of cooperation."[126] In other words, systems of international cooperation were necessary not to generate generic or short term apparitions of "corporate sentiment"—not just *a* corporate sentiment—but, rather, to draw forth its underlying and authentic form—*the* corporate sentiment.

But something else about Zimmern's spiritually conceived notion distinguished it both from Murray's understanding of Liberal spirit and from other understandings of international mind. International mind expressed, for Zimmern, both the permanent features of "sober reason" and a more mobile capacity to resolve seemingly opposing concepts, institutions, and the emotions of nationalism at a higher level of rationality. As Zimmern's writings demonstrate, the international mind was simultaneously the product of purposeful, reasonable action on the part of individuals and states and a divine engine of progress, a "higher life."[127] It would thus bring humanity "into harmony with the great moral forces which rule the destinies of mankind" forces, which Zimmern insisted were perfectly compatible with differences in both national cultures and varying levels of political status. At this moment Zimmern's internationalism begins to take on the characteristics of his own form of "oddly transposed" Hegelianism.

By extending the concept of Spirit beyond the state, Zimmern simultaneously expanded the Hegelian elements implicit in his social theory and fashioned an approach to internationalism that was, in one key respect, radically un-Hegelian. For Hegel, organized and peaceful relations between states—such as those envisioned by Kant—were impossible because the state itself concretized the "ultimate expression of Mind in the world."[128] In this sense, no power greater than the state, no extra-state organization capable of adjudicating international disputes, could exist. For Hegel, then, the unfolding of "*World* Spirit" ironically ended at the institutional boundaries of the state. At the core of this conviction lay Hegel's assertion that in relationship to others, states should be considered *individuals*. Hegel thus argued that sovereignty did not arise from the "formless mass" of the people as mere collectivity, but grew from the inside out, "as an inwardly developed, genuinely organic totality."[129] Thus for Hegel, "sovereignty at home" implied that the state itself had

---

[126] Zimmern, "The Future of Democracy," *University of Buffalo Studies* 8(2) (1930): 105.

[127] Zimmern, *Nationality and Government*, 77.

[128] Hegel, *Philosophy of Right*, 333.

[129] In an interesting Hobbesian twist, this "organic totality" was apparent in the actual person of the sovereign, the monarch, who then became the "real existence" of the "personality of the whole." [Hegel, *Philosophy of Right*, par. 279].

"individuality," which then manifested itself vis--vis other states.[130] And just as individuals in Hegel's civil society required recognition of their autonomy, so too did states have to "secure recognition from others."[131] Thus, in Hegel's view, attempts at international cooperation were always doomed to failure.

Zimmern, by contrast, argued that states themselves were only one particular manifestation of the "world as a whole." International relations, he maintained, "in their full extent involve not merely a knowledge of the relations between states but also of the relations between *peoples*."[132] Thus, a world organized along the principles of the international mind would literally teem with the movement of *people* who were sometimes organized and sometimes not. Individuals, non-state organizations, nationals without states, and capital were constantly moving within and beyond states, actively engaging that whole of which the state was only a part. Ultimately, this emphasis on movement was possible because of the international mind itself. As the unifying presence of reason in the world, it expressed and transcended both the particular and the universal. As with Murray's One Great City, Zimmern's international mind revealed itself both in the individual as a national citizen and in the world as objective truth. Thus, Zimmern sometimes defined the international mind as an "international attitude in the national mind" but at other times as a "universal conscience."[133]

But unlike Murray's Liberal spirit, Zimmern's international mind was specifically interested in the *mobility* of the world, in what he imagined as the almost raucous interplay between individuals, states, and international organizations. While the international mind was universal, and while it insisted that all people were united by "higher law" able to "transcend the claims of nationality in a greater, a more compelling, and a more universal appeal," it simultaneously recognized that these people were different—that they came from different cultural, political, and economic backgrounds, and that they might have conflicting agendas.[134] According to Zimmern, these differences were not only desirable but necessary. The international mind and the spirituality behind it amounted to more than a hazy cosmopolitanism that erased difference in the name of an unspeci-

---

[130] Hegel, *Philosophy of Right*, par. 322. In this sense, realist theorists like Morgenthau shared with Hegel the tendency to anthropomorphize the state on a global level. In this view, the world itself becomes a kind of Hobbesian stage across which self-interested giants lumber.

[131] Hegel, *Philosophy of Right*, par. 349.

[132] Zimmern, *The League of Nations and the Rule of Law*, 5.

[133] Zimmern, "The Development of the International Mind," 1.

[134] Zimmern, "German Culture and the British Commonwealth," *The War and Democracy*, 369.

fied, international identity.[135] In contrast, Zimmern's international mind, like the idealist liberals' "unity of difference," embraced the local, the contingent, and the national, while remaining ultimately confident of their transcendence. Zimmern described what this might look like in *Nationality and Government* by drawing upon his experience with the Workers Education Association. The operating principle of the WEA, he argued, was to "seek to understand their [the workers'] distinctive corporate modes of life and thought, and so, by accepting and even welcoming their differences of experience and outlook, to penetrate through to the eternal things that unite."[136] Likewise, international relations, according to Zimmern, was similarly grounded "upon the diversity of the various human groups and the necessity for studying their interaction."[137]

One of the things that made Zimmern's work so frustrating for Carr and other realists was precisely this focus on "human groups" rather than states. Thus, for IR scholars of the realist persuasion (and, ironically, for Hegel) the anthropomorphic, sovereign state was *the* unit of international analysis. International relations thus defined were relations *between* states. In contrast, Zimmern's world was characterized by the interactions of voluntary political organizations, international capital, commonwealths of nations, international organizations like the League, states, nations, and ethnic and racial groups whose own sense of internal cohesion spilled beyond sovereign borders. In this way, Zimmern's vision recognized each of these theoretical objects as a distinct moment in the overall movement of the international mind. The flexibility of the international mind made the peaceful coexistence of these groups possible by insisting on the simultaneous and interconnected existence of states and non-state social forces (or, in Zimmern's terms, "organization across the borders of the states") and the objective spirit of the "world as a whole."[138]

Zimmern's refusal to name the definitive subject of world politics made his internationalism truly irksome to its critics. Carr, for instance, characterized Zimmern's international politics as mere fantasy based on an "incessant girding at a reality which refused to conform to utopian prescriptions."[139] In an ironic sense, however, Zimmern was actually *more* realistic than the realists in that he took for granted the fact that other "human groups" besides the state (namely, capitalists, nationalists, and

---

[135] Ibid.

[136] Zimmern, *Nationality and Government*, 65.

[137] Zimmern, "Preface," *University Teaching of International Relations: A Record of the Eleventh Session of the International Studies Conference, Prague, 1938* (Paris: International Institute of Intellectual Co-operation, League of Nations, 1939), 7.

[138] Zimmern, *The League of Nations and the Rule of Law*, 194.

[139] Carr, *The Twenty Years Crisis: 1919–1939*, 39.

international voluntary organizations) effected global politics. His theory, however, was also idealist in that the concept of "international mind" not only recognized other sources of world power but also offered to reconcile them while maintaining their distinctive characteristics. Hence, Zimmern's dialecticism amounted to more than what Carr had characterized as a kind of petty snubbing of the world's complexities; it actually spoke to the need to both acknowledge and resolve them. It could be argued, then, that Zimmern developed his internationalism precisely in response to, and not despite, the myriad power relations at work in the world following the war. Just as the massive contradictions of international capitalism and colonialism were becoming increasingly apparent, Zimmern's political theory offered a philosophical approach that allowed European intellectuals to have their cake and eat it to: to talk about the universal potential of a world organization like the League while still claiming the necessity of a colonial structure grounded in an understanding of "human groupings" at different levels of civilization.

Thus, what made Zimmern's internationalism so appealing to powerful members of the British delegation in Paris, like Lord Cecil, was his claim that one did not need to choose between state sovereignty and international cooperation or between colonialism and universalism. Instead, the international mind transcended and resolved the "unbridgeable distinctions" of the new international world order by accepting these distinctions and then locating their resolution on a higher, more spiritual plane.

. In developing this particular approach, Zimmern followed in the well-worn footsteps of his intellectual predecessors. Thinkers like Green, Bosanquet, Caird, Ritchie, and Bradley had consistently dealt with opposing ideologies by positing their social theory as a kind of middle ground, a path that wound its way between the state and the social whole, between the morally autonomous individual and the communal good, between socialism and liberal individualism. Pushing social theory to either extreme on the liberal/collectivist spectrum, they argued, would have disastrous consequences. As Edward Caird suggested in 1897, "Logically carried out, the one can be nothing less than anarchism and the other social despotism."[140] The central and unifying logic of these thinkers' philosophical vision, however, was not built on a watered down theory of compromise. The middle road was not, in this sense, paved equally with stones from opposing philosophical camps. Instead, these thinkers championed a Hegelian-influenced notion of the Spiritual Principle that allowed them seemingly to express and transcend opposing political and economic interests.[141]

---

[140] Caird, "Individualism and Socialism," 179.

[141] Thus, at the heart of idealist liberal thought lay Green's "Spiritual Principle," Henry Jones's "universal ethos," and Bosanquet's "real will," all of which promised to resolve

International mind allowed Zimmern to walk a similar path between the politics of imperialism and the insistent calls for liberation from many colonized people, allowed him to champion universalism while denying liberal equality to most of the world's people. After the war, Zimmern and many of his colleagues were forced to admit that the only way to stave off the collapse of a European-led world order was to develop a "universal" approach to world politics, which nominally gestured toward the inclusion of those colonized peoples loudly banging at the door of the League of Nations. Thus, Zimmern argued that "the essential underlying idea of the League of Nations is its *inclusiveness*. It is a new method or model for all states and its membership is intended to be universal—is, so to speak, potentially universal."[142] The Trojan Horse of *potential* universality, however, harbored within in it dialectically inflected moments of distinctiveness. Thus, much as Hegel had imagined slavery as an immoral but necessary step in the movement of Mind through history, so too did Zimmern see the world's innumerable pockets of unequal, imperialist policy as moments in the international mind's overall universalizing potential, thus explaining why the League's own standards of self-determination were not yet universally applied.

In essence, Zimmern assumed that the League, international organizations, free trade, colonial states and their colonizers—indeed everything that was "an element in the international life of the world"—functioned as a cohesive whole even though the constituent elements of that whole were currently unequal.[143] Zimmern's understanding of the international mind thus transcended differences in political autonomy while bringing all the world's peoples into "harmony with the great moral forces which rule the destinies of mankind."[144]

Immediately after the war, Zimmern argued that any system of international organization resulting from the Paris Peace Conference must be accompanied by a theory of internationalism that spoke to the "great moral forces." For Zimmern, "international mind" served this purpose well. It not only provided the League with a connection to a higher cause; it gave it a language for articulating a vision of the common good which was not in fact "common" to all.[145] The war and the post-war colonial settlement brought into sharp relief the political and economic differences

---

negatively opposed concepts in a manner that was both particular to the individual and universally true. In Bradley's metaphysical language, "Spirit is the unity of the manifold . . . The universal here is immanent in the parts. [Bradley, *Appearance and Reality: A Metaphysical Essay*, 441–42].

[142] Zimmern, *The League of Nations and the Rule of Law*, 2.

[143] Zimmern, "Development of the International Mind," 5.

[144] Zimmern, *The War and Democracy*, 2.

[145] Ibid., 372.

between the colonizer and colonized, between European and non-European, and the international mind enabled Zimmern to claim that his theory spoke for both universal truth and, as he argued in 1918, the need to "diversify, to deepen and to spiritualize the common heritage of humanity."[146]

Zimmern's theory both explained political inequality and naturalized the differences between civilized and non-civilized peoples. The international mind spoke to both his own fears and those of the European leaders at the Paris Peace Conference that the world was about to be overrun by former colonials and non-Europeans, a fear not the least provoked by the presence of Japan and what Murray referred to as "a rather high proportion of small dark Latin nations" at Geneva.[147] Conceiving of the world through the dialectical lenses of the international mind allowed Zimmern to both reiterate the fixity of racial difference and the ultimate triumph of the universal. It made association with non-Europeans not only safe but enriching. Thus, cultures could comingle at Geneva, and the international mind was ultimately triumphant. But the moment of difference, of ethnic, racial, and political distinctiveness, was preserved—at least for the time being.

Zimmern imagined these differences in explicitly national terms. In many ways, as chapter 4 demonstrates, this reliance on the nation as the final arbitrator of difference arose from Zimmern's idealist liberal inability to resolve that most basic of relationships between the League as a potentially coercive institution and the international mind as a spiritual, dialectical principle. The result was a system of internationalism based on an odd division of labor between the "machine" of the League, the "organic" will of the world's people, and the "group-morality" of the national family. In yet another ironic return to the politics of his intellectual forebears, Zimmern's conception of international organization ultimately resembled an oddly premodern patchwork of interconnected family relations rather than a liberal order based on the universal equality of individuals.

CONCLUSION

An almost evangelical drive to spiritualize the world characterized Murray's and Zimmern's approaches to internationalism throughout the inter-war era. In the end, because the changes they called for were situated

---

[146] Zimmern, *Nationality and Government*, 86.

[147] Murray in a 1920 letter to General Smuts. Murray was serving as a South African delegate to the League Assembly at the time. [See Wilson, *Gilbert Murray, OM*, 288].

almost entirely within the realm of Spirit, Murray's and Zimmern's internationalisms made very few challenges to the pre-war status quo even while claiming to radically transform it. As chapter 4 details, despite the change of venue from the domestic to the global stage, both Murray's Liberal spirit and Zimmern's international mind still trailed behind them all the philosophical and political tensions implicit in the Oxford liberals' approach to Spirit. These tensions became most painfully obvious when Murray's and Zimmern's faith in transcendence confronted the worldly reality of the League of Nations.

CHAPTER FOUR

Nationhood, World Order, and the One Great City of Men and Gods

As ALFRED ZIMMERN REMEMBERED THEM, the early Foreign Office meetings that convened to discuss the impending creation of a League of Nations Covenant were generally confusing. Most notably, recalled Zimmern, he and his colleagues struggled with Woodrow Wilson's insistence that the future League of Nations "reserve the right to take any action that may be deemed wise and effectual to safeguard the peace of nations." What constituted "wise and effectual," Zimmern wondered, and just *who* was going to "prevent war?"[1] In the end, he mused, "There were many godfathers round the cradle; but none was ready with the appropriate name."[2]

For Zimmern and Murray, determining exactly *who* and *what* the League was turned out to be a very slippery endeavor. Both men viewed the destructive legacy of World War One as living proof that uncontrolled individualism or the "massed and organized selfishness" of states could lead to violence on a global scale.[3] In response, they proposed an approach to international relations premised on the unifying power of a higher Liberal spirit or international mind. Both men also believed, however, that the international mind could not perform its unifying mission in a vacuum, but had to be fostered by an international organization capable of educating the world to its meaning and channeling those "great moral forces which rule the destinies of mankind."[4]

But Murray's and Zimmern's feelings about the League of Nations as an institution were also colored by a liberal fear of state power. In this sense, although confident of the existence of a higher spirit at work in the world, they were less confident about its relationship to the organizational practices of the League of Nations itself. Thus, Murray and Zimmern argued that while their conceptions of Liberal spirit and international mind were somehow related to the bureaucratic workings of the League, they worried, in a style typical of their Oxford progenitors, about imbuing

[1] Zimmern, *The League of Nations and the Rule of Law*, 236.
[2] Ibid., 277.
[3] Murray, *The Ordeal of This Generation*, 190.
[4] Zimmern, "Introduction," *The War and Democracy*, 2.

a potentially coercive League with the full moral authority of Spirit. To do so, they argued, would potentially lead to the creation of an authoritarian body that might trample on the sovereignty of individual states. And so while they were vocal in their support for a post-war world in which the state was not the sole focus of international politics—a world made up of states and "organization across the borders of the states"—they simultaneously refused to challenge the ultimate right of European and imperial states, as individual entities, to assert their will.[5] Such a challenge might result in the unthinkable situation of the "civilized" nations of the world being obliged to share power with non-white and former colonial states. In sum, Murray and Zimmern refused to imagine a League that was even a loose approximation of what Zimmern termed a "super-state."[6]

As a result, the relationship between Murray's and Zimmern's policy prescriptions for the League as an institution and their sense of the world as a unified spiritual whole remained mired in ambiguity throughout the twenty years of the League's active existence. In the end, just as both men had struggled to hold together the loose ends of a domestic political theory that was neither fully liberal nor fully idealist, so too did they struggle to make coherent a similar view of international relations, one that approximated neither the mechanical workings of the liberal state writ large nor the spirituality of a global community united by the universal movement of Spirit. This struggle became one of the defining features of their work.

In contrast to their constant efforts to paint a coherent picture of the League of Nations (even years after its inception) stood these thinkers' crystalline vision of the world as an organic cosmos. For Murray and Zimmern, any successful post-war theory of internationalism had to speak to the inherent sociability of the world's people and the natural processes of a divinely inspired global order. Just as both men grounded their understandings of Liberal spirit in the underlying *reality* of that Spirit, so too did they argue that international society *existed* as an almost living, breathing entity. In this context, it was no wonder that Zimmern imagined himself a mere godfather beside the cradle of the post-war peace; in his mind, the baby of international cooperation had already been reborn through the painful labor of war. Perhaps this unwavering belief in the preexisting reality of a divinely inspired international community (what Murray termed a "cosmos" and Zimmern an "organism") explains why Murray and Zimmern often described their work with the League of Nations in necessary but peripheral terms, as though it did not constitute international society itself but merely accounted for its care and feeding.

[5] Zimmern, *The League of Nations and the Rule of Law*, 194.
[6] Ibid., 282.

Chapter 4 argues that Murray's and Zimmern's emphatic insistence on the organic workings of world society was a supplement for these thinkers' equally emphatic rejection of a world state and, in this sense, strongly resembled their own approaches to liberalism in a domestic context and the way an earlier generation of Oxford intellectuals had turned away from state power toward organic notions of the social whole. Thus, for first generation Oxford idealist liberals like Bosanquet and Ritchie, the state was legitimate insofar as it related to a *preexisting* "social organism." In Bosanquet's words, the relationship of society to the state "is like that by which a tree makes its wood, or a living body deposits its skeleton. The work of the State is *de facto* for the most part . . . setting its *imprimatur,* the seal of its force, on what more flexible activities or the mere progress of life have wrought out in long years of adventurous experiment or silent growth."[7] Likewise, for Murray and Zimmern, the League of Nations was, in the end, an institutional expression—what Murray referred to as a "representation"—of the global body politic, that natural social order that had been experiencing its own form of "silent growth" through the gradual emergence of an "organic citizenship" among the world's people.[8]

In this way, Murray and Zimmern elided the difficult question of where to locate Liberal spirit or the international mind. From within their idealist liberal framework, identifying spirit too closely with the institution of the League of Nations (or any international authority) would imbue it with a corrosive power politics and ultimately undermine its transcendent and conciliatory effect on the world. And yet they realized that the very sociable nature of their approaches to spirit necessitated a location, a grounding in some form of community that made the "freedom to serve" a possibility for everyone. For both men this was found in the organically conceived form of global community that they believed lay at the heart of all efforts at international organization, a community ultimately distinct from the League itself.

This similarity aside, Murray and Zimmern imagined the contours of their international societies differently, in ways that reflected their individual approaches to spirit on an international scale. Murray advocated for the existence of world cosmos, an idea he attributed to the Greeks and that he defined by using both metaphysical and natural language. In strikingly Platonic terms Murray argued that world cosmos (or the true form of global sociality) existed on a higher spiritual plane but was simultaneously embodied in the natural movements of the heavens and the normal

---

[7] Bosanquet, *The Philosophical Theory of the State*, xxxviii.
[8] Zimmern, "German Culture and the British Commonwealth," 379.

functions of a "healthy" world order.[9] When people of good will put their efforts into first discovering (or *re*discovering) and then nurturing this spiritual/natural form of social and political organization, they actualized the One Great City of Men and Gods on earth. Human beings in the era of the League of Nations, Murray argued, must strive to create a world that most closely approximated the divine form of world cosmos and reject all that did not conform to that vision.[10]

But, as we shall see, it is clear from Murray's writings on world cosmos that the form of order it represented was hardly novel, not even, in Carr's sense, "utopian." Rather, world order for Murray implied the path of least resistance; it required no revolution, and demanded no major changes in the political or economic status quo. Murray was, in fact, remarkably nostalgic for the old, pre-war international system led by the Great Powers and imperials states, Britain chief among them. The war, in this context, was a wrenching disjuncture from a clearly understood form of social cohesion and, ironically given Murray's commitment to the League of Nations system, the best thing statesmen and world inhabitants of the post-war era could do was to return to that well-understood way of living. "Cosmos has been succeeded by chaos," Murray continued to lament, ten years after the formation of the League, "and we must eventually find our Cosmos again."[11]

At the same time, Murray also wrote his work on international relations as a call to challenge the status quo, to theorize an international society that required a major shift from what he imagined as an outdated form of political organization based on maintaining the balance of power between imperial states toward a form of cooperative collective security. As a liberal reformer, he consistently maintained that he wanted to see the pre-war international order overturned in favor of a more open "democratic idea."[12] But Murray's consistent longing for *place*—that is, a place to posit the spirit of international cooperation other than the League—coupled with his aversion to power politics and a deep and abiding fear of both colonial nationalism and Bolshevism ultimately compelled him to embrace a moralized form of the pre-war order, a "kinder, gentler"

---

[9] Murray, "A Survey of Recent World Affairs," 10.

[10] Murray traced this idea not only to Plato himself but also to the British liberals. "Plato, Aristotle and the Stoics, St. Augustine and Thomas Aquinas, Kant and J.S. Mill, and Comte and T.H. Green," Murray maintained, conveniently omitting Hegel from this list, "all argue or assume that there exists in some sense a Cosmos or Divine Order; that what is good is in harmony with this Order and what is bad is in discord against it." [Murray, "Satanism and World Order," 9].

[11] Murray, *The Ordeal of This Generation*, 190.

[12] Murray, *The League of Nations and the Democratic Idea* (Oxford: Oxford University Press, 1918).

version of Great Power and imperial domination that, as with his conception of "order" on a domestic level, was notably pre-liberal in its commitment to a social hierarchy based on natural distinctions between leaders and led.[13]

Zimmern's understanding of world society differed from Murray's in a number of ways. It was strikingly more organic than Murray's in that Zimmern never failed to describe his world "organism" with a kind of naturalist's zeal as a living body. Likewise, while Murray's understanding of cosmos rested on the constantly articulated differences between civilized and non-civilized peoples (the forces of order versus the forces of chaos), Zimmern's conception of difference was much more complicated and reflected his overall more dialectical notion of international mind. For Zimmern, unique *national* communities constituted the international organism. Nations in distinction from states, he argued, provided world society with its greatest source of moral energy. Much as Oxford idealist liberals of the preceding generation had imagined the family as a discrete cell within the social body, so too did Zimmern envision a world body comprised of individual national families. Within the explicitly domestic walls of these families of mankind, global sociality was first nourished, and ordinary citizens were first schooled in the ways of the international mind.[14]

For Zimmern, one had only to look at the evils of Bolshevism or the cosmopolitan Levantine to understand the "moral degradation the loss of nationality involves."[15] In this context, both the transnational aspirations of the Bolshevik and the mobility of the Levantine merchant—whose Middle Eastern origins were obscured by his travels—were always described in the most materialist and shallow of terms.[16] Fixed nationalities, by contrast, literally rooted human beings in the good earth of a moral home. Zimmern thus argued that the international community must nourish nationalities, in all their diversity, and the League itself must work to promote appropriately *internationalist* nationalisms. And yet only through those lessons taught within the nation was internationalism itself brought to fruition. In essence, according to Zimmern, appreciating the differences between nations and fully experiencing the power of one's own patriotism was a prerequisite to being a full citizen of the world. To truly experience the international mind, to live in what he described as "a room with the windows open on a wide prospect over the world," one

[13] Murray, *Satanism and World Order*, 40.

[14] Zimmern, *Nationality and Government*, 36.

[15] Zimmern, *Nationality and Government*, 52.

[16] The term "Levantine" refers to someone from the "Levant," a region that today includes Syria, Lebanon, and Israel, but has historically also included Egypt and the Mediterranean. Zimmern's use of the "Levantine" example will be discussed later in this chapter.

must first go back to the nation, to that place "of old custom, of reverence, of home."[17]

As chapter 6 maintains, Zimmern's language of family and Murray's equally natural understanding of order both naturalized economic and imperial power relations and ultimately propelled both men toward an international political agenda strikingly conservative in its ends despite it reformist beginnings. Chapter 4 explores on an international scale the antinomies of Murray's and Zimmern's liberalisms that led up to such conservative conclusions about the international body politic. The first section investigates the philosophical tension inherent in their under-standing of the relationship between the League of Nations and the move-ment of Liberal spirit and the international mind. The second section ar-gues that these thinkers responded to their own conflicted approach to the League system by turning toward organic and naturalistic explanations of global society as a means to both legitimize international cooperation and compensate for the League's lack of coercive power. The third section examines Murray's understanding of world order and the central role of nationhood in Zimmern's internationalist imaginary. In so doing, it sets the stage for the final chapter's more extensive analysis of how both men's ideas of international society worked to smooth over the power discrepan-cies at the heart of the post-war peace.

A Liberal Problem: Spirit and World Statehood

In Murray's opinion, the early days of the League of Nations movement in Britain tended toward the fanatical fringe. Otherwise completely rea-sonable people, he argued, concluded during the war that the only way to prevent war in the future was to create an international organization capable of independently enforcing international law. Even H. G. Wells, Murray grumbled, caught up in the "crude international ideas of the day," allowed himself to "go off in the direction of a World State with an over-whelming army, which would abolish all diplomacy, all foreign offices, and, in some cases, all national parliaments, and content itself with com-pelling everybody to do right, or off with their heads if they objected."[18] As Murray's words suggest, anything that resembled a world state was, he imagined, necessarily authoritarian and repressive. An inherent con-nection existed, Murray implied, between the mere existence of an inter-

---

[17] Zimmern, "The Development of the International Mind," 3; Zimmern, *Nationality and Government*, 78.

[18] Bodl. MS Gilbert Murray (241), fols. 26–27. (Typescript account of the origins of the League of Nations with corrections by Murray, 1922.)

national body with any measure of coercive force and the destruction of all local politics and liberal rights. Zimmern wholeheartedly agreed with this conclusion, arguing in 1918 that if any post-war international organization was "framed in accordance with a Constitution which binds its representatives to accept its decision and obey its Government, then the World-state, with a World Executive, will already have come into being. There will be no more war, but only Rebellion and Treason."[19]

In many respects, Murray's and Zimmern's understandings of world statehood as necessarily repressive can be seen as an extension of their attitudes toward liberal statehood in general. Just as the internal tension between an idealist notion of spirit and a liberal wariness toward state power in their domestic political theories resulted in two conflicted, even incoherent, accounts of the liberal state, so too was their fervent rejection of world statehood the result of an inability to reconcile international spirit with international authority. Equating Liberal spirit or the international mind with world statehood would, by necessity, sully it with power politics. Circumstances particular to the post-war era, however also intensified these scholars' anxiety toward statehood on a global level. As noted in chapter 2, Murray's and Zimmern's liberalisms were significantly more anti-statist than those of most nineteenth-century Oxford liberals, primarily as a result of forced conscription at home and Prussianism abroad.[20] In addition, the Bolshevik Revolution and early signs of imperial collapse convinced both men of the distinct possibility that the more "modern-minded states and communities of the world" might lose their grip on authoritative world power and let it slip into the hands of "politically immature peoples"—ex-colonials and socialists.[21] In his 1919 Foreign Office memorandum encouraging the British delegation to create a League with limited coercive abilities, for instance, Zimmern argued, "We have to look forward to a period when Bolshevism—or the religion of the international class war—will be a prominent factor in European policy, and may at any time seize the reigns of power in States which are, or desire to become, member of the League."[22] In response to the specter of a League of Nations controlled by the Soviets, both men translated their heightened fear of the state into vociferous rejections of a "super-state." The idea of a super-state was implicitly authoritarian for these thinkers in a way that the domestic state was not. While their domestic political theories were rife with contradictions in regard to the state, they never

---

[19] Zimmern, *Nationality and Government*, 27.

[20] Freeden, *Liberalism Divided*; see chapter 2, "The War on Liberalism."

[21] Zimmern, "Introduction," *The War and Democracy*, 7.

[22] Zimmern, "Foreign Office Memorandum," *The League of Nations and the Rule of Law*, 220.

argued against its necessity. Rather, they tended to write around it, assuming the state's presence but avoiding its power. In an international context, however, Murray and Zimmern argued successfully for a League with *no* coercive capacity whatsoever. Any attempt to make the League remotely like a state, they insisted, would come at the price of individual liberty and state sovereignty.

And yet this picture is complicated by another schizophrenic trend that runs throughout both Murray's and Zimmern's thinking on sovereignty: their decision to challenge status quo assumptions about the preservation of "outward" sovereignty one minute and their complete unwillingness to do so the next.[23] In this sense, neither Murray nor Zimmern fits neatly into the general tendency of League historians to pit supporters of a "traditional conception of sovereignty" against "internationalists."[24] While a number of prominent internationalists (most famously, Laski and Hobson) were openly critical of the notion of sovereignty, Murray's and Zimmern's approach was much more internally at odds with itself.

Both men agreed that the unchecked ability of the Great Powers to wage war on one another had been in some way responsible for the war. Creating a just and peaceful post-war order meant somehow challenging what Murray termed "our modern anarchy," the idea that individual states had infinite rights with regard to other states.[25] Thus, for Murray, states that agreed to live together peacefully had to agree to give up at least a portion of their sovereignty. "We had to demand," he argued in a retrospective on his work with the League of Nations Union, "at least one vital reduction of sovereignty; the nations must agree in the first place to renounce war among themselves and, in the second place, to use their united strength to defend any unoffending member against an aggressive attack."[26] But for Murray, this renunciation was always, by necessity, voluntary and the creation of a world power capable of forcing states to abjure their right to wage war would be intolerable. This approach makes considerable sense giving Murray's emphatic belief in the power of Liberal spirit to transform the world. Hence, for Murray, in a correctly ordered world (a world wherein all states accepted the dictates of Liberal

[23] For an excellent analysis of "inward" and "outward" notions of sovereignty, see Ken Conca, "Environmental Protection, International Norms, and State Sovereignty," *Beyond Westphalia? State Sovereignty and International Intervention*, ed. Gene Lyons and Michael Mastanduno. (Baltimore: The John Hopkins University Press, 1995).

[24] See for instance, Gary Ostrower, *The League of Nations From 1919–1929* (Garden City Park, NY: Avery, 1996), 110–11; David Hunter Miller, *The Geneva Protocol* (New York: Macmillan, 1925); Michael Dockrill and J. Douglas Goold, *Peace Without Promise* (Hamden, CT: Archon, 1981).

[25] Murray, *Liberality and Civilization*, 62.

[26] Murray, "The League of Nations, the First Experiment," 66.

spirit as revealed to them by the Committee on International Cooperation and other such experts associated with the League), there was no need for coercion. In the rare case in which disputes arose over territory or economic practices, states would willingly cede their sovereign right of war and adhere to this dispassionate advice.

But while Murray was able to imagine a situation in which the absolute right to sovereignty might be somewhat compromised with regard to other European states (albeit only within a voluntary framework), he was completely appalled by the idea that British sovereignty (particularly with regard to the Empire) might be similarly challenged. In perhaps the only instance in his vast writings on international relations in which he used the word "foreigner" in anything other than ironic sense, Murray argued in his speech to the annual meeting of the League of Nations Union General Council in 1924 that calling in "foreigners" to settle disputes within the Empire was completely intolerable.[27] Comparing the conflict between the Great Britain and the Irish Free State to "a dispute between the French Central government and Alsace-Lorraine" was a "gross exaggeration."[28] While it might make sense for the French government to follow the suggestions of League experts with regard to a territory that it considered its own, for the British government to make a similar concession would present a serious threat to its own internal cohesion, a cohesion that Murray imagined in the most naturalistic of terms. Thus he argued in language resounding with the pro-imperial exuberance of the Round Table Society, that "the British Empire is a thing by itself. It is a new growth and it is not exactly like any other growth that has hitherto existed in the world." All internal disputes, then, disputes presumably having to do with self-determination of British colonials, must be dealt with internally, according to Murray, by "the best legal brains in the Empire."[29]

What seemed most threatening to Murray was precisely this possibility, that an India or an Egypt might petition the League of Nations to intervene on its behalf. Recall that for Murray, any and all movement toward the breakup of Empire fell into the category of the Satanic, the selfish, the disintegrating drive toward world anarchy. "Men in many parts of the world," Murray thus argued in 1924, "some even as close to us as Ireland—are daily giving up their lives to the sacred cause of hatred, even a hopeless hatred, against us, and the World Order which we embody."[30] Sovereign challenges made by colonials were inherently destructive not

---

[27] Murray, *The League of Nations Union Policy: an Address delivered at a Meeting of the General Assembly of the League of Nations Union, Dec. 19, 1924* (Geneva: League of Nations Union, 1924), 8.

[28] Ibid.

[29] Ibid.

[30] Murray, *Satanim and World Order*, 34.

only because they elevated the less politically mature people of the world to an equal status with Europeans, but also because they were messy, sometimes violent, and hopelessly chaotic.

Like Murray, Zimmern's experiences with the empire shaped his understanding of sovereignty, but, unlike Murray, Zimmern was painstakingly careful to use the word "commonwealth." Zimmern's attachment to the idea of commonwealth appears in his writings after 1913 and coincides with the beginning of his involvement with the Round Table Society. Along with Lionel Curtis, Zimmern was one of the leading forces behind a major rethinking of the society's mission in the years just before and during World War One. At this time, thinkers like Curtis (along with other members of the society's "London Group," which included Zimmern, Phillip Kerr, and Ramsey Muir) began working on a number of papers for circulation that focused on something Curtis called the "principle of commonwealth." The ideas behind this principle were developed largely in reaction to the growing anti-statism of British liberals, a sentiment that was itself a reaction to Prussianism and Bolshevism. In other words, liberals associated with the Round Table Society felt they needed to reconcile their increasing discomfort with the language of state authority—a language that, by necessity, dominated the discourse of a far flung imperial edifice held together by military coercion—and their support for an ethical empire.

From the beginning, Zimmern played a central role in recasting the society's conception of empire in terms of a supposedly less centralized commonwealth. Indeed, his own work on *The Greek Commonwealth* was widely read by Round Table members who were interested in his interpretation of Greek citizenship and its relationship to what he claimed were the largely communal, not state-centered, ethics of Athenian life.[31] In the end, in a classically Oxford liberal move, Zimmern, Curtis, and their colleagues forged an alternative ideology of empire that appeared to decenter the role of the imperial state. In a manner highly reminiscent of Bosanquet's and Ritchie's relocation of moral authority from the state to the social organism, key thinkers of the Round Table argued that the empire ought to be conceived of as a living community with a shared sense of cultural and moral ends rather than as a collection of dependencies organized around the centripetal pull of a powerful state.[32]

In his writings on internationalism more generally, Zimmern frequently used the British Commonwealth as a functioning example of the type of

---

[31] Indeed, Curtis's 1915 article, "The Project Of Commonwealth," referred frequently to Zimmern's conception of Athenian citizenship. [See Kendle, *The Round Table Movement*, 171].

[32] Kendle, *The Round Table Movement*, 172.

polity he believed best characterized the modern world, a polity "less rigid than a federation but more intimate than an alliance." The commonwealth proved to the world, he argued, that a different kind of state was possible—a "composite" state of various nationalities with differing levels of self-government, ranging from the almost complete autonomy of the "white dominions" to the total imperial control of British Africa.[33] This composite state functioned, Zimmern repeatedly maintained despite vast evidence to the contrary, as a "free union" of consenting states and thus proved the folly of the "vague nineteenth-century shibboleth" that "every nation has a right to be a sovereign state."[34] Nations in the commonwealth, Zimmern argued, could have all of their cultural needs met while the more competent imperial "motherland" took care of their political and economic policies [35]

And yet while Zimmern believed that the sheer existence of the commonwealth might demonstrate the absurdity of the logic behind the "right" to national self determination, both he and Murray also insisted that the empire itself, as a political unit, as a state in toto, was supremely sovereign. Sovereignty, therefore, was something to be enjoyed by the imperial European powers, the "white dominions," the United States, Japan, and, only reluctantly, those formerly colonized states that had declared their independence far in advance of the war (primarily, those in Latin America). A variety of other post-war developments no doubt also pushed Murray and Zimmern in this direction, not least the widely held post-1917 opinion that state sovereignty and the right to self-determination were necessary to oppose Bolshevism, a revolutionary ideology that, in the words of Susan Buck-Morss, not only challenged class disctinctions but "ignored state boundaries."[36] Championing sovereignty in the face of Bolshevism also became part and parcel of these thinkers' response to more radical British internationalists like Hobson and Laski who openly questioned the effectiveness of an international institution that accepted the inviolability of the sovereign state. The response of Zimmern and his colleagues to thinkers like Laski and Hobson was always defiantly and determinedly liberal. Yes, the creation of a world state and the "abrogation" of sovereignty might bring about world peace, but at what price? While Hobson's idea of a world state might not be "intrinsically impossible," argued Zimmern in 1918, the "real difficulty is to establish free world government—to ensure universal peace without the universal sacrifice of liberty."[37]

[33] Bodl. Ms. Zimmern (135), fol. 124.
[34] Zimmern, "Nationalism and Internationalism," 89.
[35] Zimmern, "The Ethics of Empire," *The Round Table* (1913): 494.
[36] Susan Buck-Morss, "Passports," *Documents* 3 (Summer, 1993): 75.
[37] Zimmern, *Nationality and Government*, 39.

Thus, even though they both believed that states at the least had to voluntarily give up their right to make war against each other, Murray and Zimmern ended up being fierce adherents to a rather realist looking notion: the idea that states, like individuals, had a legitimate interests in their own survival and a simultaneous right to reject and repel the directives of other states. According to Zimmern, "the essence of a State is that it is sovereign and takes orders from no one above it."[38] The League of Nations, as envisioned by Murray and Zimmern, both before and after ratification of the covenant in 1919, could only press but never fully challenge sovereignty. According to Zimmern, it must ultimately approximate "a system of cooperation between independent, or, if you like, sovereign authorities."[39] The League was thus imagined by two of its most powerful intellectuals framers not as a challenge to post-war state relations as decided in Versailles, but merely as another not quite clearly defined but somehow powerful presence in the world. Zimmern perhaps put it best when he described political relations in an era of internationalism as a game of chess. "The coming of the League of Nations has put a queen on that board" he argued in 1926, "and the movements of that queen now dominate the whole board and the whole game, although there are certain movements the queen, by the rules of the game, is unable to perform."[40] Chief among these movements was anything that resembled the actions of a state.

And yet their insistence that the League of Nations not challenge the fundamental power relations between states ran directly counter to their cry for a radical transformation of "the international anarchy which led to the War."[41] The new world order was not supposed to be about power politics, not supposed to rely on what Murray termed the old "method of healing all wrong by killing or hitting somebody."[42] Rather, the Paris Peace Conference was to usher in an era of rationality in international relations. For Zimmern, the process of creating a peaceful world "*assumes* a new spirit in the whole field of international politics. It presupposes a transformation of Power politics into Responsibility politics."[43] Likewise, as their deep commitment to the notions of Liberal spirit and the international mind suggests, this sense of responsibility was to transcend state boundaries. In these terms, an end to power politics necessarily implied an "extension of the sense of social responsibility across the

---

[38] Ibid.
[39] Zimmern, *The Future of Democracy*, 99.
[40] Zimmern, "The Development of the International Mind," 6.
[41] Murray, "Then and Now," *From the League to the U.N.*, 18.
[42] Murray, *Satanism and World Order*, 35.
[43] Zimmern, *The League of Nations and the Rule of Law*, 285.

frontiers of the state."[44] In this world vision, individuals and "voluntary, non-governmental organizations" took on a central role in the construction of world peace.[45]

As fearful as they were of a super-state and challenges to state sovereignty, Murray and Zimmern were also emphatic in their insistence that some institutional mechanism should exist above and beyond states to help make international politics more rational. In Murray's words, creating a peaceful global community "without any common guidance" was impossible. Rather, what the world needed was the construction of "some organization or machinery which would represent the unity of the world."[46] For both Murray and Zimmern, this "machinery" should focus its efforts on cultivating a class of dispassionate and rational international relations experts who would meet in Geneva and arrive at solutions to international conflicts that adhered most closely to the vision of global cooperation espoused by the League. Again, in this context, the League's relatively minor Institute for Intellectual Cooperation loomed large in the minds of both men. Through its publications, summer schools, and conferences, Zimmern argued in 1926, the institute hoped to cultivate a "body of persons in all countries" for whom internationalist thinking became "not merely a habit but a need."[47] Once created, this international intelligentsia would be set up as a permanent part of the League's bureaucratic organization. Solutions to world problems (ranging from the status of ethnic minorities to the opium trade to the "traffic in women and children") were first to be formulated within discrete "bodies of experts" created by the League's institutional apparatus. It was then up to member states to accept the solutions of these experts. In the words of Zimmern, "The only hope of the survival of our civilization lies in the existence of such a body of students of international relations and in the willingness of the free peoples to accept their leadership."[48]

The philosophical and political tensions between Murray's and Zimmern's fears of a world state, commitment to state sovereignty, belief in the universal, power of Spirit, and the logistical need for international organization, shattered their approaches to the League of Nations into many of the same liberal and idealist fragments that they had so desperately tried to piece back together in their domestic political theories. Thus,

[44] Zimmern, "The Problems of Collective Security," *Neutrality and Collective Security,* ed. Quincy Wright (Chicago: University of Chicago Press, 1936), 28.

[45] Zimmern, *The League of Nations and the Rule of Law,* 282.

[46] Murray, "A Survey of Recent World Affairs," 2.

[47] Zimmern, "The League and International Intellectual Co-operation," and "The Development of the International Mind," *Problems of Peace* 5 (1927): 149.

[48] Zimmern, "The Problems of Collective Security," 87.

in their most idealist moments, Murray and Zimmern imagined a world united by the transcendent power of Liberal spirit and international mind. In their most liberal moments, opposition to a super-state compelled them to champion the rights of the individual sovereign state against the world authority. The result of this fundamental contradiction was the development of a profoundly schizophrenic approach to the League of Nations. On the one hand, these thinkers wanted the League *to be a part* of the gradual unfolding of Liberal Spirit the world. On the other, they wanted a League institution that was absolutely distinct from the spirituality of the international mind. The League was thus supposed to be inherently spiritual and merely mechanical, both implicit in and foreign to the emergence of international mind in the global community.

For the most part Murray and Zimmern tried to address these contradictions by vacillating blithely between spiritual and bureaucratic depictions of the League. Murray's works, in particular, swung wildly in their portrayals of a League that was detached and bureaucratic to one that was deeply spiritual. Thus, in 1919 Murray argued that the League should not be considered an "alliance" between states but rather "constitutes chiefly a way of behaviour."[49] In other words, the actual mechanism of the League paled in comparison to the spirit of the endeavor. One year later, Murray had changed his tune slightly and was arguing for a League with its own moral (and gendered) personality. "The League is not an alliance" he continued to maintain in the *Problems of Foreign Policy*. Rather, "she is asked only to sit in council with other nations . . . to face the vast problems which now confront mankind and which the rest of us have pledged ourselves to face in the spirit of peace and justice."[50] In a speech given that same year, Murray painted a slightly less anthropomorphic picture of the League. Here the League was a largely bureaucratic collection of like thinking people, an "assembly of able men drawn from all quarters of the globe united by a professional interest in the welfare, concord, and wise guidance of the world as a whole."[51] At the same time, Murray was fascinated by something he referred to as "League spirit," a way of behavior that consistently put the good of the whole above the "forces of uncontrolled and irresponsible covetousness" at work in the world.[52] In this sense, the League actually reflected (or in Murray's earlier words, "represented") the movement of Liberal spirit,

[49] Murray, "The Problem of Nationality," *Proceedings of the Aristotelean Society, 1919–1920*, 259.
[50] Murray, *The Problem of Foreign Policy*, xvi.
[51] Murray, "Orbis Terrestris," 197–98.
[52] Ibid., 196.

of true international cooperation. Ultimately, he argued, the League possessed a "spiritual background without which it could not live."[53]

Zimmern's characterizations of the League were often equally mixed. Thus, throughout his most influential book, *The League of Nations and the Rule of Law*, Zimmern referred to the League as a "Co-operative Society," as a "Concert," as a "machine," and an "organism." Although the League was already over fifteen years old when he wrote the book, a clear definition of the League had yet to gel for Zimmern. In the end, he resorted to the almost dialectical language of his Oxford origins and painted a picture of a League that was more than a multi-lateral treaty and less than a super state.

> The League, in fact, lies in an intermediate zone between these two extremes. Or, to use a more fitting image, it swings between these two poles, drawing nearer sometimes to the one, sometimes to the other, but never remaining fixed. And the direction and force of these oscillations are due, not to anything inherent in the League itself, not to its constitution or (except in a wholly minor degree) its so-called 'Civil service', but to the attitude and policies of its component states, particularly of the Great Powers. What the League *is*, at any given moment, is determined in fact by the degree of willingness on the part of the powers to co-operate with one another.[54]

The capacity of the League to organize world affairs had nothing to do with its own institutional construction but was contingent upon the cooperative spirit of its state members, upon their willingness to participate in the international mind, to recognize that their own interests were "bound up with the interests of the whole enterprise."[55] This required that participants in the League think of it not in state terms but "in terms of something more flexible and more subtle."[56]

One of the problems with insisting on a "subtle" League was that none of its supporters seemed capable of explaining its inadequacies. Because the League's purpose was unclear from the outset, it became almost impossible to explain its failures. Murray and Zimmern, who had seen their conflicted visions of the League institutionalized in the Covenant, seemed genuinely perplexed by the League's inability to adequately address the global economic depression of the 1930s or to keep member states from violating one another's territory. When they did acknowledge

---

[53] Murray, *The World and the League: An Address Delivered at the Annual Meeting of the League of Nations Union General Council, June 17th, 1924.* (Geneva: League of Nations Union, 1924.)

[54] Zimmern, *The League of Nations and the Rule of Law*, 281.

[55] Ibid., 283.

[56] Zimmern, "The New International Outlook," 16.

the League's failings, they tended not to blame the League itself but, again, a lack of global will. Thus, in 1933 Murray argued that the 1932 World Economic Conference had broken down not because of something inherently insecure about the League or because of the contemporary economic practice of capitalism but because of a "lack of world spirit."[57] In 1936, Zimmern noted that despite the rise of fascism, the Italian invasion of Ethiopia, the Japanese invasion of Manchuria, and the world economic collapse, the League continued to be an "indispensable agency for the life of the modern world," although he seemed singularly incapable of explaining to his readers why this was so.[58]

Leftist critics of the League system were more explicit about the its ultimate failure. The League could not survive, according to Konni Zilliacus, precisely because of its subtlety (what Zilliacus called its "elasticity"), which he translated into the framers' unwillingness to make it a seat of authority in the world. The result was an international institution that, in Zilliacus's words, was "an adjunct of, rather than an alternative to, the old diplomacy, so that the world, instead of becoming safe for democracy . . . once more becomes safe for the old order by reverting to international anarchy, power politics and an arms race."[59] Likewise, Laski argued before his audience at the Geneva Summer School in 1926 that the only way to ensure world peace was to take "the League of Nations very much farther than it has at present gone" by giving it the ability to actually enforce international law.[60] In one of their many joint attempts to save the League during the 1930s, Zilliacus and Laski released a pamphlet entitled *The Dying Peace* in which they pleaded with their audience to make a choice "between international government and international anarchy." "Unless" argued Laski in the preface, "we vindicate within a brief period the paramount claims of the League to the allegiance of its members, with all that this paramountcy implies, it is difficult to see any prospect of avoiding disaster."[61]

But for Murray and Zimmern, making the League more like a government would run contrary to its spiritual nature. They thus argued successfully for a League of Nations that stood apart from the machinations of governments, governments which were invariably, according to Murray, possessed by selfishness.[62] Instead, they envisioned a League that would

[57] Murray, "A Survey of Recent World Affairs," 5.

[58] Zimmern, *The League of Nations and the Rule of Law*, 7.

[59] Zilliacus, *Mirror of the Past*, 310.

[60] Laski, "International Government and National Sovereignty," *Problems of Peace: Lectures Delivered at the Geneva Institute of International Relations: 1926*, 299.

[61] Laski, "Preface," *The Dying Peace* (London: The New Statesman and Nation, 1933.)

[62] Murray, *The Ordeal of This Generation*, 191.

rise above the world like a living symbol of international cooperation, a flag fluttering in the wind, a *representation* "of the unity of the world." As Zimmern described it, the League "looks forward to abiding results, not through the mechanical cooperation of governments, but through the growth of an organic citizenship, through the education of the nations themselves to a sense of common duty and common life." Because this movement toward a "common life" was part of an inevitable civilizing process, its slow pace did not worry Zimmern. "We must," he argued, "take the old slow high road of civilization, not the short cut across the field."[63]

In essence, for Murray and Zimmern the League was most powerful when it gestured toward a future in which conflicts between states did not exist and the international mind reigned supreme. In Zimmern's words, participation or non-participation in the League offered states a simple choice "between cooperation or exile from the world's life: between internationalism or monasticism: between an effort to Hellenization, by whatever means may be at hand, or acquiescence in catastrophe and a return to the Dark Ages."[64] Ultimately, for Murray and Zimmern, the greatest power that the League of Nations could wield was symbolic.

For Zilliacus, this belief in the power of symbolism was inherently disingenuous, a grand concession to conservative and capitalist forces. "The Peace Conference liberals" he argued, "in defense to the obduracy of conservatism and plutocracy, agreed to a very low minimum of obligations in the Covenant . . . [and then] took comfort in believing in a brilliant future for the moral forces that they were uneasily aware had been badly defeated at the Peace Conference."[65] But it is not so clear as Zilliacus implies that "Peace Conference liberals" like Murray and Zimmern were either cognizant that they had agreed to give something up when they constructed their anti-state approach to the League or "uneasily" aware that these "moral forces" had somehow been defeated. Well before the peace conference, Murray and Zimmern were adamant in their insistence that the League not possess any actual coercive power. Their position on this never wavered throughout the inter-war period. More importantly, however, as chapter 3 demonstrated, Murray and Zimmern were firmly committed, in the tradition of the Oxford idealist liberals, the notion that the *real* was the *rational*. Thus, for these thinkers, the slow unfolding of moral, internationalist forces in the world and the symbolic expression

---

[63] Zimmern, *Nationality and Government*, 29. It was this very notion which conditioned the League's own approach to the mandate system; that is, to the eventual and supposed "maturation" of the colonies.

[64] Zimmern, *The Study of International Relations*, 19.

[65] Zilliacus, *Mirror of the Past*, 310.

of these forces in Geneva were not meaningless, not some cynical gesture to rescue the League project from political obscurity. Instead, Murray and Zimmern believed, throughout their years of association with the League, that states gathered together in Geneva in the spirit of cooperation were in fact expressing, bit by bit, the underlying reality of "that impalpable, Something."[66]

And yet in their more bureaucratic moments, these thinkers also argued that the League had no particular moral character of its own, that "as an organization" it was "only enlightening in so far as it points beyond itself to the forces in the mind of man upon which its own future and that of our present-day civilization depend."[67] As Zimmern argued, "that Something does not reside in a tabernacle at Geneva. It is communicated to Geneva by the peoples of the Member States."[68] In other words, as an institution the League itself carried no moral weight and instead served as a mere conduit for the international mind. In Zimmern's words, "I do not mean to say that Geneva is going to become a centre of all politics; I do not think it will . . . but, I think this place will henceforward supply the conditions for the thinking out of such policies and the stimulus which will lead to their being thought out."[69] Institutionally then, the League was to restrict itself to being "a focus and centre for thought," a place "to pool the best brains of all nations for the common service of all."[70] In spatial terms, the League was that "room with the windows open on a wide prospect over the world," but the room itself stood empty.[71] The League was not to act as a kind of neutral third party. It was not to pass moral judgment. In fact, in this particular vision of the League, no greater moral subject existed at Geneva, only what Zimmern termed the "maximum of cooperation between governments at any given moment."[72]

Murray and Zimmern used their positions of power within the Foreign Office, the Liberal Party, and the League of Nations Union to ensure that Geneva remained an empty room. The international organization created by the 1919 Covenant was a somewhat uncomfortable combination of powerful language and powerless institutions. For instance, Article 16 of the covenant at once deemed economic sanctions against aggressive member states "compulsory" and military measures to curb this aggression

---

[66] Zimmern, *The League of Nations and the Rule of Law*, 289.

[67] Ibid., 9.

[68] Ibid., 289.

[69] Zimmern, "The Development of the International Mind," 7.

[70] Zimmern, *The League of Nations and the Rule of Law*, 5; Murray, *The Ordeal of This Generation*, 193.

[71] Zimmern, "The Development of the International Mind," 3.

[72] Zimmern, *The League of Nations and the Rule of Law*, 9.

"optional."[73] In addition, the principle of unanimity governed the League Assembly, thus making it virtually impossible for a majority of states to enforce their will on a wayward member.[74] In sum, two of the League's most influential intellectual founders purposely envisioned it as institutionally powerless, a fact which later prompted Carr to describe the League as a "body politic without a policy."[75] A more accurate description however might be Gertrude Stein's Oakland: At Geneva, there was no there there. The body politic was instead located beyond the League, in the organic totality of the world cosmos.

AN ORGANIC SOLUTION: WORLD COSMOS AND THE GLOBAL ORGANISM

Murray's and Zimmern's political liberalism teetered perpetually on the cusp between an idealist understanding of Spirit inherited from their Oxford progenitors and a more orthodox liberal fear of state authority, also inherited from these same thinkers. In a domestic context, their writings on the state were filled with contradictory understandings of the state's role in creating the material conditions necessary to make the truly spiritual liberal order possible, contradictions that ultimately drove them to locate the moral foundations of liberal community in a vision of *society* that existed, both men insisted, *in distinction from* the state. Similarly, Murray's and Zimmern's work on the League was characterized by equally contradictory impulses that also compelled them toward the social. In the context of international relations, however, their particular understanding of international society was almost entirely novel. No one, until this time, had ever tried to theorize the perseity of an international society as anything more than the cooperation of individual states working toward internal enlightenment. In arguing for an international body politic that was more than the sum of its parts, where fraternal bonds of duty transcended the boundaries of states themselves, and which essen-

[73] *League Covenant*, Article 16, Paragraphs 1 and 2, [from Miller, *The Drafting of the Covenant*, vol. 1]. Subsequently, the possibility of economic sanctions was itself undermined by a report on the applications of the principles of the Covenant submitted to the Assembly in 1938 which stated that there was "general agreement" among League members that economic sanctions not be binding. [See League Document A.74.1938.VII, in *Records of the Nineteenth Ordinary Session of the Assembly, Minutes of the Sixth Committee* (Geneva : League of Nations Press, 1920–1938), 102].

[74] For instance, a hostile state could always vote down any proposed joint military action, which is precisely what occurred in 1931 and 1933 with the Japanese invasion of Manchuria and the Italian invasion of Ethiopia. [See Sobel, "The League of Nations Covenant and the United Nations Charter; An Analysis of Two International Constitutions," *Constitutional Political Economy* 5(2) (1994), 177].

[75] Carr, *The Twenty Years' Crisis*, 8.

tially *predated* the League, Zimmern and Murray were making a heretofore unheard of claim. As such, much of their work on international society was motivated by the desire to *prove* the existence of this society. In a philosophical move strikingly similar to the way idealist liberal thinkers had turned to organicism to explain the essential qualities of society itself, so too did Murray and Zimmern draw upon the conceptual language of nature, the movement of the cosmos, and the intricacies of the organic world to claim the absolute existence of the global social whole.

That both men would draw upon such imagery is hardly surprising. Turn of the century liberals of all stripes employed the terminology of the natural sciences and Social Darwinism to describe everything from the state's inimical relation to society, to the essentially social characteristics of all human beings, to the fundamental differences between British and Prussian society.[76] Indeed, throughout the war and well into the 1920s, the relationship among the state, the "unitary social order," and the natural, biological world continued to inspire lively debate within liberal and idealist intellectual societies and journals.[77] Murray and Zimmern, however, tended to use the language of nature in a manner much more consistent with that of an earlier generation of Oxford idealist liberals. As Bosanquet, Muirhead, and Ritchie had employed organic language to establish the existence of a social whole that, in effect, replaced the state as an agent that logically preceded its members, so too did Murray and Zimmern build their understanding of global society on naturalistic foundations that supposedly predated formal international institutions.

Like their intellectual predecessors, Murray and Zimmern believed that human beings were inherently social, connected by deep, spiritual bonds of fellowship. "Man is a social animal," Zimmern argued in 1916, noting that "in the life of our fellows, in the Common Weal, we live and move and have our being."[78] For Zimmern, this sociability amounted to more than cultural habit and the common need for survival. Rather, he maintained that human sociality rested in a very basic instinct, and thus, "the principles that regulate human association are inherent in the nature of

---

[76] Thus, Hobson argued during the war that in "opposition to the Prussian State, which is absolutely centralized in its power and control, the British state is organic in the sense that it is a free corporation of cells and organs which, while contributing to the life of the organism, preserve also their private liberties and ends [Hobson, *Democracy After the War* (London: George Allen and Unwin, 1918), 164–65].

[77] See for instance, H.J.W. Hetherington, "The Conception of a Unitary Social Order," and L. T. Hobhouse, "Physical, Biological and Psychological Categories," *Proceedings of the Aristotelian Society* 18 (1917–18): 286–316, 468–78; Lloyd Morgan, "A Concept of the Organism, Emergent and Resultant," *Proceedings of the Aristotelian Society* 27 (1926–27): 141–76.

[78] Zimmern, "Progress in Government," 162.

man."[79] Murray agreed, explaining the progress of humankind in explicitly evolutionary terms that echoed his commitment to the importance of duty and sacrifice.

> Long before you get as high as mankind the unit becomes a group, struggling partly indeed against other groups, but chiefly against the difficulties of the environment. Inside the group—and sometimes even between groups—there is a need for social qualities, for co-operation, for mutual help, for self sacrifice.[80]

According to Murray, this movement to widen the circle of social responsibility was an inevitable byproduct of the maturation of the species. "That form of growth," he maintained, "not mere struggle for life, is the normal mode of human Evolution." Murray argued that the expansion of social feeling contained a self-generating element such that these feelings inevitably, unless disrupted by unnatural events like war, extended "their boundaries farther and farther."[81] For both Murray and Zimmern, the increases and improvements in global communication and trade before 1914 proved that the world was already moving toward common social understanding before it was interrupted by World War One. Years later, on the brink of a Second World War, Zimmern still looked to the First as a kind of cosmic disjuncture between humans and their natural tendency to expand their social parameters, insisting that rather than being inherent in the nature of humanity (as Reinhold Niebuhr would later argue), "the violence so characteristic of the younger generation in certain countries is a legacy, perhaps a temporary legacy, from the war."[82]

In this context, both men argued frequently that the League of Nations was itself a natural extension of humanity's tendency toward social cohesion. In these terms, the League was more than a mere bureaucracy; it was an integral "element," according to Zimmern, "in the international life of the world."[83] For Zimmern, in particular, the emergence of the League gestured toward the ongoing movement of worldwide social evolution. The expansion of global society, argued Zimmern, was happening through natural, unplanned, spontaneous processes. Recognizing and encouraging this spontaneous movement, he explained in an early lecture on Greek civilization, is what made the Greeks unique.[84] Thwarting "all

---

[79] Ibid., 167.

[80] Murray, *Liberality and Civilization*, 41.

[81] Ibid., 42.

[82] Zimmern, "Liberty, Democracy, and the Movement towards World Order," *Problems of Peace: Lectures Delivered at the Geneva Institute of International Relations: 1935* (Oxford: Oxford University Press, 1936), 150.

[83] Zimmern, "The Development of the International Mind," 5.

[84] Bodl. M.S. Zimmern (135) fol. 89.

spontaneous or unauthorized associations," he argued during the war, made the Prussians repressive.[85] Forging the bonds of human conscience on an international scale, Zimmern concluded, required the cultivation of unofficial "international contacts" that would "promote understanding and an organic relationship."[86] For Zimmern, the League was at its most natural when it sought to cultivate these kinds of relationships, thus "creating the opportunity for international understanding" rather than forcing such understanding on the world from a position of authority.[87]

At the same time, however, and particularly toward the beginning of the League of Nations movement, Murray and Zimmern worried about the possibility of a world state arising out of this otherwise natural and spontaneous movement toward international organization. The contrasting metaphor of the League as a "machine," which appears throughout their writings, expressed this liberal anxiety particularly well and demonstrates the extent to which their internationalisms sought to divest the League of any authenticating claim to authority. While both men sometimes referred to the League in organic, social terms, at other times they used impersonal, technical language to describe it as a kind of engineering wonder, a well-oiled machine purring to itself at Geneva as it quietly processed the world's queries. Zimmern thus argued in retrospect that when they initially envisioned the League, the authors of the Covenant (appearing more like engineers than godfathers) merely "aimed at providing the machinery" to prevent war, and if a "breakdown" in the international system should "nevertheless occur, it would be in no way attributable to the lack of adequate machinery."[88] According to Zimmern, the architects of the covenant intended that same machinery to serve as a clearing house for ideas and thus to help fashion the "disinterested good will" necessary to process the conflicting interests of the global community. Essentially, this particular vision of the League cast it in mechanical not spiritual or organic terms, and thus—much like the orthodox liberal view of the state—stripped it of any moral characteristics of its own. This League was no spontaneous expression of human society, but rather an automated response to world conflict.

At times, the tension between the idea of the League as an authentic expression of the international organism and a disinterested machine would rupture and the metaphors collide. During a 1926 lecture, for in-

---

[85] Zimmern, *Nationality and Government*, 13.

[86] Zimmern, *Education and International Good Will; The Sixth Earl Grey Memorial Lecture, Delivered at King's Hall, Armstrong College, New Castle-On-Tyne, on April 25, 1924* (Oxford: Oxford Univ. Press, 1924), 5.

[87] Ibid.

[88] Zimmern, *The League of Nations and the Rule of Law*, 1.

stance, Zimmern swung from one sentence to the next between descriptions of the League as an "extraordinarily good machine" and as a "living organic agency," finally arriving at a definition of the League as "simply a living organic mechanism."[89] Zimmern quickly concluded this thought by apologizing to his audience, noting that "I hope I am not mixing my metaphors."[90] But Zimmern's apology—that is, his recognition of fact that he *was* mixing his metaphors—offers the reader a striking glimpse into the competing claims at the heart of his internationalism. For Zimmern, the relationship between the mechanical and the organic, between the disinterested state and the moral whole of the world, never resolved, remaining a mixed metaphor. This was no proto-cyborg theory, no glimpse into a future co-mingling of the biological and the technological but simply what Foucault would call "disparity," the ragged edges of two theoretical worldviews that refused to coalesce.

Murray and Zimmern responded to their own intractable theoretical binaries by embracing with even greater enthusiasm the language of nature. Such a move allowed them to resolve their own contradictory understandings of the League as a technically powerless, bureaucratic institution and the League as a powerful, organic expression of universal humanity and Liberal spirit by locating the soul of international cooperation elsewhere, in social rather than state relationships. Thus, the global society that both men theorized in the most natural of terms predated and undergirded the work of the League. Within this nascent social organism, spontaneous "international contacts" were supposedly transformed into the adamantine bonds of brotherhood, bonds that would themselves vivify the emerging Great Society.[91]

Both men presumed that the chrysalis of this Great Society lay just beneath the surface of contemporary politics, and that theorizing internationalism entailed a sustained study of these elements and their natural guiding processes. Murray's understanding of these processes originated in his interpretation of the Greeks, and it was specifically from Greek cosmology that he took his understanding of world cosmos. "The Greeks," he argued in 1933, "invented that word 'cosmos' when they discovered that the stars in their orbits, the sun and the moon, were all obeying a law and that the orbit of each planet was part of the tremendous world order."[92] For Murray, the "eternal laws" that governed this idea of a world cosmos were "obedient to the purpose and intelligence of God" and stood in opposition to the forces of "Chaos or Disorder."[93] Making

---

[89] Zimmern, "The New International Outlook," 26.
[90] Ibid.
[91] Zimmern, *Nationality and Government*, 23.
[92] Murray, "A Survey of Recent World Affairs," 2.
[93] Murray, "The Cult of Violence," *From the League to the U.N.*, 59.

the world a less chaotic, more divinely ordered realm meant tapping into the eternal laws that guide us.

And yet Murray's understanding of Greek cosmology was more complicated than this. He was clearly aware that the Greeks based their notion of cosmos on an incorrect interpretation of the universe, a *weltanschauung* in which "earth was the physical center."[94] But that it was grounded in an incorrect science did not make the notion of cosmos any less meaningful for modern society, Murray argued. "Of course their belief was erroneous, and ours, we hope, is based on real knowledge," he stated in 1920.[95] But the problem with a real knowledge that dislocated the earth from the center of the universe, Murray insisted, was that it divested the earth itself of the divine. "The earth," he continued, "has become comparatively small, limited, well ascertained and, I may almost say, rational." Since the Enlightenment, Murray continued, philosophers had come to believe that they could address difficult questions of moral and political theory through direct observation, without the guidance of an overall cosmology, a coherent, divinely inspired, moral world order. This was precisely the kind of thinking that had led to the chaos and nihilism of the war. Murray argued that philosophers, diplomats, internationalists, and statesmen alike must counter these factious impulses by turning back to that ancient understanding of cosmos, but in a manner that brought the new scientific sensibilities to bear. Thus, he maintained, scientific discoveries and exploration had indeed made the world smaller, ensuring that we "now know the stuff the earth is made up, its various strata, their qualities and their comparative age, we see the rivers and the mountain ranges in terms of intelligible processes."[96] But this expansion of knowledge, he insisted, now made it possible to root the spiritual cosmos in physical fact, to resurrect the old cosmology in a manner that was both divinely inspired and scientifically observable, to "begin to say in a clearer sense than was possible to the ancients 'nothing that is human is alien to me.' "[97]

Thus, Murray employed the conceptual language of both idealism and naturalism when theorizing the existence of a global cosmos that he believed offered the post-war world its best chance to live peacefully in the presence of the divine. Policies generated by either the League of Nations or its state members that were in harmony with this vision of cosmos were good, while those that deviated were reckless and Satanic.[98] When the

[94] Murray, "Orbis Terrestris," 184.

[95] Ibid., 186.

[96] Ibid.

[97] Ibid., 186.

[98] Murray, *Satanism and World Order*, 9.

world was peaceful, the cosmos was in good health. When the world sunk into economic or political crisis, the cosmos was sickly. The League failed to stop the Japanese invasion of Manchuria, Murray argued, not because it was limited by its own sanctions policy but rather because the "infirm world order in which the great shock had just fallen was in weak health and did not react healthily and normally."[99] Murray constantly insisted, throughout his career as he watched the League system rise and ultimately fall, that a world organized along an orderly understanding of divine cosmos was "natural," "healthy," and "normal," and that deviations from this natural form of cosmic coherence had radical and dangerous consequences. Again, to illustrate this, Murray turned to the example of the Greeks. The Sophists, he argued during the Second World War, "made a great point of the difference between Law or Convention on the one hand and Nature on the other."[100] In dislocating law from the natural order of the world, Murray went on to argue, the Sophists became relativists, arguing that "morals were just invented by the weak to protect themselves against the strong."[101] Such thinking had led to the Peloponnesian War, Murray concluded. Modern sophists (and these included, according to Murray, figures as diverse as Hitler, Marx, and Hobbes) had all helped divorce nature and law from each other, leading inevitably to violent conflict. Returning to a world ordered along the lines of a moral cosmos required, for Murray, that internationalists and statesmen alike treat world problems as symptoms of an unhealthy body denied its natural remedies. Thus, in 1933 Murray described the world suffering from an economic crisis as "a patient suffering from a complicated disease due in large part, though not entirely, to alcoholism."[102] In other words, overindulgence and moral nihilism. Curing the patient required a return to a natural moral equilibrium.

Murray's use in this instance of the body as an analogy for the world cosmos was somewhat unusual for his work. For the most part, his naturalism was rooted in the pre-Copernican imagery of cosmic order. Zimmern, by contrast, constantly used the metaphor of the body to describe a world that, he argued during the First World War, had "already, in many respects, become a single organism."[103] This was a much more developmental conception of global society than Murray's cosmos. Rather than arising from a great cosmic plan, from the timeless relationship between nature and the divine, Zimmern's world organism *evolved* through seem-

---

[99] Murray, "A Survey of Recent World Affairs," 10.
[100] Bodl. MS Gilbert Murray (436) fols. 127–128.
[101] Ibid., fol. 128.
[102] Murray, "Epilogue," *The Evolution of World Peace*, 202.
[103] Zimmern, "Progress in Government," 164.

ingly natural processes, from the gradual accretion of international contacts between states and individuals. The more that states and individuals forged synaptic connections among themselves, the more truly alive the international organism became. Nothing illustrates this better than Zimmern's consistent use of the metaphor of the nervous system to describe the growing interconnectedness of the world. In many ways, Zimmern's use of this metaphor is a testament to the consistency of his organicism throughout the inter-war era. Thus, in 1918 Zimmern described the movement of international communications and capital as flowing through a "single world nervous system."[104] In 1926 he located the dynamics of a "moving, changing world" within "the adequate functioning of this international nervous system."[105] By 1928 this world body had taken on even more biological qualities as "trade and industry" were supposed to "respond," like efficient limbs and organs, to the "reactions of a single, world wide nervous system."[106] For Zimmern, the peaceful functioning of the world depended on the existence of a natural, organic movement that, like the processes of the human body, both evolved and awaited discovery and explanation.

In this sense, Zimmern saw himself in the exact opposite role of Hegel's anatomist "whose occupation, be it remembered, is not with the living body but with the corpse."[107] Instead, for Zimmern, League internationalists were physicians, "godfathers," whose job it was to uncover the heretofore mysterious workings of the social body, to prescribe treatment, to offer advice, and to protect it from what he vaguely described as "barbarians" and "the forces and passions that divide and embitter mankind."[108] Truly discerning the courses of the world organism meant correctly diagnosing which elements within it were static and which were dynamic. International relations must thus, "like medicine," take into account not just the mobile but the stationary qualities of the world body. "Many a surgeon" Zimmern argued "has failed to save a patient's life because, in ensuring the 'success' of his operation, he overlooked certain permanent elements in his constitution."[109]

This faith in the workings of an organic world body and a naturally inspired world cosmos made it possible for Murray and Zimmern to insist, even in the absence of an international organization with coercive authority, that harmonious and peaceful relationships between the world's

---

[104] Zimmern, *Nationality and Government*, 23.

[105] Zimmern, "The New International Outlook," 22.

[106] Zimmern, "German Culture and the British Commonwealth," 327.

[107] Hegel, *Logic*, par. 135R.

[108] Zimmern, *The Study of International Relations*, 18; Zimmern, "Introduction," *The War and Democracy*, 11.

[109] Zimmern, *Learning and Leadership*, 15.

peoples were not only a probable but also a natural outcome of a smoothly functioning "international nervous system," and a "healthy" world order. And at the heart of this natural move toward internationalism were those permanent elements in the world's constitution. In other words, as with their idealist liberal understanding of the social more broadly, Murray and Zimmern both believed that international society was also ordered, that it too had its traditions, that it was comprised of permanent relationships between people, and that these relationships were structured through particular types of institutions. For Murray, these relationships could be found in the natural, hierarchical order between governed and governing races; for Zimmern, in nations, the families of mankind.

An Organic Solution: World Order and the Families of Mankind

In their broader political theory, both Murray and Zimmern argued that the power of liberal spirit to reconcile freedom with fraternity, rights with responsibilities, difference with universality, functioned not through the authoritative structure of the state but within local societies, community relations, and a shared awareness of cultural traditions. For instance, Zimmern believed that the moral, liberal community could thrive only in a society in which individuals understood themselves in relation both to their distinct class experiences and to those common cultural traditions that provided cross-class forms of social identification, traditions ranging from "the universally recognized distinction between mere man and gentleman" to a shared liking for bacon and eggs.[110] Community institutions and social relationships both men argued, allowed people to truly live the transformative power of a liberal spirituality through their duty to others and their connections to the social whole. In a basic way, their emerging theories of international society mirrored this commitment to grounding liberal spirit in traditional social relationships, what Murray termed "the social order of the world."[111]

Murray used the term "world order" throughout his career in two different but related contexts. On the one hand, he sometimes described it as a completely new conception of world organization, one consciously based on tidiness. Again, recall that for Murray, few things were more distressing about the post-war world than the mess, the political and economic "chaos" engendered by both the war itself and the selfish impulses

---

[110] Bodl. MS Zimmern (135), fols. 24, 25.
[111] Murray, *The World and the League*, 7.

of most states. Order, by contrast, implied the creation of an organized world system that was politically and economically structured around a true picture of the whole as interpreted by experts. For instance, in an ordered world, Murray maintained, states and industrialists would "take the advice of the economists of the world" and work with each other to "get some world order into economics" rather than simply following what appeared to be their own interests.[112] The result would be a neater, more smoothly functioning international system. Here, once again, Murray betrayed both his classical and idealist roots, as well as his Oxford training. These experts were not simply specialists whose work focused on particular aspects of the global economy. Rather, Murray imagined them as proper students of the *Literae Humaniores*, men and women whose work led them to toward "some coherent Whole of knowledge."[113]

In his commitment to a cosmologically inspired vision of the whole, however, Murray also made it clear that "order" implied something more than functionality. Dictators and Prussians of all stripes had their own idea of order, but these ideas were characterized first and foremost by power and coercion. By contrast, Murray described his notion of order as a moral code whose principles governed the most basic of human interactions. Thus, in 1934, at the height of what seemed an economic depression that no one could control, Murray appealed to a group of students to save the world by taking control of themselves, to "save Liberty by restoring Order in your public action, your thinking, and your individual lives."[114] In this instance, "order" implied a way of life, and thus had to be embraced voluntarily. Likewise, sovereign states' own moral sensibilities, not the coercive practices of a super-state, must compel them to accept this ordered vision of the world. Again, however, as Murray's exhortation to save Liberty implies, this vision of a voluntary order also entailed a particular conception of liberalism as a spiritual principle that transcended seemingly divergent concepts like freedom and duty. "As free institutions are compatible with social order," Murray continued, "so freedom of thought and speech and consciousness and daily living are compatible with the good social life."[115] On an international level, "good life" and "world order" were essentially the same.

For Murray, an ordered world was a peaceful world, a controllable world, a world capable of repelling distressing contingencies like war, economic crises, and revolution. "There are always lawless and dishonest men in every large community," Murray observed in 1921, "who make

---

[112] Murray, "A Survey of Recent World Affairs," 4.
[113] Bodl. Ms Murray (418), fol. 179.
[114] Murray, "The Cult of Violence (1934)," 59.
[115] Ibid., 59.

a profit out of their neighbors extremity, who use advertisements to stifle truth, who jeer at all that is higher than themselves. But in a good social order they are not influential."[116] Murray thus understood the reestablishment of world order after the First World War as a way of stabilizing world politics. Revolutions, in this context, were always suspect because they were aimed at overthrowing order and, therefore, were naturally short lived. "It must be remembered," Murray maintained, "that in general tendency, order lasts and disorder does not; revolutions do not last."[117] In short, for Murray, when individuals and states took the central idea of liberal altruism to heart, when they imagined the world as an "ordered whole, in which every individual had his due share both of privilege and of service," they could create a lasting approximation of "the One Great City, not a discordant jumble of Greek and barbarian, slave or free."[118]

Murray's words in this context might leave one with the impression that his vision of world order was somehow radically egalitarian—that gone would be the traditional difference between legitimate citizens and barbarians, feudal distinctions between the free and the indentured. But this was not consistently the case, and it takes no more than a brief glance through Murray's collected writings on internationalism to see the conservative, almost reactionary elements simultaneously implicit in this notion of world order. Murray's internationalism might have been grounded on what he described as the "ultimate Fraternity of Mankind," but it also adhered closely to a pre-war imperial politics. "World Order," in this sense, implied tradition, and above all, traditional forms of global hierarchy, which were, like the global cosmos itself, natural. As Murray argued in *Satanism and World Order*

> Surely there is something wrong in that whole conception of human life which implies that each man should be a masterless, unattached and independent being. It would be almost truer to say that no man is happy until he has a master, or at least a leader to admire and serve and follow. That is the way in which all societies naturally organize themselves, from boys at school to political parties and social groups. As far as I can see, it is the only principle on which brotherhood can be based among beings who differ so widely as human beings do in intellect, in will power or in strength. I do not think it is true that no nation is good enough in this qualified sense to be another's master. The World Order does imply leaders and led, governors and governed; in extreme cases it does imply the use of force.[119]

---

[116] Murray, *The Problem of Foreign Policy*, xv.
[117] Murray, "A Survey of Recent World Affairs," 9.
[118] Murray, *Liberality and Civilization*, 43.
[119] Murray, *Satanism and The World Order*, 40.

For Murray then, order also necessitated rank. In this almost ecclesiastical approach to international politics, distinctions between the world's peoples—between masters and servants, leaders and led, governors and governed—were fixed categories of political organization. The new society that Murray imagined emerging out of the ashes of the war was not really new at all. Even its innovations (including the League of Nations and its system of voluntary collective security) asked the Allies to give up very little in terms of colonial power and economic practices. Imperial governance must continue, Murray argued, for the good of the entire global order and in the name of this order he was willing to sacrifice his own expressed dislike for power politics. "World Order" thus implied not only hierarchy; when dealing with Bolsheviks, revolutionaries, and "native races" colonial governments' use of force was legitimized.[120]

In one sense, Murray's attitude toward world order can be explained simply in terms of his sentimental attachment to both a domestic and international system dominated by the "traditions of Liberal England."[121] For Murray, the British Commonwealth should have been, by virtue of these traditions, the lynch pin of the entire League system. "As every one knows who has cared to read my writings," he thus argued in 1921, "I look to the League of Nations as the main hope of the world, and to the British Commonwealth as the mainstay of the League of Nations."[122] Like many British intellectuals of his generation, Murray continued to hold an abiding faith in the civilizing mission of the empire and the "incalculable benefits" it had conferred upon its colonies: "the benefit of protection from invasion, of comparative protection from plague and famine, of social order, of administrative justice, to say nothing of roads and railways, and the enlivening force of Western knowledge."[123] The rise of nationalist movements in the colonies and the challenges posed by Germany and the Soviet Union to British economic and military power terrified Murray, and throughout his career he could only understand these movements in the most basic terms of good versus evil. "The spirit that I have called Satanism," he thus argued in 1924, "the spirit which rejoices in any widespread disaster which is also a disaster to the world's rulers, is perhaps more rife today than it has been for over a thousand years. It is felt to some extent against all ordered Governments, but chiefly against all imperial Governments, and it is directed more widely and intensely against Great Britain than against any other Power."[124] Murray reacted to this upset of

---

[120] Murray, "Orbis Terrestris," 195.
[121] Murray, *The Problem of Foreign Policy*, xvi.
[122] Ibid.
[123] Ibid., 76.
[124] Murray, *Satanism and World Order*, 33.

global hierarchy by articulating, in ever stronger language as the interwar period progressed, an increasingly moral picture of the colonial world order, all the while reflecting with a kind of desperate nostalgia on the "agreed cosmology" of the Victorians.[125]

And yet Murray's deep attachment to a hierarchical social order cannot be explained away as simple conservatism, first and foremost, because Murray considered himself a liberal progressive, a supporter of reformist political agendas at home and abroad. In this sense, Murray argued that imperial governments must be liberal and must rule by the good will of their colonial members, and that this "good will in its turn depended upon equal law, good government, and good faith."[126] But, again, this very phrase suggests that "liberalism" meant something different for Murray than it did for either its orthodox founders or for the new liberals. "Liberalism" for Murray meant "faith," a belief in the resolving power of Spirit as lived through community. Murray's notion of liberalism thus demanded a community in which to root itself, and much of his theorizing about international politics was aimed at articulating both what this community should look like (the One Great City of Men and Gods) and why it was inevitable given the workings of cosmos.

At the same time, Murray was acutely aware that he was asking people to make a leap of faith about this community, a form of social cohesion that, while it might exist in a higher form, did not yet occupy a space in the world. Unlike the British Commonwealth or the United States, which were both held together by "a community of laws, traditions, history, and language," this new community had no traditions. "Our task was far harder" Murray maintained in a retrospective on his role in the League's founding, "to make a new society out of nations among whom no such community existed, a society in which potential enemies would sit in peace at the same table and gradually learn to co-operate."[127] Murray's decision to base this notion of community on a preexisting international order makes considerable sense. Here was a man who believed profoundly that the loss of the traditional values of self-sacrifice and duty had led to breakdown of the international system and the Great War. Tyrants and criminals only gained power, he argued, "in a society which, in external conduct, is losing its traditional standards and inwardly, in the words of Tolstoy's great condemnation, has forgotten God."[128] Traditions and faith were necessary for liberal morality to be lived, Murray's

---

[125] Murray, "Then and Now," 18.
[126] Murray, *The Problem of Foreign Policy*, xvi.
[127] Murray, "The League of Nations, The First Experiment," 78.
[128] Murray, *The Problem of Foreign Policy*, xv.

political theory postulated. Therefore, traditional forms of international order had to be maintained for that morality to be lived on a global level.

Zimmern similarly invested his theory of internationalism in the notion of lived tradition, but, unlike Murray, he chose to qualify it not through the idea of world order per se but in relation to the most natural constituent parts of that order: national communities. Zimmern's decision to focus his internationalist thinking on the moral qualities of nations (as distinct from states) seems to have developed initially out of both his particularly dialectical conception of international mind as a form of "unity in difference" and his growing conviction—which coincided with his writing of the *Greek Commonwealth* and his deepening involvement with the Round Table Society—that the British Empire offered the world one of the most perfect organic examples of this unity. But, again unlike Murray, the continued survival of the empire in and of itself did not seem to move Zimmern as much as the *idea* behind it. As a "living body which lives through the organic union and free activity of its several national members," Zimmern argued, the empire was most powerful as a symbolic embodiment of the type of political community he believed should serve as a model for the post-war world.[129]

Not coincidentally, Zimmern's understanding of international relations as premised on the moralizing power of national communities also emerged simultaneously with the solidification of the national ideal in Europe. As Hobsbawm has argued, the explosion of nationalist movements in Europe during the First World War was a culmination of long-simmering nineteenth-century sensibilities.[130] Explanations for the rise of European nationalism during the nineteenth century vary, ranging from Hobsbawm's understanding of the liberal state's response to industrialization, to Benedict Anderson's focus on print technologies, to Etienne Balibar's analysis of European communities' and their desire to distinguish themselves from colonized subjects, from "'southern populations' (Turks, Arabs, Blacks.)"[131] While they may emphasize different points of departure for the historical emergence of nationalism in Europe, however, each of these theorists agree that "nationalism" itself implies what Gellner defines as the "general social conditions [which] make for standardized, homogenous, centrally sustained high culture, pervading entire

---

[129] Zimmern, *Nationality and Government*, 29.

[130] Eric Hobsbawm, *Nations and Nationalism Since 1780* (Cambridge: Cambridge University Press, 1993), 93.

[131] Anderson, *Imagined Communities*, 67–82; Balibar and Wallerstein, *Race, Nation, Class*, 105.

populations and not just elite minorities."[132] In other words, national cultures were now assumed to unite across class lines within a particular
spatialized unit rather than descending downward from an imperial center and spreading outward to encompass a conceivably infinite geographi-
cal area. During the First World War, the politicized identification of European peoples with specific, geographically defined "national cultures"
increased as the result of official, wartime mobilization by states (what
Hobsbawm terms the "merger of state patriotism with non-state nationalism") and through the Allies' strategy of fomenting nationalist revolutions
within the colonial holdings of the Axis powers.[133]

Zimmern's decision to choose the nation as a privileged site of moral
unity also reflected a trend the idealist liberals of a previous generation
had already established. Bosanquet, for instance, argued that the "highest
gifts of humanity have hitherto, at any rate, sprung from localized
minds . . . the greatest gifts are still to be, as they have been, achievements
of diversely identified life centres."[134] Bosanquet's use of the term "life
centre" also rings true with his distinctly familial definition of the nation.
As argued in chapter 1, the identification of the national community
with the family writ large was also part of the idealist liberals' tendency
to elide the distinction between family and society, to simultaneously establish a theory of the family that was distinct from the state and yet
served as a model for the nation as a whole. Thus, in *The Philosophical
Theory of the State*, Bosanquet argued that the nuclear family must be
protected from both the state and the larger society because, as "an ethical
idea . . . the monogamous family . . . has a unique place in the structure
of the citizen mind."[135] And yet, "in a modern nation," Bosanquet insisted, "the atmosphere of the family is not confined to the actual family.
The common dwelling place, history, and tradition, the common language
and common literature, give a colour of affection to the everyday citizen-
consciousness, which is to the nation what family affection is in the home
circle."[136]

Zimmern's internationalism echoed these sentiments almost in their entirety. While one can see rudiments of his approach to the relationship
between nationhood and international society in lectures going back as
far as 1905, Zimmern first fully elaborated these ideas in 1918's *National-*

[132] Ernest Gellner, *Nations and Nationalism* (Ithaca: Cornell University Press, 1983), 55.
For Anderson, this development implied a shift from a conception of the "social group" as
"centripetal and hierarchical" to one which was "boundary-oriented and horizontal."[An-
derson, *Imagined Communities*, 15].
    [133] Hobsbawm, *Nations and Nationalism Since 1780*, 93.
    [134] Bosanquet, "The Function of the State in Promoting the Unity of Mankind," 297–98.
    [135] Bosanquet, *Philosophical Theory of the State*, 279.
    [136] Ibid., 273.

ity and Government.[137] The international theory as developed in this seminal text entailed four key assumptions. First, Zimmern maintained that natural differences between people could only be understood in national terms. Second, he argued that these national differences were necessary for both the creation of global society and the true progress of humanity. Third, Zimmern identified nations as distinctly *familial* units. Fourth, Zimmern assumed that, like families, nations produced the spiritual and moral energy necessary both to animate the social organism and to ensure international cooperation.

In notably Hegelian terms, Zimmern argued that nations performed the same functions in the ethical development of the individual-engaged-with-the-world as the did the family in the ethical maturity of the individual-engaged-with-the-state. In other words, nations, like families, facilitated that process whereby world citizens recognized other nationalities as both distinct from and inherently similar to themselves by giving them a moral focus, a resting place, a space from which to interact with the "life of the world" from a position of safety.[138] Although not necessarily ethnically coherent, once a people had reached a certain level of "corporate self consciousness," once they had begun to feel particularly intensely and intimately about their "home country," they took on those natural "sentiments" and "qualities" that distinguished them from all groups and provided for them the unquestioning love and security of home.[139]

Ultimately, the particular qualities produced by the intensity and intimacy of the nation distinguished it from all others social institutions. In addition, these qualities made each nation uniquely suited to meet the moral and spiritual needs of its citizens. Thus, Zimmern maintained that "true internationalism is the contact between nations in their highest and best and *most distinctive* representatives and manifestations."[140] For Zimmern, nations at their most distinctive were also the most spiritual, and true internationalism implied that individuals both engage that spirit in themselves and appreciate it in others. In Zimmern's words,

> Any fool can book a ticket for a foreign country, just as any fool can learn Esperanto. But contacts so established effect nothing. . . . It is through a deeper exploration and enjoyment of the infinite treasures of the word's nationalities,

---

[137] See Bodl. Ms. Zimmern (135). This box contains a number of relevant early lectures given between 1900 and 1905. In particular, "United Britain" (fols. 124–169) and "Thucydides the Imperialist" (fols. 98–117).

[138] See Hegel's theory of "the corporation" in *The Philosophy of Right*, trans. T. M. Knox (London: Oxford University Press, 1967). The "life of the world" was a favorite phrase of Zimmern's and it reappeared throughout his work.

[139] Zimmern, *Nationality and Government*, 52.

[140] Zimmern, "Nationalism and Internationalism," *The Prospects of Democracy*, 93.

by men and women whose vision has been trained and sensibilities refined because they themselves are intimately bound up with a nation of their own, that an enduring network of internationalism will some day be knit and a harmony of understanding established in a world of unassailable diversity.[141]

Zimmern also argued that nations were *natural* and *spiritual* entities, the most organic, germinal elements of the international organism. Thus, the sensibilities of nations and states come across as quite different in his work, mirroring almost exactly the Enlightenment dichotomy between passion and reason, subjectivity and objectivity, nature and civilization. "Nationality, like religion," Zimmern argued, "is subjective; Statehood is objective. Nationality is psychological; statehood is political. Nationality is a condition of mind; Statehood is a condition in law. Nationality is a spiritual possession; Statehood is an enforceable obligation. Nationality is a way of feeling, thinking and living; Statehood is a condition inseparable from all civilized ways of living."[142] Feelings within nations, Zimmern argued, were based on "instinctive tendencies and primary emotions" rooted in "the half-conscious assumptions and dim feelings of life in a community."[143] In Zimmern's word, "nationalism is not a mere fashion and foible . . . but springs from deep roots buried in man's inherited nature."[144]

This metaphorical equation between the nation-as-natural-and-subjective and the nation as-intimate-and-familial was hardly incidental for Zimmern. Rather, nations were so uniquely moral precisely because of their familial qualities. Within the nation, within this home saturated with genuine, natural intimacy, internationally minded individuals first learned to respect themselves and others. For Zimmern, the nation functioned as "a school of character and self-respect." World citizens, he maintained, learned respect for others in the *international* community only through their prima facie awareness of and respect for themselves as part of a *national* communities.[145] Zimmern's internationalism thus necessitated that *every* person in the world have a place to call home. Likewise, his theory also required that individual nations have distinct spatial identities, that they occupy "a definite home country." While this identity did not necessarily entail sovereignty, it did necessitate "an actual strip of land associated with the nationality, a territorial centre where the flame of nationality is kept alight."[146]

---

[141] Ibid., 93.
[142] Zimmern, *Nationality and Government*, 51.
[143] Ibid., 348.
[144] Ibid., 99.
[145] Ibid., 54.
[146] Ibid., 84.

Just as an earlier generation of idealist liberals had argued that any shift in the fundamental composition of the nuclear family would have dire consequences for the morality of the nation, so too did Zimmern argue that the loss or rejection of one's national homeland would lead inexorably to moral decay. To illustrate this point, Zimmern turned to the rootless "Levantine lounger" to provide his readers with the ultimate spectacle of the "moral degradation the loss of nationality involves."[147] While the term "Levantine" has historically been used to describe a person from the Levant—an unspecified region that included Lebanon, Syria, and Palestine—it also encompassed southern Europe. In essence, the Levant specifically addresses an area of constant cultural and economic contact between Europe and the Middles East.[148] In historic terms, the very word "Levant" implied movement, cultural exchange, and the buzz of economic activity. By the time Zimmern was writing *Nationality and Government*, however, Americans were using the term "Levantine merchant" as a pejorative to describe a person of Lebanese or Syrian ancestry working as peddlers.[149] Since pack peddling was a particularly popular occupation for Lebanese and Syrian immigrants in the United States, and since Zimmern visited there extensively before the war, that Zimmern used the "Levantine" to exemplify all that was wrong with cosmopolitanism—with the rejection of national identity in favor of material gains, with the decision to embrace an occupation and lifestyle which was necessarily *transnational*—is perhaps not surprising.

The rootlessness of these Levantine merchants (coupled with their unspecified "Near-Eastern" origins) made them potent examples "of the spiritual degradation which befalls men who have pursued . . . cosmopolitanism and lost contact with their own national spiritual heritage."[150] Zimmern did all that he could to highlight not only the moral degradation of his Levantine, but also what he considered the banality of cosmopolitanism through descriptions of "drab" Levantine seaports and the "greasy American passports" of merchants he encountered there. In sum, Zimmern used the phrase "Levantine merchant" similarly to anti-Semitic evocations of the "wandering Jew." While Zimmern's intentions with regard to this similarity are unclear, both Jews and Levantines would have served the same derisive metaphorical purpose: both were defined by a diasporic, transnational ethnic identity and both were assumed to be driven by

[147] Ibid., 52.

[148] Lawrence Ziring, *The Middle East: A Political Dictionary* (Santa Barbara, CA: ABC-CLIO, 1992), 19.

[149] Alixa Naff, *Becoming American: The Early Arab Immigrant Experience* (Philadelphia: University of Pennsylvania Press, 1985), chapter 4.

[150] Zimmern, *Nationality and Government*, 52.

material greed.[151] Likewise, Zimmern regarded Bolshevism as similarly amoral because, as an ideology, it too refused to respect the rootedness of nations and was driven by a materialist (rather than spiritual) theory of world history. In Zimmern's mind, both the Levantine merchant and the Bolshevik had given up the spirituality of their national heritage for a vulgar materialism. Nationality, in this respect, was "a safeguard of self respect against the insidious onslaughts of a materialistic cosmopolitanism."[152]

For Zimmern, internationalism did not imply forgoing national identity but rather "inter-communication between the families of mankind."[153] Not only was cosmopolitanism undesirable, but it was also ultimately untenable; national sentiment, like all natural forces, could not be suppressed. Indeed, according to Zimmern, "Nationalism thwarted, perverted, and unsatisfied . . . is one of the festering sores of our time."[154] Instead, he maintained, nationalism must be channeled and guided to take on a more internationalist form. Thus, as Zimmern saw it, one of the most important missions of the League of Nations was to create an institutional framework wherein the true aspirations of nationalism could flourish. At the same time, the League of Nations must somehow discourage individual nations from falling prey to dictators bent on warping the nobility of national sentiment to their own ends. In sum, the League, in its educative capacity, was to encourage nationalism that was consistent with the goal of internationalism. Thus, Zimmern argued that the League's educational mission could best be defined "as a process of harmonization between the inner and the outer," between the national home and the international world.[155] "Nationality," he insisted "rightly regarded, is not a political but an educational conception."[156]

In Zimmern's internationalist imaginary, nations were moral, life-giving, spiritual entities. "Nationalism rightly understood and cherished," he argued, "is a great uplifting and life giving force, a bulwark alike against chauvinism and against materialism—against all the decivilising impersonal forces which harass and degrade the minds and souls of modern men."[157] The most natural, animating, and spiritual component of the great global organism thus resided in the "living spirit of patriotism."[158]

---

[151] This is complicated by Zimmern's clearly conflicted feelings about his father's Judaism.

[152] Zimmern, *Nationality and Government*, 53.

[153] Ibid., 38.

[154] Ibid., 101.

[155] Zimmern, *Learning and Leadership*, 30.

[156] Zimmern, *Nationality and Government*, 53.

[157] Ibid., 100.

[158] Zimmern, "The Ethics of Empire," 497.

Within nations, individuals first learned to love, just as wise men through-out the ages have "loved their home land as they loved their parents."[159] This was a primordial love, the kind that tied human beings to the great natural cycles of life. For some inter-war theorists of internationalism such as Nicholas Murray Butler, the pathos of nationhood, its sheer emo-tional violability, made it inherently suspect. To stand as a rational indi-vidual in the face of a wave of nationalist sentiment was, for Murray Butler, "the mark of a real man."[160] In contrast, Zimmern's more idealist tendencies made it possible for him to steadfastly refuse to position him-self on either side of the passion/reason dichotomy, and to assume that while the nation might be prone to irrationality, its very naturalness, its passion, and its familiarity were in fact necessary to the ultimate triumph of the international mind in the world. According to Zimmern, "the road to Internationalism lies through Nationalism; and no category or ideal of Internationalism can be helpful . . . unless it is based on a right under-standing of the place which national sentiment occupies and must always occupy in the life of mankind."[161]

At this moment, in his negotiation between the universal and the na-tional, Zimmern reveals his true idealist colors. Internationalism, he as-sumed, was capable of speaking both to those national characteristics that differentiated human beings from one another and to those "eternal things which unite, to the rock bottom level of our common humanity."[162] Internationalism was both transcendent and situated, organic and me-chanical. Internationalism, as a theory and a way of life, entailed both spiritual relations and the day-to-day workings of the League in Geneva. Like his Oxford forbears, Zimmern refused to acknowledge the "old op-position" between individual and society, or nationalism and internation-alism, insisting instead upon the necessity and dignity of both as well as their eventual resolution within the international mind.

As we shall see, what gets lost in Zimmern's understanding of nations as families is an analysis of power relationships. For Zimmern, national-ism was familial; the family, loving. The more national sentiment grew within a community, the more loving and inclusive its politics. In this way, Zimmern's understanding of international relations seems, at times, stunningly naive as he continued to insist, long after Mussolini's march on Rome and the Nazi's rise to power, that nationalism supplied the key to world peace.

---

[159] Zimmern, *Nationality and Government*, 100.
[160] Murray Butler, *The International Mind*, 98.
[161] Zimmern, *Nationality and Government*, 62.
[162] Ibid.

CONCLUSION

For Murray and Zimmern, the dream of post-war internationalism vacillated between two poles. On the one hand, they were committed to a transformation of the old international order, which they characterized as anarchic, rife with power politics and secret diplomacy. In this transformative vision, the League of Nations played a central role in reshaping the contours of a peaceful world. On the other hand, both men were deeply fearful of radical changes in the world economic and political system wrought by the war—the rise of socialism at home and abroad, and the slow splintering of the imperial edifice. Viewed in this light, the League of Nations became potentially threatening, a state-like organization that must be divested of any independent authority. In the grand tradition of the Oxford idealist liberals, their internationalism walked a middle way between these two extremes by claiming both the transformative power of a radical social movement and the rootedness of a political cause grounded in a world community characterized both by its own traditions and by the traditions of its national participants. At the same time, Murray's and Zimmern's turn toward the more authentic qualities of the international whole forced them to reject key liberal assumptions about equality and universality. Chapter 5 argues that Murray and Zimmern championed an approach to international society that not only naturalized state sovereignty and the economic status quo but also served to obscure some of the more radical and egalitarian proposals of their peers. As chapter 5 suggests, we can only begin to calculate the long-term effects of this hegemony.

CHAPTER FIVE

Sovereignty and the Liberal Shadow

THE INTERNATIONAL ORGANIZING Committee, a special committee appointed by the 1919 Paris Peace Conference, officially drafted the Covenant of the League of Nations after the war.[1] Although representatives on the committee came from the five Great Powers (Britain, France, the United States, Italy, and Japan) and nine less influential states (Belgium, Brazil, China, Portugal, Serbia, Greece, Poland, Czechoslovakia, and Romania), from the beginning the drafting of the covenant was, in the words of Inis Claude, a "predominantly Anglo-American enterprise."[2] In the mid-1930s, Zimmern's recollections of that period went even further by describing the final draft of the Covenant as a "British framework together with a number of Wilsonian policies."[3] These comments are true insofar as it was largely British liberals who laid out the structural possibilities and limitations for the League.[4] In fact, on a number of key points, the final version of the covenant closely resembled documents drawn up by liberal-dominated, pro-League organizations or by liberals associated with the Foreign Office. Thus, arguably, British liberals, in the words of one editorialist of the day, did "the hard constructive thinking which made the League of Nations possible."[5]

The story of the intellectual origins of the League of Nations in Britain has already been told. Henry Winkler and George Egerton in particular have carefully traced the movement of specific proposals for a League of Nations from their development by individuals and groups during the war, through their integration into the 1918 report of the Phillimore Committee, and into the draft proposals prepared by the Foreign Office (which were eventually approved by the imperial war cabinet and presented as part of the British negotiating position in Paris).[6] Many of these proposals were incorporated almost unchanged into the covenant

---

[1] Inis Claude, *Swords Into Plowshares: The Problems and Progress of International Organization* (New York: Random House, 1956), 37.

[2] Ibid., 38.

[3] Zimmern, *The League of Nations and the Rule of Law*, 239.

[4] Conservative MP Lord Robert Cecil was one among several notable exceptions.

[5] "A False Step at Geneva," *Nation and Athenaeum*, Oct. 11, 1924, p. 42. This influence was expanded even further once the American delegation pulled out of the League project.

[6] Most importantly, Henry Winkler's *The League of Nations Movement in Great Britain* (New Brunswick: Rutgers University Press, 1952), and George Egerton's, *Great Britain and*

itself.[7] The goal of this chapter is not to rearticulate this narrative but rather to locate Zimmern and Murray within its context and demonstrate how both men came to influence the two institutions that ultimately held such sway with the British delegation at Paris: the League of Nations Union and the Foreign Office. The final internationalist vision preferred by the delegation ultimately shied away from anything resembling a world state. In contrast to the coetaneous movements for international government in Britain and America, supporters of this approach focused their efforts on a plan for creating an international community united by moral and symbolic rather than coercive criteria. This form of internationalism relied heavily on precisely the kind of moral, spiritual, and organic arguments put forth by Murray and Zimmern rather than requiring the Great Powers to sacrifice even a fraction of their sovereignty.

The first section focuses on the origins of the League of Nations movement in Britain, Murray's and Zimmern's connections to this movement, and their impact on the formulation of the League of Nations Covenant. It also examines the long-term influence of Murray's and Zimmern's particularly pro-League form of internationalism on the disciplinary development of IR in Britain between the wars. The second section explores more closely what about their particularly idealist liberal form of internationalism made it so attractive to members of the ruling coalition in Britain and to a generation of liberal thinkers. In particular, it examines how both men's analyses of international politics ultimately occluded responses to world conflicts that insisted on a more critical examination of the free market and state sovereignty. It does this by comparing their approach to that of their friend and colleague, the liberal socialist Harold Laski. The final section looks more closely at the long-term impact of the approach to sovereignty which Murray and Zimmern were so instrumental in consolidating during the inter-war period. It argues that this approach, this historical artifact, continues to generate scholarly disconnects between deconstructive critiques of sovereignty, critical democratic theory, and international ethics, disconnects that make it appear impossible to reconfigure democracy even in the face of global economic integration and the emergence of a transnational peace movement. The chapter ultimately suggests that the obfuscating quality of their liberalism—a quality that made it seem unnecessary to challenge the fixity of sovereignty—lives on as one of Murray's and Zimmern's most potent and troubling legacies.

---

the League of Nations: Strategy, Politics, and International Organization, 1914–1919 (Chapel Hill: North Carolina University Press, 1978).

[7] Peter Yearwood, " 'On the Safe and Right Lines': The Lloyd George Government and the Origins of the League of Nations, 1916–1918," *The Historical Journal* 32 (1989): 132.

LEAGUE INTERNATIONALISM AND THE TWENTY YEARS CRISIS IN BRITAIN

In George Egerton's words, by 1918, "the league of nations idea stood at the center of the ideological response of British and American liberalism to the tragedy of modern war and the fear of revolution."[8] Well before 1918, however, support for some kind of international league to promote peace had already taken hold among the majority of British liberals. During the war, many of these thinkers were organized into pro-League societies and intellectual circles that sought to influence the coalition government and the British public by producing a plethora of policy schemes aimed at the construction of a post-war league of nations.

The earliest rumblings of support for the league of nations idea in Britain became audible shortly after the onset of the war when a group of left-leaning and pacifist liberals (including Hobson, Norman Angell, and H. N. Brailsford) founded an anti-war organization known as the Union of Democratic Control (UDC) Included in the UDC's "Cardinal Points" was a commitment not only to arms reduction as a requirement of the peace settlement but also to the establishment of an international council aimed at promoting "an abiding peace."[9] Shortly thereafter, members of the UDC and other intellectuals formed the Bryce group to study more specific recommendations for the construction of this abiding peace. The scheme the group ultimately adopted stipulated that the six Great Powers of Europe, the United States, and Japan enter into a treaty arrangement. A court of arbitration at The Hague with the mandate to enforce reparations and sanctions was to handle disputes between member states.[10] This emphasis on international law was also apparent in the Fabian Society's favored proposal (authored by Leonard Woolfe) that appeared shortly after the publication of the Bryce Group's findings.[11]

Ultimately, however, although elements of both the Bryce and the Fabian plans made their way into the British draft covenant, more conservative (yet still liberal) organizations like the League of Nations Society (LNS) had the most influence on the Foreign Office. Although membership between the UDC and the LNS overlapped, ideologically the LNS (of which Murray and Zimmern were both founding members) touted itself as a centrist organization occupying a position somewhere between the UDC and conservative foes of the League idea. The LNS initially strove to blend these two approaches through a theory of internationalism

[8] Egerton, *Great Britain and the League of Nations*, 62.
[9] Ibid., 6.
[10] Ibid., 9.
[11] Ibid., 15.

grounded in the principles of diplomacy and open discussion, the formation of an international body to facilitate this discussion and to set international moral standards, and the expansion of international law. At the
same time, this vision flatly rejected the authority of a world state. Thus,
while the society's scheme ultimately reflected the Bryce and Fabian plans
in its focus on The Hague and the establishment of a permanent court of
justice, it was more cautious in its approach to the enforcement of the
court's decisions. For instance, while the Bryce plan called on signatory
nations to use economic and military force to exact reparations from belligerents, the society's proposals made no provisions whatsoever for the
enforcement of international law.[12]

Other, decidedly more anti-world-state organizations also had an impact on the formation of the covenant. In particular, the influence of the
pro-imperialist Round Table Society expanded significantly after the editor of its magazine, Philip Kerr, became Lloyd George's private secretary.[13]
The group with perhaps the closest ties to Oxford, the Round Table Society was established at New College in the mid 1880s by Alfred Milner,
and many of its members were self-proclaimed disciples of T. H. Green.[14]
In general, the group primarily aimed to develop and elaborate the moral
discourse that accompanied Britain's continuing imperial expansion.
Long-time member Zimmern perhaps best expressed the Round Table's
core tenet in his 1913 when he argued that if "the British Empire is destined to endure, it will be only as the guardian of the moral welfare of its
peoples. Faith in this mission alone can justify the effort to further its
consolidation."[15] Throughout the war, the Round Table's magazine reflected this emphasis on morality, community, and an improved imperialism, arguing that the main job of any new league would be to create the
international conditions where "right and not might shall prevail in the
world."[16] These thinkers stressed an approach to the league that maintained the status quo, one that both protected Britain's imperial interests
and was itself modeled after the society's sanguine portrayal of the commonwealth.

By 1918, the coalition government had begun to explore the possibility
of a creating a league of nations in earnest, prompted in large part by the
force of public opinion. Woodrow Wilson's Fourteen Points had recently
become wildly popular in Britain, a popularity that the coalition government did not hesitate to use to justify its war effort despite their very real

---

[12] Bodl. MS Alfred Zimmern (82). (Appendix: "Recent Schemes of Federation," by Rt.
Hon. Lord Phillimore.)

[13] Yearwood, "On the Safe and Right Lines," 144.

[14] Kendle, *The Round Table Movement*, 18.

[15] Zimmern, "Ethics of Empire," 484.

[16] Yearwood, "On the Safe and Right Lines," 144.

imperial trepidations about Wilson's commitment to a policy of "national self-determination."[17] Once the Germans appealed to Wilson for a peace based on the Fourteen Points, the government found itself in the awkward position of having to accept the inevitability of some sort of post-war international league to prevent war without having yet developed an official opinion about what this league ought to look like.[18] Lloyd George and his colleagues were clear, however, about what the League of Nations should *not* look like. For key members of the Foreign Office and high-ranking players in the ruling coalition, any international organization to emerge out of the war must ensure that British imperial sovereignty (and specifically, British naval power) remained intact.[19] In addition, it must also protect free trade and colonial expansion, exclude the Soviet Union, and, in the words of Lloyd George, "offer Europe an alternative to Bolshevism."[20]

The report of the Phillimore Committee betrays this bias against league schemes that required any weakening of British sovereignty. Inspired by deputy foreign secretary and unflagging league supporter Lord Robert Cecil, the Phillimore Committee was established by Lloyd George in 1918 to study the various league proposals that had accumulated during the war. The draft convention that they submitted to the government was, according to David Hunter Miller, "the first formulation of League of Nations suggestions in a definite text under [British] Governmental direction."[21] From the outset, the Phillimore Committee's report was hostile to any proposal that hinted at the creation of an extra-state organization with juridical or military power.[22] The plan upon which they ultimately agreed carefully avoided the appearance of a super-state by rejecting the necessity for a permanent international body with an existence at all independent of member states.

While the scheme the government finally adopted went beyond the Phillimore Committee's suggestions and called for an independent league, the

[17] Allen Sharpe, "The Genie that Would Not Go Back Into the Bottle: National Self Determination and the Legacy of the First World War and the Peace Settlement," *Europe and Ethnicity*, eds. Seamus Dunn and T. G. Fraser (London: Routledge, 1996), 11.

[18] Egerton, *Great Britain and the League of Nations*, 80.

[19] Zilliacus, *Mirror of the Past*, 239.

[20] Lloyd George, "Some Considerations for the Peace Conference Before They Finally Draft their Terms" [in Zilliacus, *Mirror of the Past*, 224].

[21] David Hunter Miller, *The Drafting of the Covenant*, vol. 1 (New York: G. P Putnam's Sons, 1928), 3.

[22] In its lengthy analysis of the Fabian, Bryce, the LNS, the UDC, and American and French league plans, the report itself consistently dismissed the idea of an "international authority" as untenable. They painted the Fabian scheme in decidedly fanatical terms as similar "to the paper constitutions which the Abbe Sieys used from time to time to produce during the French Revolutionary Period." [Bodl. MS Alfred Zimmern (82). (Phillimore Report, Appendix, p.15)].

version of the covenant the British delegation presented in Paris maintained the Phillimore Committee's skepticism toward committing sovereign states to the authority of such an organization. For all intents and purposes, the government ultimately proposed establishing a league that wielded moral authority alone, accompanied by a weak system of collective security. In many of its key assumptions, this approach to league internationalism mirrored almost exactly ideas that Murray and Zimmern had developed.

That Murray and Zimmern would become influential players in the coalition government's effort to draft a post-war peace makes considerable sense given both the influence of Greenian social theory on the Liberal Party toward the end of the nineteenth century (culminating with Asquith's election in 1906) and both men's association with the Liberals before and during the war.[23] Murray, for instance, was such an establishment figure within the Asquith government that he often referred to himself as a "party hack."[24] Zimmern also worked with the Liberal government before the war, serving as an inspector of the National Board of Education from 1912 to 1915.[25] By the time war was declared in 1914, both men had already situated themselves as somewhat influential persons in relation to the government and were thus poised to join other liberal intellectuals in helping the Lloyd George Coalition develop its approach toward a post-war peace.

Zimmern had the most direct influence on the government during this period through his positions first in the Ministry of Reconstruction and then in the Political Intelligence Department of the Foreign Office. In the latter post, he came to the attention of Lloyd George in the thick of the 1918 election, when the Liberals were eager to shore up the party's position on the creation of the League of Nations.[26] The Foreign Office placed Zimmern in charge of a League of Nations section during which time he authored what came to be known in late 1918 as the "Foreign Office Memorandum." This document, along with the suggestions of the Phillimore Committee, laid the foundations for the famous "Cecil Draft," which the British delegation took to Paris in 1919.[27]

Zimmern's Foreign Office Memorandum spelled out the official British objection to Woodrow Wilson's "more ambitious ideas" for a League of Nations with potentially coercive powers, specifically Wilson's desire to include "guarantees" in the covenant that would require states to respond forcefully to the unlawful actions of both member and non-member

[23] Pugh, *The Making of Modern British Politics*, 112.

[24] West, *Gilbert Murray: A Life*, 150.

[25] Markwell, "Sir Alfred Zimmern Revisited," 280.

[26] Paul Rich, "Reinventing Peace: David Davies, Alfred Zimmern and Liberal Internationalism in Interwar Britain," *International Relations* 16 (2002): 119.

[27] Markwell, "Sir Alfred Zimmern Revisited," 280.

states.[28] Zimmern took issue with the language of "guarantees," arguing that such a commitment would unacceptably infringe upon state sovereignty. Instead, Zimmern echoed the Phillimore Committee's contention that the League of Nations ought to be based on the voluntary actions of sovereign states alone.[29] His memorandum also agreed with the Phillimore report in its insistence that state sovereignty ultimately "precluded long-term engagements," that is, precluded the creation of an international council comprised of member states perpetually in session. At the same time, however, Zimmern's report elaborated the basic structural requirements for a permanent international organization that would be primarily responsible for judicial, administrative, and investigatory activities.[30] Further, in the tradition of Phillip Kerr, Lionel Curtis, and other prominent members of the Round Table Society, Zimmern's report maintained that this international organization should approximate less a centrally organized bureaucracy than a loosely associated version of the British Commonwealth.[31] The Foreign Office Memorandum thus ultimately argued that any post-war arrangement of international relations ought to resemble a voluntary community of states and consist of regular conferences between leaders from all the Great Powers. Zimmern went on to suggest that such a league might be modeled on the 1815 Concert of Europe.[32]

In toto, the memorandum reads in classic Zimmern style as a juggling of compromises, a kind of complex meliorism that depended more on the assertion of international organization than on the specific (often conflicting) details of how to bring this organization about. Yet despite its lack of clarity—or maybe precisely because of it—when Robert Cecil became the head of the Foreign Office League of Nations Section in October of 1918, he chose Zimmern's memorandum as a foundation from which to work and had its various organizational suggestions summarized in a "Brief Conspectus of League of Nations Organizations." This draft, later known as the "Cecil Plan," went with Cecil and the delegation to Paris in early 1919 where they presented it to the Americans. This meeting between Cecil's committee and the American delegation produced the Hurst Miller draft, a combination of American suggestions and British

[28] Long and Wilson, *Thinkers of the Twenty Years Crisis*, 82. According to Paul Rich, the proposals embodied in this draft "did much to weaken some of the idealism of Woodrow Wilson's plan and to limit the League's role to one where it was an expansion of the concert of Europe." [Rich, "Reinventing Peace," 120].

[29] In fact, according to Zimmern, the League ought to be subject to renewed consideration by sovereign member states every two to four years. [Egerton, *Great Britain and the League of Nations*, 94].

[30] Egerton, *Great Britain and the League of Nations*, 96.

[31] Zimmern was a member of the Round Table Society from 1913. Along with Curtis, he was one of the leading forces behind a major rethinking of the Society's mission in the years just before World War One. [Kendle, *The Round Table Movement*, 172].

[32] An idea he attributed directly to Murray. [Zimmern, *Nationality and Government*, 24].

concerns, which substantially reduced the powers of the league from those originally articulated in Wilson's Fourteen Points.[33] In particular, the British delegation insisted that the league's commitment to "preserve as against external aggression the territorial integrity and existing political independence of all State members of the League" be understood as a "principle" rather than an "obligation."[34] In this way, Zimmern's draft significantly altered the original American plan in a direction favored by the Lloyd George government, members of the Round Table Society, and the newly formed League of Nations Union

The League of Nations Union (LNU) was created in 1919 when the League of Nations Society merged with the more conservative League of Free Nations. Formed in July of 1918, the League of Free Nations was considerably more anti-German and pro-war than the LNS. Lowes Dickinson would later describe them as "ardent supporters of the war, and good haters of Germany."[35] By October 1918, however, the armistice with Germany had become a reality. The focus of the British and Allied press now turned from condemnations of German militarism to the British elections that Lloyd George had called, elections that were widely regarded as a mandate on the league idea. That month, the LNS and the League of Free Nations agreed to merge and join their efforts to "give moral support to the League."[36]

Many leaders in the LNS used the merger as an excuse to purge the organization of its more radical members, among them, Murray. Murray had drafted an influential document in September of 1914 supporting the war and by 1918 he and a number of his colleagues had begun to believe that even though it was formed in opposition to the UDC, the LNS was itself becoming too radical, that it was in danger of being overrun by leftists, labourites, and other "pacifist faddists."[37] As what *Gnoman* would later describe "the principle architect of the League of Nations

---

[33] Zimmern, *The League of Nations and the Rule of Law*, 195. A letter to Zimmern from Eustace Perry with the British Delegation in Paris in 1919 makes it clear that most of the American representatives at the conference were equally worried about what was seen as a kind of abstract utopianism on Wilson's part. "All our American friends share our views very completely," Perry relayed to Zimmern, "if they could only get the President to take sufficient account of the actual facts of international relations and prevent him from confining himself to academic principles."[Bodl. MS Alfred Zimmern (16) fol. 2].

[34] Zimmern, *The League of Nations and the Rule of Law*, 242.

[35] G. Lowes Dickinson, *The Autobiography of G. Lowes Dickinson, and Other Unpublished Writings*, ed. Dennis Proctor (London: Duckworth, 1973), 191.

[36] Bodl. MS Gilbert Murray (11) fol. 50 (*Proceedings of the British Acadamy*, J.A.K. Thompson, p. 253).

[37] Gary Messinger, *British Propaganda and the State in the First World War* (Manchester: Manchester University Press, 1992), 36; Wilson, *Gilbert Murray OM*, 254. Other signatories of Murray's pro-war document included Henry Jones, Sir Arthur Conan Doyle, H. G. Wells, and Rudyard Kipling.

Union," Murray used the merger to transform the organization into some-thing that appeared more respectable.[38] During those early years, Murray worked constantly for the LNU. Then, after coming home from his stint as the South African delegate to the League in the early 1920s, he became chairman, a position he would hold from 1923 until 1938. According to his biographer, Murray's appointment as chairman represented a final defeat "for the U.D.C. and radical members of the L.N.S."[39] During his tenure, he exercised a considerable amount of sway over the official goals of the organization.[40] In his own words, he was the man "principally re-sponsible for the policy of the League of Nations Union."[41]

In lending its moral support to the League, the LNU was extremely successful. After the merger, it continued the public education campaign begun by the UDC and the LNS, only this time with the explicit support of the Liberal Party, which, given the post-war expansion of the franchise, viewed the issue as necessary to its success at the polls.[42] After the election, the frenzied pace of the LNU's educational agenda continued as the Paris Peace Conference drew near, although the organiztion's focus leaned more toward its other equally important mandate: to solidify, through its research committees, an approach to international organization that would directly influence the Paris Peace process.[43] Since, as Murray put it, such an approach ought to be grounded in "moral force" rather than in the coercive power of an extra-national state, the LNU ultimately pro-duced a set of policy suggestions based on expanding opportunities for states to discuss international issues.[44] Indeed, in a memorandum entitled "Comments on the Covenant" issued by the executive in February 1919, the LNU argued that the draft covenant it supported proceeded upon the assumption "that if disputants are forced to meet and talk some way of settlement will always be found."[45]

Because of his close friendship with Cecil, Murray played a significant role in extending the influence of the LNU, particularly after January 1919, when Cecil asked him to become a member of a small advisory committee created both to "discuss the draft schemes on which we are working in Paris and to supply us with the criticisms and suggestions of it on the various aspects of the subject."[46] Murray thus became one of a

---

[38] Bodl. MS Gilbert Murray (11) fol. 3 (*Gnoman*, 1957).

[39] Wilson, *Gilbert Murray, OM*, 254.

[40] Ibid., 251.

[41] Bodl. MS Gilbert Murray (242) fol. 110c (undated letter).

[42] Egerton, *Great Britain and the League of Nations*, 92.

[43] As Murray later recollected, "at one time we held more than a thousand meetings a year." [Murray, *The League of Nations Movement*, 7].

[44] Ibid., 8.

[45] Bodl. MS Murray (180) fols. 97–98.

[46] Ibid., fols. 4–5 (letter from Cecil to Murray, January 4, 1919).

few key advisors in Britain to whom Cecil turned with questions and requests during the February negotiations. While Cecil was in France, the two men were in almost constant communication, and Cecil frequently either asked Murray for the LNU's input on particular issues or requested that Murray help him drum up support for a proposal upon which he knew the leaders of the LNU would agree.[47] As a result, by the time the League of Nations published its official covenant in early 1919, the document had been so thoroughly saturated with LNU ideals that the group itself declared it to be "a long step—perhaps the longest possible for the time being—in the right direction," and observed approvingly that the "the main provisions of the Covenant are in accord with the policy of the Union."[48]

Through their membership in both official and voluntary organizations during the war, Murray and Zimmern played essential roles in wresting the impetus for a league of nations from the early "pacifist faddists" like Angel, Hobson, and Woolfe, and moving it toward a more conservative approach to sovereignty. Their particular vision of liberal internationalism and the "moral forces" associated with it allowed them to embrace a League Covenant with policy prescriptions that did little more than advance the status quo.

In addition, as both key players in the creation of British league policy and respected academics, Zimmern and Murray exerted an enormous intellectual influence over the academic study of IR in Britain. They also played an essential role in shoring up what many observers of disciplinary history such as Jim Vasquez and Hedley Bull have referred to as the liberal or idealist stage in the development of twentieth-century IR.[49] According to these scholars, IR in Britain between the wars was characterized by a belief in the cooperative power of the League of Nations, collective secu-

[47] In an undated letter labeled "Private and Personal," Cecil asks Murray to help in toning down the LNU's rhetoric with regard to "minorities." He asks Murray to "use your influence with the Union on these lines to secure efficiency by moderation and circumspection."[Bodl. MS. Gilbert Murray (242) fol. 6]. Cecil's letters during this period also frequently refer to documents he had altered or proposals he had made that were based on Murray's suggestions. At the same time, Cecil clearly needed not only the expertise of the LNU but their influence as well to help him press his ideas on both Liberal and Conservative governments throughout the 1920s. See for instance Bodl. MS Gilbert Murray (189) fol. 93 (letter from Cecil)].

[48] League of Nations Union, "Observations on the Draft Covenant of the League of Nations, by the Research Committee of the League of Nations Union," (Feb. 1919) [Egerton, *Great Britain and the League of Nations*, 143]. Bodl. MS Gilbert Murray (180) fols. 97–98.

[49] See, for instance, John Vasquez, *The Power of Power Politics, A Critique* (New Brunswick: Rutgers University Press, 1985); Hedley Bull, "The Theory of International Politics, 1919–1969," *The Aberystwyth Papers: International Politics 1919–1969* (London: Oxford University Press, 1972); Torbjorn Knutsen, "Interwar Politics: The Twenty Years Crisis," *A History of International Relations Theory* (Manchester: Manchester University Press, 1997).

rity, and international law along with a general conviction that, in Bull's words, the "system of international relations that had given rise to the First World War was capable of being transformed into a fundamentally more peaceful and just world order."[50] A spate of recent works by scholars such as Peter Wilson, David Long, and Brian Schmidt have challenged this monolithic approach, and have argued instead that these idealists were more diverse in their thinking than scholars have commonly assumed. But it remains true that a number of key academic positions within Britain were defined specifically in relation to the League of Nations and the system of international organization upon which it was based.[51]

Thus, while this book agrees with Long, Wilson, and Schmidt that idealism between the wars was significantly more wide ranging than its critics have given it credit for, it maintains that one version of IR (a version closely associated with a particularly rosy reading of the league) held more institutional sway than did other approaches. When Oxford announced the establishment of its first independent professorship of IR in 1931, for example, it urged potential applicants to "bear in mind that the underlying motive of the Donor is the furtherance of International Peace in accordance with the deliberations and decisions of the League of Nations at Geneva."[52] And as influential participants in the process that inevitably resulted in the League of Nations Covenant, Murray and Zimmern not only were from the beginning closely associated with an approach to IR that addressed the form of international governance associated with the League as the primary subject of analysis, but also helped institutionalize this approach within the British academy between the wars.

Murray, for instance, played a key role in defining the Oxford position, and Zimmern was the first person to occupy it.[53] Between the wars, both men continued to wield this kind of influence over the fledgling discipline, pushing the intellectual pursuit of IR toward "training the younger generation to regard international co-operation as a normal method of conducting world affairs" at a number of different universities and scholarly organizations including Oxford, the University of London, the Geneva School of International Relations, and the League's own Committee of

---

[50] Bull, "The Theory of International Politics," 34.

[51] See, for example, the recent works of Brian Schmidt and Peter Wilson, in particular, Wilson's 1998 article "The Myth of the 'First Great Debate," *Review of International Studies* 24 (1998), and Schmidt's "Lessons from the Past: Reassessing the Interwar Disciplinary History of International Relations," *International Studies Quarterly* 42 (1998).

[52] J. P. Dunbabin, "The League of Nations' Place in the International System," *The Historical Association* (Oxford: Oxford University Press, 1993), 421.

[53] Murray's role in defining this position and the eventual hiring of Zimmern is documented in a number of interesting correspondences between Murray, Philip Baker, Toynbee, and Zimmern himself. See Bodl. MS Gilbert Murray (391), fols., 2–5, 9, 10, 37, 38, 55–57, 60–67.

Intellectual Co-operation.[54] They did this through two very distinct professional paths. Murray remained a Classics scholar at Oxford, influencing the discipline largely through his involvement with voluntary organizations and his extensive informal contacts. By contrast, Zimmern left off the study of Classics almost entirely in 1909 to take a variety of different academic positions in IR, beginning in 1919 when he became the first professor of IR in the world at the University of Aberystwyth.

Despite Murray's decision to remain a professor of Greek and Zimmern's more transient career as an IR scholar, however, both men spent a considerable amount of time shuttling back and forth between the academy and League-associated institutions and voluntary organizations in Britain and Geneva. Their commitment both to the League as an institution and to the intellectual pursuit of IR represents an important aspect of inter-war idealism that has escaped the notice of many disciplinary historians. Knutsen, Smith, and Hollis, for instance, are fairly typical in attributing the pro-League tendencies of inter-war IR scholars almost entirely to the legacy of World War One and the force of Wilson's Fourteen Points, as though these two factors alone were enough to generate two decades of League-oriented scholarship.[55] In so doing, they fail to recognize the vigilance of those pro-League academics, like Murray and Zimmern, whose constant movement between the academy, League organizations, and the League itself helped push the emerging discipline in a distinctly pro-League direction.

Murray, for instance, served as a delegate to the League for the second and third meetings of the assembly.[56] Along with Zimmern, Murray was also instrumental in establishing the League's Institute for Intellectual Co-operation in 1923 and was for years actively involved with the Advisory Committee on the League of Nations Teaching. Finally, through their personal influence, Murray and Cecil shaped a number of key university positions in Britain to conform to the LNU's vision of IR. In particular, with the appointment of Zimmern and others to key positions at Oxford, Murray and Cecil transformed Oxford's fledgling department into what Ernest Bramstei has described as a "stronghold of academic pioneers of collective security."[57]

Zimmern spent a great deal of his academic life moving between university and League appointments, ultimately establishing himself both as one of the most powerful intellectual influences over IR and as a guiding light

---

[54] Murray, *Liberality and Civilization*, 83.

[55] See Hollis and Smith, *Explaining and Understanding International Relations*, and Knutsen, *A History of International Relations Theory*.

[56] Wilson, *Gilbert Murray OM*, 250.

[57] Ernest Bramstei, "Apostles of Collective Security: The LNY and its Functions," *The Australian Journal of Politics and History* 13 (1967): 351.

of the idealist approach to world politics. While a young fellow at Oxford before 1910, he influenced a number of students who would go on to play key roles in British international politics, including Arnold Toynbee, Reginald Coupland, and several future members of the Round Table Society.[58] As noted above, in 1919 he was appointed to the Wilson chair of international politics at Aberystwyth.[59] At the same time, Zimmern was attending the first sessions of the League at Geneva and helping found the Institute of International Affairs in London.[60] Two years later, Zimmern established a summer school for international studies in Geneva known as the Geneva Institute for International Relations. Zimmern solidified his predominance (and the primacy of the League) in the discipline with his appointment to the Oxford Chair in 1933.

Through their personal connections Murray and Zimmern thus pushed their agendas on both the League of Nations Covenant itself and on the study of IR. But beyond these personal connections lies the more important question: what was it about their particular pro-League forms of internationalisms that made them so successful and so appealing not only to representatives of the government (like Lloyd George and Cecil) but to the liberal academic establishment more generally? This book argues that the answer can be found in the way their liberalisms successfully hid from sight the power relations behind many of the inter-war world's most intense economic, political, and cultural conflicts. At the same time, their approach made it possible for many contemporary British liberals to invest themselves in a form of international political change without cost, in what appeared to be a radically new approach to politics that on a basic level refused to challenge the fundamental assumptions of the pre-war international system—especially the supremacy of sovereign statehood in international politics.

THE LIBERAL SHADOW

In the *Twenty Years Crisis*, Carr aimed one of his most pointed criticisms of the interwar idealists at their inability to adequately diagnose political problems. For Carr, the faith of thinkers like Zimmern in the liberal "harmony of interests" doctrine resulted in a kind of stubborn utopianism that then prevented them from treating political and moral purpose as anything but fact. As a result, they were completely unable to see the

---

[58] See Toynbee's account of Zimmern in *Acquaintances*, 48–61. See also, Carroll Quigley, *The Anglo-American Establishment*, 89.

[59] Long and Wilson, *The Twenty Years Crisis*, 79.

[60] Markwell, "Sir Alfred Zimmern Revisisted," 280.

world as it really was. "The American Declaration of Independence claims that 'all men are created equal,' " observed Carr by way of explanation, ". . . yet it is a matter of common observation that all men are not created equal in the United States."[61] Such an unwillingness to let go of fantasy prevented utopian thinkers from implementing their political agendas. Carr's observations do not exactly ring true, however, with regard to Murray and Zimmern. While both men bore the unmistakable stamp of utopianism insofar as they believed in an ideal type of world order, they were also much more prescient in their ability to identify the sources of international conflict than Carr gave utopians credit for. The problem with Murray's and Zimmern's internationalism lay not in their unwillingness to identify the world problems that made international cooperation difficult but in their inability to consider the motivation behind these problems as anything other than mulish selfishness or the solution to such selfishness as anything other than a sterile reordering of pre-war order. In other words, as this section argues, Murray's and Zimmern's impotence in this regard arose not from a liberally produced utopianism that kept them from identifying world conflict but from a liberalism that adumbrated the power relations behind these conflicts.

Murray's and Zimmern's observations of the main problems of international relations were not only startling in their accuracy but remain eerily relevant today. For example, both men were quite critical of the fact that capital was increasingly transnational in its purview while political organization remained firmly wedded to the sovereign nation state. They argued that such an imbalance led to the development of international cartels, trade conflict, and a general inability by states and political activists to curb exploitative economic practices throughout the world. Murray and Zimmern also argued that one of the primary causes of war in the world resided in the sovereign "right" of nations to wage war, a situation that ultimately devolved into international anarchy. Thus, in contrast to Carr, this book suggests that Murray and Zimmern were never *prevented* from seeing the problems of the world by the hulking edifice of their utopian visions. Neither man was so enamored with his ideal image of international organization (as the living embodiment of the One Great City of Men and Gods, or the smooth functioning of the international organism) as to be completely blinded to the workings of power politics. Where Murray's and Zimmern's analyses fall curiously flat is in their understanding of the origins of the conflicts they identify as central to contemporary world politics and in their prescriptive solutions to such problems. Again,

[61] Carr, *The Twenty Years Crisis*, 12.

however, the shadow in this case was cast by neither man's utopianism but, rather, by their liberalism.

For instance, while both men were worried by the unchecked pace of capitalist expansion in relation to what appeared to be the stymied growth of international community, neither was willing to concede that significantly regulating either the domestic or international economy might be necessary. Again, this unwillingness sprang from a deep-seated liberal discomfort with challenging certain free market assumptions. As chapters 3 and 4 have argued, Murray's and Zimmern's works were consistently shot through with deeply ambivalent attitudes toward free market capitalism—worried cynicism, wide-eyed appreciation, condemnation of the "harmony of interests" doctrine—that culminated in a general unwillingness to support a state-regulated economy. Their political theories largely avoided these competing concerns by elegantly switching the focus of liberalism from the economically driven individual and his or her freedom to the possibility of transcendence and particularly the superceding of class interest in the name of universal social good. Again, as with Green, Bosanquet, and their cohort, Murray and Zimmern linked this transcendence to the unfolding of Spirit through the world. The lack of Spirit, the lack of that communal understanding that compelled individuals to work for the good of others, was missing in the current form of world economic organization. The job of concerned citizens, statesmen, and the League of Nations was, for Murray, to bring "a cosmos into the world economic life," or, in Zimmern's words, to make the world "really interdependent in its spiritual relations just in the same way it is in its material and economic relations."[62] Infuse the capitalist economy with spirituality and the need for state regulation on a domestic scale disappeared, and creating extra-state institutions with a mandate to regulate international capital become unnecessary.

This basic refusal to imagine the relationship between the state and capital as anything other than antagonistic, and their conviction that any antagonisms that did exist between the operations of the market and the public good could be addressed through an enhanced notion of public spirit alone, meant that Murray's and Zimmern's liberalisms successfully concealed the very real connections between the state and the interests of capital. And yet by the early 1920s, neither Murray nor Zimmern could claim ignorance of political theories that elaborated these connections. Indeed, throughout this era, both British socialists and Murray's and Zimmern's more socialistically inclined liberal brethren (and often good

[62] Murray, "A Survey of Recent World Affairs," 4; Zimmern, "The New International Outlook," 22.

friends) were busy articulating the state's implicit relationship to class privilege.

Harold Laski, for instance, a long-time acquaintance of Murray's and good friend of Zimmern's, was particularly vocal in this regard. From the very beginning, Laski was among the most radical of the inter-war liberals. In particular, he insisted upon "the abrogation of the idea of sovereignty in international affairs," thus pusing the envelope of what even left-leaning scholars and activists like Hobson and Woolf were willing to accept.[63] Laski's virulence about sovereignty is hardly surprising given that he began developing his critique long before most of these pro-League thinkers had started to imagine a world in which international cooperation was the norm. While living in theUnited States, he wrote several articles that specifically examined the issue of sovereignty from a pluralist perspective, and he continued to write extensively about the subject after his return to England in the early 1920s.[64]

Laski's domestic and international politics—his concern with issues of economic justice and democracy and his passionate work for international cooperation and against imperialism—were linked by this central analysis of sovereignty. As a liberal socialist who was both wary of state authority and critical of capital, Laski based his critique on the idea that modern forms of liberal state sovereignty concealed the state's relationship to economic and social power. Despite the insistence by many liberals (including T. H. Green, Laski argued) that the state stands against both the rights of the individuals and the market, the simple fact of the matter was, according to Laski, that "from the standpoint of international relations the true heart of the state is its government; and the unity it represents is not so much the interests of it's subject as the whole of that part which dominates the economic life of its members."[65] As a liberal, this frightened Laski immensely. The "temptation to make the state a unity," Laski argued, made it prone to authoritarian action aimed with particular vengeance against its weakest members.[66] As a socialist, Laski argued that the apparent *unity* of the liberal state (in which all citizens and economic classes are fairly represented by one government, a government that supposedly stood in opposition to capital) conveniently hid from sight not only the relationship of the state to the "economic life" that dominated

---

[63] Harold Laski, "International Government and National Sovereignty," *Problems of Peace: Lectures*, 289.

[64] See "The Personality of the State," *The Nation* July 22, 1915, 101, and "The Apotheosis of the State," *The New Republic* July 22, 1916, 7.

[65] Harold Laski, "Foundations of Sovereignty," *Foundations of Sovereignty and Other Essays* (Free Port, NY: Books for Libraries Press, 1921), 27.

[66] Harold Laski, "The Sovereignty of the State," *Studies in the Problems of Sovereignty* (New Haven: Yale University Press, 1917), 1.

its members but also the "complex of interests which struggle among themselves for survival."[67] In sum, the liberal doctrine of state sovereignty successfully masked class conflict by transforming the state into a unity.

Laski also saw an implicit connection between domestic sovereignty and international politics. By obscuring internal class struggle and then projecting the state into the world as one unitary and coherent society, sovereignty effectively concealed the shared interests of workers in different states and the inherently transnational qualities of capital itself. Asking sovereign states (who were, in effect, representatives of their own home-grown capitalists interests) to solve international economic problems was, in Laski's mind, akin to leaving the wolf to guard the hen house. The *effects* of international capital were felt by individuals all over the world, but sovereign states, with deep connections to their own privileged classes, could not be trusted to think universally, to act for the good of all people. In Laski's words

> If there is one outstanding fact in the modern world it is that the fact of a world market has made a world economy, and that everything that interferes with the movement of that world economy is so much taken from the prosperity of the world, and by that amount so much taken from the standard of life of the people. Things that are shared in common by one nation and another can only be decided in common by one nation and another. . . . The national sovereignty that makes up its mind that its tariff laws or its immigration laws, or what you will, are matters upon which its own unaided and uncontradicted word is the final decision in the making of the ultimate result is thereby a traitor to the unification that we need.[68]

Laski responded to these "traitors" by calling for an international system of governance in which it was impossible for the "privileged class which determines the habits of the state" to "use that power in the international field both to consolidate and reinforce their authority."[69] Laski's feelings about how to bring this about evolved over his career. During the early to mid-1920s, his work on international politics and economic reform focused on this issue of sovereignty alone. Real international change in both the economic and political realms could only come about, Laski maintained, if state representatives at the League of Nations or some other international organization were prevented from speaking as the unitary voice of their people. Rather, an emboldened form of world state might

---

[67] Laski, "Foundations of Sovereignty," 27.

[68] Harold Laski, "International Government and National Sovereignty," 293.

[69] Harold Laski, "The Economic Foundations of Peace," *The Intelligent Man's Way to Prevent War*, ed. Leonard Woolf (London: Victor Gollancz, 1933), 545. Essays by Norman Angell, Gilbert Murray, and Lord Cecil also appear in this same volume.

allow individual political states to voice their opinion but, in the end, "there would be no room for separate sovereignties."[70] As the 1930s progressed, Laski combined this approach to international government with an increasingly virulent critique of capitalism. The "high road to peace," Laski now argued, could only be reached in light of a structural transformation of the global economy and the creation of a world order of socialist societies. This global society would be in a position, he insisted, "to consider its economic problems upon a basis of genuine mutuality and good will."[71]

Laski also saw a clear connection between sovereignty, imperialism, and the possibility of international democracy. Sovereign states acted in the interests of their own elite classes, he argued; because these classes supported imperial expansion, liberal states had to fold imperialism into their own ostensibly democratic frameworks to drive the "habits of imperialism into the national unity."[72] The contradictions between a formal commitment to universal equality and democracy at home and inequality and authoritarianism in the colonies produced instabilities, which Laski termed "cleavages," within the state's discursive understanding of itself. As a result, according to Laski, official and unofficial imperialist ideologies based on "pseudo-scientific biology" or notions of white burden proliferated.[73] And, in Laski's words, "a society which denies equality within is bound by the logic of its nature to deny it also abroad." In sum, sovereign democratic states' own internal logic of "unity" drove them to develop ideologies that justified imperial expansion but that ran counter to their own formal commitments to equality. International democracy was untenable through the League of Nations, according to Laski, as long as the "internal constitution of its members" was rooted in inequality. The only remedy, Laski argued, was to expose the relationship between capital and sovereignty so that "sovereignty was no longer a cloak for that interest."[74]

Neither Murray nor Zimmern could accept such a radical response to the deep-seated connection between state sovereignty and transnational capital because neither man's liberalism connected state interests with power politics, Laski's interests of the privileged class. Nowhere is this more clearly demonstrated then in Zimmern's analysis of the relationship between the international economy and the League of Nations. Again, however, Zimmern was acutely perceptive in pinpointing the economic

---

[70] Harold Laski, *A Grammar of Politics* (London: George Allen and Unwin, 1963 [1938]).

[71] Laski, "The Economic Foundations of Peace," 543.

[72] Ibid., 527.

[73] Ibid.

[74] Ibid., 543.

and political problems that arose when "private international organization" (the worldwide economy) was allowed to function "in a vacuum."[75]
He frequently noted the irony of the fact that, in some ways, economic
integration had brought the current world "organism" or community into
existence, had "created the rudiments of a world wide πόλις (*polis*)."[76]
And yet, sovereignty itself prevented ordinary citizens from fully experiencing the world as an integrated community or nascent polis. The inherent disconnect experienced by ordinary citizens between their material
lives (shaped as they were by an international economy) and the political,
intellectual, and emotional restrictions placed on them by sovereign statehood worried Zimmern most intensely.

> We are born into a world of economic internationalism and political national-
> ism or, to speak more correctly, localism. Our bodies are fed, clothed, and cared
> for from the uttermost parts of the earth; but our minds dwell within limits
> fixed by local system of instruction, entitled national system of education, in
> which prejudice, superstition, and even deliberate falsification may play a pre-
> dominant part.[77]

In other words, the political limitations of national sovereignty not only
obscured the rapidly integrating nature of the world social whole but also
fostered feelings of nationalism and xenophobia within states.

Zimmern was also acutely aware that leaving the world's economic
processes purely in the hands of transnational private interests could have
negative effects on workers whose means of democratic appeal were still
limited to national governments. At several points in his career, Zimmern
appeared on the verge of suggesting that the League or some other form
of international *public* organization be given the necessary political tools
to sanction and modify the workings of capital. No "clear-headed individualist in the twentieth century," he argued in 1936, would "desire to allow
the economic process to be entirely immune from social control."[78] Indeed, Zimmern was emphatic in his conviction that if "you desire that the
destinies of civilization should be publicly controlled in a lawful manner,
you must contrive some public organization to keep pace with the private
organization."[79] His writings on the subject, however, make clear that he
never intended this "public organization" to enforce the "lawful manner"
in which the "destinies of mankind" were realized. Just as he once theorized a domestic economy guided by moral workings of communal and

---

[75] Zimmern, *America and Europe and Other Essays*, 98.
[76] Zimmern, *Quo Vadimus?* 6.
[77] Ibid., 11–12.
[78] Zimmern, "The Problem of Collective Security," 31.
[79] Zimmern, *America and Europe and Other Essays*, 99.

public interest alone, so now did Zimmern imagine that this international form of economic "social control" would be almost entirely voluntary. In this context, the League needed no independent policing power over capital because, by its sheer existence, it provided the world with an opportunity to witness the global community in action, to peek over the fence into the neighbor's yard. The League of Nations thus provided the venue for a moral, global conversation about the economy that would inevitably lead to the good of the whole.

As with his domestic example, however, the actual details of the policy-making activity behind this global conversation (and its relationship to the League) bedeviled Zimmern. Zimmern came closest to detailing how workers might take advantage of the league system in 1926, when a student at the University of Buffalo pressed him on the subject. Zimmern responded by explaining that if "workers want to amend what is unjust in the capitalist system, the only way that they can do it is by associating themselves with the League of Nations and using that organization for making their views known. They will not get 100 percent of what they ask—nobody ever does—but they have an extraordinarily good machine, an international machine, for carrying out their objects."[80] But he only ever briefly articulated how the League "machine" made this "carrying out" possible. In fact, his descriptions of the machine itself (the workings of those economic and labor committees associated with the League) never entirely made clear how the League was to challenge the economic policies of individual states or the practices of international capital. Zimmern's writings often made it appear that the International Labor Organization and the Financial Committee were able to generate fair economic policy through their sheer existence alone.

Additionally, when Zimmern *did* describe how League committees addressed economic or labor issues, he completely refused to consider that the representatives of sovereign states at the League might be influenced by the interest of capital. Indeed, Zimmern not only accepted but even celebrated that, within the League's Financial Committee, a representative from the Bank of England "sits at the right" of the British delegate.[81] As a result, these committees' deliberations, as he described them, seemed remarkably open to manipulation by the forces of economic integration that simultaneously intrigued and worried him. Zimmern suggested in 1929, for instance, that the International Labor Organization carried out its mandate by largely ignoring the traditional political norms and institutions associated with democratic states. Instead, the organization was at its finest, argued Zimmern, when it was breaking down the "old rigid

---

[80] Zimmern, "The New International Outlook," 18.
[81] Ibid.

distinction between that which is official and that which is non-official" between elected representatives and "non official bodies, employers and workingmen's associations."[82] It never seems to have crossed Zimmern's mind that the public organization meant to counterbalance the private organization of capital ought not to include representatives of capital, that in fact these two classes might have antithetical, irreconcilable interests. Thus, not only did Zimmern's solution to the disconnect between private and public internationalism fail to explain how the League was to enforce the public good against the will of capital, but private interests still largely influenced the *means* by which the public good was established in the first place.

Zimmern's unwillingness or inability to see this as a problem makes considerable sense given the structure of his liberalism. For Zimmern, the essence of a liberal polity, whether national or international, was spiritual. The transcendent and conciliatory impulses of the international mind ultimately underscored the movement toward international community. In this context, the job of the League of Nations must therefore be to strengthen those communal bonds that would make life in the international polity more just for everyone. This theory once again masterfully obscured the myriad power relationships at work beneath the transcendent practices of liberalism. By making workers and representatives of capital equal partners in constructing the good of the whole, Zimmern's theory effectively neutralized the very real conflicts between them. In addition, Zimmern's emphasis on the voluntary, self regulating power of the international community and those cooperative institutions assembled at Geneva made it possible for him to assert that the good of the global public could be achieved in the absence of a broader challenge to state sovereignty. Finally, Zimmern's emphasis on the informal "unofficial" quality of the League's work stripped from its committees the necessity to function democratically.

The ultimate irony is that both Murray and Zimmern had emerged from the war as critics of unfettered sovereignty (particularly of the right of sovereign states to declare war) and supporters of what Murray termed the "democratic idea" at the heart of the League of Nations. Each man put considerable faith in a world community that they imagined as a densely populated and vibrant society, a City of Man and Gods in which state boundaries were meaningless in the face of the "ultimate fraternity of mankind." At times, both men sounded like veritable champions of international government. Murray, for instance, argued in 1933 that an excess of sovereignty—which he envisioned as curable by the creation of a

---

[82] Zimmern, *America and Europe and Other Essays*, 102.

"world government"—made the current "world cosmos" infirm. [83] Likewise, Zimmern's works on the inherent separation of nationhood from statehood and his commitment to the composite nature of the commonwealth were replete with the desire to address "the problem of law and order for the world" in a way that sometimes skimmed strikingly close to an international extension of state power. [84]

And yet, although Zimmern and Murray had initially openly acknowledged sovereignty as a problem, both men settled upon internationalist theories characterized by their vociferous refusal to challenge sovereignty at its most basic level. Their idealist liberal form of internationalism was particularly adept at reconciling this discrepancy by refocusing liberalism itself. Both men claimed that liberalism was ultimately characterized by the relationship between freedom and fraternity, and the transcendent power of Spirit. Once a general adherence to Liberal spirit transformed the world, the organized power of inter-state or super-state politics was no longer necessary to achieve internationalist goals.

The irony here, of course, is that Murray and Zimmern developed a liberal social theory that undermined their own stated political project. In this sense, as much as they might have wanted to challenge liberal theory and practice to make it more socially responsible on both a global and domestic level, they were in the end hamstrung by their own uncritical commitments to free trade and their unwillingness to challenge the relationship of the liberal state to capital. Their internationalism thus insisted that international political reform could be achieved even if the structural forces behind the world's looming tensions were left firmly in place. Such an approach made it possible for the state representatives who ultimately crafted the League of Nations system to ignore the international theory of thinkers and activists like Laski, who not only insisted that these larger issues be addressed but who vocally expressed his doubts that such a system could act in the best interests of the world's citizens.

THE LIBERAL SHADOW TODAY

The liberal shadow cast by Murray and Zimmern over the problematic of sovereignty has had a number of long-term discursive effects on current academic thinking about international politics. On the one hand, it has helped solidify the sovereign state as the unit of analysis within the discipline of IR. While standard realist accounts of inter-war "idealist" ap-

---

[83] Murray, "A Survey of Recent World Affairs," 2.

[84] See for instance his discussion of sovereignty and law in "The Problem of Collective Security," 14–16.

proaches to internationalism have remained both skeptical and hege-monic since the end of the Second World War, mainstream IR still largely assumes the core tenets of this liberal philosophy as far as the sanctity of sovereignty is concerned. Within the discipline, most academic propo-nents of both "idealist" and "realist" accounts of the world agree on this point, despite the growing amount of research being done on transna-tional movements and global integration. As Saskia Sassen notes in *Glob-alization and Its Discontents*, the literature on transnational economic processes is still "profoundly rooted in the nation-state as the ultimate unit for analysis."[85] Ironically, in terms of sovereignty, the "twenty years crisis" has been a far more prolix phenomenon than realists have under-stood it to be.

On the other hand, the ossification of the category of "sovereign state-hood" within IR has also seriously limited the extent to which political theorists have been willing to push their conceptions of democracy, a phe-nomenon keenly felt in the paucity of critical democratic theory that seri-ously considers an expansion of democratic practices beyond sovereign statehood. This is true of even those political theorists committed to ex-ploring the obfuscating political effects of collective identity. Political the-orists such as Lisa Disch have done stellar work on how the discourse of national interest (what Disch terms "symbolically inclusive rhetoric") can obscure the very real social and political differences of experience at the heart of domestic policy issues.[86] Likewise, Sheldon Wolin considers the relationship between the identity-generating mien of American constitu-tionalism and the legitimacy this sense of collectivity confers upon the state. Wolin's feelings on the anti-democratic nature of this "alchemy of authority" echo Laski's in his concern that "the identity given to the col-lectivity by those who exercise power will reflect the needs of power rather than the political possibilities of a complex collectivity; it will be a collec-tivity devoted to consolidating *unum* rather than to encouraging *plures*."[87] In the end, however, neither Disch nor Wolin identify their work as an explicit critique of sovereignty, and, while both trouble the relation-ship between the state and national identity on a domestic level, neither questions the fixity of statehood as *the* spatial determinant of democratic possibility. In other words, their thinking about democracy necessarily ends at the internal borders of the state. And this is fairly typical. Within

[85] Saskia Sassen, *Globalization and Its Discontents* (New York: The New Press, 1998), 212.

[86] See Lisa Disch, "Publicity-Stunt Participation and Sound Bite Polemics: the Health Care Debate 1993–94," *Journal of Health Politics, Policy, and Law* 21 (1996).

[87] Sheldon Wolin, "Collective Identity and Constitutional Power," *The Presence of the Past: Essays on the State and the Constitution* (Baltimore: The Johns Hopkins University Press, 1989), 13.

the current corpus of works on democratic political theory, virtually no one seeks to combine a critical reading of collective identity/sovereignty with a radically expanded approach to democratic politics. Indeed, most political scientists since Laski seem to have lost the ability or desire to imagine how the current global public sphere might be emboldened with the democratic tools necessary to transform a global politics still controlled by sovereign states and international capital into a global politics controlled by world citizens.

But the issue of sovereignty has not been entirely ignored within the discipline. In fact, over the last ten years the increasing disconnect between the actual processes of economic integration and standard IR descants on sovereignty has spawned a growing movement of post-structuralists seeking to critically unpack the conceptual framework of sovereignty as both a historically situated and continually contested discursive terrain. In *Simulating Sovereignty*, for instance, Cynthia Weber borrows Foucault's basic refusal to "solve" the question of sovereignty as it is continually posed in contemporary debates concerning norms of intervention. Rather, she approaches the questions that swirl around the discourse of intervention as consistently reinscribing and reconstructing the notion of sovereignty itself "by positing a sovereign state with boundaries that might be violated."[88] Viewing sovereignty as an inherently contested site of knowledge production (rather than as a fixed fact or a problem that must be solved) allows Weber to develop a critique of sovereignty that focuses on the way the concept blinds us to its own historicity and simultaneously renders the state's ability (indeed, its right) to "represent" a people both unproblematic and a priori. Roxanne Doty makes a similar theoretical move in her work by drawing upon post-structuralist international relations literature to problematize the supposedly unambiguous relationship between nationhood and sovereignty. In her article "Sovereignty and the Nation," Doty maintains that rather than arising naturally from an already clearly demarcated nation, sovereign authority functions to fix the more ambiguous qualities of collective identity into an unquestioned inside/outside dichotomy.[89] The fixity of this dichotomy, she argues, can and does then lead to the creation of hegemonic anti-immigrant discourses and exclusionary practices on the part of the state.

In the end, both Weber and Doty raise a number of concerns about sovereignty that almost exactly mirror those articulated by Laski, particu-

[88] Cynthia Weber, *Simulating Sovereignty: Intervention, the State, and Symbolic Exchange* (Cambridge: Cambridge University Press, 1995), 4.

[89] Roxanne Doty, "Sovereignty and the Nation," *State Sovereignty as a Social Construct*, ed. Thomas Biersteker and Cynthia Weber (Cambridge: Cambridge University Press, 1996), 122.

larly their focus on the discursive power of sovereignty to transform the historically complicated and ambiguous boundaries between human communities into discrete political unities that then legitimate state authority. But neither of them transform their deconstructive arguments into the kind of constructive thinking about democracy that Laski saw as so important to his project. Both authors continually stress the need to *destabilize* the univocal character of sovereignty, to unpack and expose its more obfuscating characteristics, but neither projects beyond these critiques to elaborate a moral vision of global society, to theorize a kind of democratic polity capable of replacing the eviscerated concept of sovereignty itself.

This is often also true of international ethicists who *are* interested in elaborating positive democratic solutions to world problems, but for entirely different reasons. While these thinkers are concerned with constructing arguments aimed at expanding democratic accountability on a global level, they often acknowledge the limitations of sovereignty but ultimately refuse to think beyond the concept itself. Thomas Pogge's works on international economic justice and the need to democratize meta-state institutions like the European Union, for instance, tend to begin (like Murray's and Zimmern's writings) with a serious nod to the role sovereignty plays in structuring global inequality or hindering democracy. Thus, in "Economic Justice and National Borders," Pogge makes the compelling argument that economic inequality on a world scale is exacerbated by the fact that any government (regardless of whether it came to power democratically) is recognized as legitimate by international loan or development organizations like the World Bank and institutions of international governance, such as the United Nations. The logic of sovereignty thus makes it possible for *any kind* of state to claim to represent "a people" in the international arena. International recognition then grants these governments certain economic privileges, including the privilege to "dispose freely of the natural resources of the country" and "to borrow in the country's name."[90] This combination of what Pogge terms the "international resource privilege" and the "international borrowing privilege" ultimately encourages the proliferation of undemocratic and corrupt regimes in resource rich but economically underdeveloped countries by giving corrupt and authoritarian governments virtually unlimited proprietary rights over the countries' resources. At the same time, these regimes can borrow funds from international lending institutions, run up huge debts, and then straddle the next—potentially democratic—government with those debts.[91]

---

[90] Thomas Pogge, "Economic Justice and National Borders," *Revision* 22(2) (1999): 29.
[91] Ibid.

Because corrupt, undemocratic regimes are more interested in their own survival than in the good of their people, reasons Pogge, they will inevitably sell their country's recourses cheaply (in a global economic environment eager to depress these prices) and keep the profits rather than redistributing them, thus leading to further inequalities of wealth between developed and underdeveloped states. Improving the material well-being of the vast majority of the world's people thus entails the elimination of that system of anti-democratic incentives embedded in the international recourse privilege and the international borrowing privilege. This could be accomplished, argues Pogge, by assigning such privileges only to "democratically legitimated governments."[92]

At this point Pogge's previous capacity to think critically about the logic of sovereignty (particularly his Laskian observation that the privileges of sovereignty transform all types of government into the legitimate mouthpieces of their people) begins to give way to an unexamined, Kantian faith in the ability and desire of democratic states to behave morally (indeed, altruistically) in an international context. For Pogge, committees of jurists associated with the United Nations ought to generate the criteria by which democratically legitimated governments should be judged. And yet, Pogge never challenges the fact that the United Nations is itself composed of *sovereign* state members, not all of whom of are democracies. More importantly, for our purposes, Pogge never questions the desire of democratic states themselves to support fledgling democracies in the third world. And yet he also spends a great deal of his argument carefully articulating the dynamics of a world economic system in which economically developed states, corporations, and first-world consumers alike have a vested interest in paying as little as possible for developing countries' raw materials. In Pogge's words, the international resource privilege guarantees first world nations "a reliable and steady supply of resources because we can acquire such ownership rights from anyone who happens to exercise effective power" which then "greatly reduces the price we pay for these resources."[93]

To assume that these states would have an interest in promoting democracy in the developing world, one would also have to assume that democratic states do not take the interests of their own economic elites (and international capital) into account when constructing foreign policy. Current world economic and political events suggest otherwise—a phenomenon best exemplified by the Bush administration's virtual give away of $1.7 billion in contracts to the Halliburton Corporation in spring 2003. One would also have to assume that *internal* democratic institutions

[92] Ibid., 32.
[93] Ibid., 31.

would have some influence over a state's *external* behavior, an assumption again disproved on a massive scale by the U.S. and British invasions of Iraq. In both cases, the ability of sovereign states to claim certain representational powers in the international arena allows privileged economic and political interest to wield disproportionate global influence. Pogge's inability to think *beyond* sovereignty prevents him from offering viable ethical solutions to his own well-constructed elaboration of the problem.

Pogge's analysis of the European Union's democracy deficit suffers from a similar unwillingness to challenge basic assumptions about sovereignty even as he claims a kind of ethical imperative to deal with the reality of "supranational integration."[94] Thus, Pogge accepts the European Union as a fait accompli whose "practical necessity" is beyond question in a world increasingly conditioned by "transnational externalities."[95] What bothers Pogge is that the European Union's governing institutions have been constructed by bureaucratic elites rather than through democratic processes that fully involved the participation of ordinary European citizens This elite push for transnational integration has resulted in a gradual erosion in some cases of the democratic guarantees enshrined in the constitutions of individual European states.[96] Pogge's response is not to reclaim sovereign statehood as the guarantor of democratic rights but, rather, to construct a counterfactual account of how EU institutions could have been crafted democratically from the beginning. Pogge demonstrates how a series of questions—questions that entail basic guidelines about EU institutional decision making in the realms of economic justice, foreign policy, the financial system, migration, and so on, all of which infringe on nation states' current political processes—might be presented "to the citizens of prospective member states for their judgment."[97] But it is unclear in Pogge's argument *why* the sovereign state members of the European Union would ever agree to allow these questions to be put before the people in the first place. For instance, what would make state bureaucrats willingly offer up for democratic approval a policy concerning economic justice or migration that might place restrictions on its own ability to exercise authority? Pogge assumes that sovereign states are ultimately capable of seeing beyond their own interests, or the interests of their most vocal and powerful citizens.

[94] Thomas Pogge, "Creating Supra-National Institutions Democratically: Reflections on the European Union's 'Democracy Deficit,'" *The Journal of Political Philosophy* 5(2) (1997): 182.

[95] Ibid.

[96] See in particular Pogge's discussion of the German Maastricht Verdict of 1992 (Ibid., 164–65).

[97] Ibid., 175.

My critique of Pogge does not spring out of a blanket assumption that sovereign states will always jealously guard their own power. The continued growth and expansion of the European Union and the increasing economic power of non-democratic transnational economic institutions like the World Trade Organization (what Zimmern termed "private international organization") suggest that sovereign states are often more than willing to eschew internal forms of sovereign authority in exchange for increased economic integration. This phenomenon has prompted a number of experts (of all political persuasions) to declare what liberals and Marxists had been predicting for the last one hundred fifty years: that the sovereign nation state is now really "withering away" in the face of the new world economic order.[98] And yet such an analysis sells sovereignty short by assuming that the state's goal is to get and keep power under any costs and that this remains consistent in all situations. By contrast, a more historically grounded and critical investigation into the power dynamics and economic interests at the heart of the democratic state's claim to "represent" its people (à la Laski) suggests that the modern liberal state might be only too happy to sacrifice some forms of authority in the name of an economic integration that benefits its elite. Given this interpretation, why should it come as any surprise that modern liberal states—forced to enact progressive labor and environmental laws by an increasingly concerned national public—would not be at all heartbroken to see a global economic organization with no democratic accountability impinge upon this aspect of their sovereignty?

Part of the legerdemain of liberal sovereignty as it congealed in its twentieth-century form between the wars was its ability to successfully occlude the relationship between capital and the state within the context of economic integration. In our own era, when international trade is even more tightly controlled by non-democratic transnational institutions, the grip of liberal sovereignty continues to shape even the discourses of the opposition. Not only do many anti-globalization activists reflexively employ the very logic of capital itself to justify their cause (e.g., calling for "free" and "fair" as opposed to "unfair trade"), sovereignty still largely frames their response to the creeping interpolation of international capital into the democratic politics of statehood. Even Ralph Nader, for example, argues that sovereign states are our only salvation against the irascible forces of economic integration, that the international tribunals set up by the WTO amount to "a staggering rejection of our due process and our democratic

---

[98] See, for instance, Richard Barnet and John Cavanagh, *Global Dreams: Imperial Corporations and the New World Order* (New York: Simon and Schuster, 1995).

procedures."[99] Nader never considers the possibility that the liberal democratic state (as a representation of a projected unity) might, under some circumstances, be only too happy to give up some of its internal sovereignty. He also never considers that the time might be ripe for considering a radical expansion rather than retraction of democracy, that maybe, like Laski we ought to be thinking beyond the limitations of our democratic procedures and demanding that these procedures be embodied in global, public institutions that can match the WTO in political power.

Perhaps the most staggering and long-lasting effect of that adamantine notion of sovereignty that Murray and Zimmern ultimately embraced is its persistent ability to obscure connections among radical, deconstructive critiques of sovereignty, democratic theory, and international ethics. In other words, there is almost no movement among political theorists, internationalists, or philosophers to think democracy through sovereignty, to critique sovereignty as a site of power/knowledge production and economic hegemony, and, at the same time, to theorize normative possibilities for a democratic practice with radically different boundaries. Ironically, this reluctance continues even when the contradiction between the limitations of sovereign democracy and the protest politics of an increasingly visible global public sphere are greater than ever. On the one hand, since the terrorist attacks of September 11, 2001, and the invasion of Iraq in spring 2003, the United States has ratcheted up the language of sovereignty, a phenomenon most presciently expressed in the Bush Doctrine's call for preemptive self-defense. As Bush argued in his first speech to the nation after the United States had "preemptively" invaded Iraq, the "United States of America has the sovereign authority to use force in assuring its own national security."[100] On the other hand, even as Bush administration officials were most vigorously pushing sovereignty to its logical—and simultaneously ludicrous—conclusions, activists from around the world protested these conclusions in a heretofore unheard of transnational effort, unprecedented in its coordination. The eleven million people who took to city streets across the world on February 15, 2003, and the thousands of who participated in Lysistrata productions in fifty-three different countries on March 3, 2003, gesture toward the coalescence of an increasingly well-orchestrated global peace movement.

In the end, the very terms of liberal sovereignty that Murray and Zimmern helped raise to the level of orthodoxy within IR continue to struc-

---

[99] Ralph Nader, "WTO Means Rule by Unaccountable Tribunals," *The Ralph Nader Reader* (New York: Seven Stories Press, 2000), 203.

[100] George W. Bush, "Remarks by the President in an address to the Nation, the Cross Hall, March 17," The Cross Hall, 8:01 P.M. EST. Available at http://www.whitehouse.gov/news/releases/2003/03/20030317–7.html.

ture the arguments of even the most radical critics of sovereignty and the most democratic of political theorists. And yet, as the visceral example of the international peace movement suggests, the opportunity may be ripe to reimagine world democracy, to rediscover the silenced voices of thinkers like Laski—so adamant in his commitment to an "abrogation of sovereignty" as the only ethical solution to an unjust world. The time may have come to instantiate the democratic impulses of the global public sphere by theorizing it, by combining a critical perspective on statehood and power with an ethical projection of a democratic future. Our current situation demands the realization of Laski's most radical vision: "that things which affect the world in common have got to be decided by the world in common."[101]

[101] Laski, "International Government and National Sovereignty," 295.

CHAPTER SIX

Liberal Community and the Lure of Empire

MURRAY'S AND ZIMMERN'S liberal internationalisms provide us with a highly suggestive set of lenses for analyzing contemporary political theory, in particular those theoretical approaches that seek to deepen our understanding of the relationship between liberalism and community. While both men consciously sought to reconcile liberal freedom and communal fraternity on a domestic scale, we can most clearly see the *kind* of community they thought best suited to liberal ethics and governance in their work on international relations. By audaciously claiming that international liberalism could function in the absence of a state, both men had to articulate clearly the form of international social order that would make it possible for liberal spirit to unite the world. In other words, Murray's and Zimmern's enterprise itself obliged them to find preexisting forms of social relationships that could actualize liberal duty on a global scale.

To do this, both men employed a timeworn idealist liberal strategy: they turned toward natural forms of social organization. According to Murray, true international liberality must be based on a naturally occurring world order that implied "leaders and led." For Zimmern, the liberal impulses of the international mind could be fulfilled only within those most natural constituent elements of the social organism (the national families of mankind). Thus, Murray's and Zimmern's approaches to international community demonstrated plainly and well the pitfalls facing liberals who want to nest liberal ethics and politics in social relationships—the temptation to turn political and economic power into seemingly natural forms of social order.

This is not meant to suggest, however, that the project in which Murray and Zimmern were engaged was not, in key ways, laudable. Most importantly, perhaps, it helped force one of liberalism's classic theoretical gaps to the surface. Since Locke first sidestepped the issue by grounding his theory in a form of tacit consent, many liberal theorists have simply avoided the question of political origins, accepting state and national communities as given. In Murray's and Zimmern's attempts to theorize international society from the ground up, we see the unfolding of an approach to liberalism that refused to take social relationships for granted, and instead sought to understand the connection between liberal freedom and social context. At the same time, Murray's and Zimmern's work shows all too clearly the need to ensure that these forms of fraternity adhere to liberalism's own core principles of equality. In the absence of this commitment, Murray's and Zimmern's attempts to push liberalism in a more social direction metastasized into the confused form of its own opposite: an internationalism that relied upon an economic system grounded on individual interest coupled with a pre-liberal, almost medieval understanding of a global social order that ultimately served to justify British imperialism throughout the inter-war era.

This concluding chapter explores the ways that Murray's and Zimmern's work continue to speak to both the limitations and promises of the liberal communal vision on both a global and domestic level. It begins by focusing on the current divide in political theory that largely relegates thinking about community to communitarians. It then briefly examine the work of Will Kymlicka and Yael Tamir, two liberal scholars who both reject, in Kymlicka's words, the "communitarian idea that people's ends are fixed and beyond rational revision" while at the same time demanding that liberalism itself take seriously the socializing and reciprocal aspects of community. The chapter continues with a more extensive investigation of the way Murray's and Zimmern's attempts to fuse liberalism with an enriched sense of global community ultimately naturalized a theory of world order that not only assumed massive inequality on a global scale but also camouflaged the power politics of empire. The concluding section suggests that Murray's and Zimmern's work should serve as a cautionary example for thinkers like Kymlicka and Tamir, both of whom overlook the subtle ways that their own approaches to social and national cultures similarly obscure certain anti-liberal, anti-egalitarian aspects of these cultures. In this spirit, the final section also explores some examples of the recent crusade for a return to imperial politics that liberal scholars and pundits like Michael Ignatieff, Robert Cooper, Fareed Zakaria, and Robert Kagan have mounted since September 11, 2001. It concludes that Murray's and Zimmern's liberal internationalisms demonstrate all too well the densely imbricated assumptions of hierarchy and power embedded in the contours of these modern imperialist projects, projects that claim to reconcile the liberal values of human equality and democracy with a simultaneous call to impose order on the world.

Putting Liberalism in its Place: The Context of Community

In *Multicultural Citizenship*, Will Kymlicka uses Zimmern's analysis of "composite statehood" to illustrate his point that liberals were once able to talk in a language other than that of individual rights. For Kymlicka, whose work primarily focuses on developing a dialogue between liberals and advocates for minority rights, historical precedents are especially important. Thus, he notes that for "most of the nineteenth century and the first half of the twentieth, the rights of national minorities were continually discussed and debated by the great liberal statesmen and theorists of the age."[1] According to Kymlicka, however, a convergence of post-war political changes (beginning with the failure of the League of Nations' minority policy) largely silenced a lively debate among liberals. As a result, very few contemporary liberal theorists "have explicitly discussed the rights of ethnic and national minorities."[2]

While Kymlicka is absolutely correct to acknowledge Zimmern as one of the more prominent liberal theorists of nationality, Zimmern's political theory also illustrates a liberalism concerned with more than just the issue of minority rights. Rather, the fact that late nineteenth- and early twentieth-century liberals were discussing the rights of national minorities at all points to the more basic concern that a great number of these thinkers were wrestling with; the exact relationship between communities and liberal freedom. The works of Green, Bosanquet, Ritchie, Murray, and Zimmern all reveal that the current division of labor in political theory is relatively recent. That communitarians produce the majority of today's critical thinking about community (while most liberals, simply assuming the existence of a community, focus their analysis on the individual rights) does not necessarily arise from the liberal tradition. It is, rather, a peculiar characteristic of the post-war world.

While some contemporary liberals continue this trend of avoiding or assuming the community in which their theories function, others are more explicit in their insistence that they are frankly unconcerned with developing a broader understanding of social organization. In *Political Liberalism*, for instance, John Rawls notes in his first lecture that the theory he is about to develop in greater detail assumes a "closed society"—that is, a society that members enter "only by birth" and leave "only by death," which has no relations with other societies.[3] How the particular origins and qualities of this society (its foundational myths, its understanding of itself) might affect liberal politics within its closed borders is unimportant for elaborating a theory of liberal justice, Rawls implies. Rawls remained unbothered by the apparent contradiction between depending on a theory that is at its most basic level universal and then assuming that it only works within closed exclusive societies in his more recent "restatement" of the theory of justice, *Justice as Fairness*.

---

[1] Will Kymlicka. *Multicultural Citizenship* (Oxford: Oxford University Press, 1995), 49. (His discussion of Zimmern appears on page 55.)

[2] Ibid., 49.

[3] John Rawls, *Political Liberalism* (New York: Columbia University Press, 1993), 9.

Other liberal theorists, such as Ronald Dworkin, have argued that liberalism ought to be more concerned with thinking through the relationship between social institutions and the practice of liberalism, although he is consistently vague about why this concern is warranted. In his article "Liberal Community," Dworkin spends a considerable amount of time trying to define community in liberal terms, ultimately settling upon a definition that takes the "collective agency" of its citizens as fundamental.[4] For Dworkin, a particular nation or a state is distinct from other nations or states because the individuals associated with it engage in constitutive "collective acts." Such a definition assumes that the state is, in his words, a "decent, democratic political community."[5] In sum, when citizens within this democratic community come together to vote, when their legislature, executive, or judiciary makes legal decisions in their names, one "distinct legal person" is created. To illustrate this, Dworkin argues that the "United States [as a legal person] rather than particular officials and soldiers, fought in Vietnam."[6]

On a basic level, Dworkin's definition reveals an unspoken assumption (common among liberal theorists in the United States) that one can generalize from the experience of America. But in less obvious terms, Dworkin's example also fails in the case of other liberal democratic societies. Dworkin could not have chosen a worse example than war to demonstrate the community-creating qualities of democratic citizenship. Within most modern liberal states, decisions concerning national security are typically made not through democratic channels but through executive power alone. In the United States, the electoral system ensures that up to nearly half (or, as in the Presidential election of 2000, *over* half) of the voting citizens may not have voted for the sitting president and, thus, would have had no voice in the construction of the "legal person" who fought in Vietnam. Moreover, wartime is typically seen as a period during which democratic rights can be legitimately suspended. Finally, nothing reveals the non-liberal underbelly of national community as does war. During war, citizens are called upon to make sacrifices not for democracy alone but for "our way of life," for mom and apple pie, for things that are not rooted in collective political acts but in a pre-political understandings of what makes us different from other societies.

Communitarian critics of liberalism have long argued that this refusal to define the constituents of the very community upon which the "collec-

---

[4] Ronald Dworkin, "Liberal Community," *Communitarianism and Individualism*, eds. Shlomo Avineri and Avner De-Shalit (Oxford: Oxford University Press,1992), 212.

[5] Dworkin, "Liberal Community," 213.

[6] Ibid. (brackets mine).

tive acts" of a liberal society are grounded reveals a larger flaw in the logic of liberal theory as a whole: namely, that liberalism is epistemologically dependent upon an unarticulated notion of community that implies mutual obligation. Rawls assumes, Michael Sandel argues, that members of his "closed society" have some kind of inchoate connection to one another, some sense of themselves as a cohesive group. As such, Sandel maintains that Rawls's theory of liberal justice depends upon a preexisting network of moral ties among citizens that make the practices of distributive justice possible.[7]

Jack Crittenden echoes this line of thinking in his discussion of liberalism's historically impoverished notion of the "unencumbered self." Drawing upon communitarian critiques of liberal individualism, he suggests that the individual with whom liberalism is concerned is not unencumbered but is already socially constituted by his or her relationship to both a community and an implicit sense of communal obligation. For Crittenden, understanding the nature of what he refers to as the "compound" individual necessarily means understanding the nature of the community itself.[8] And in a community, he argues, "relationships precede obligations." In other words, Crittenden maintains (in direct contrast to Dworkin) that neither the conscious moral nor political acts of a citizenry are enough to explain communal cohesion. Instead, he argues, communal obligations "arise out of the members' own sense of identity."[9] Not only is the individual of liberal theory already socially constituted by a community, that particular community is constructed from preexisting relationships of identity and organization.

Most communitarian critiques of liberalism's unspoken dependence on communal ties end here, however. Theorists like Charles Taylor and Alasdair MacIntrye who are rooted firmly in the communitarian tradition develop ethical arguments about the relationship of the socially constituted individual to the collective conception of the good rather than analyzing the nature of this collectivity.[10] In essence, communitarianism largely fails to develop any real political analysis of the very communities whose necessity it insists upon.

---

[7] Michael Sandel. "The Procedural Republic and the Unencumbered Self," *Communitarianism and Individualism*, 22.

[8] Jack Crittenden, *Beyond Individualism: Reconstituting the Liberal Self* (Oxford: Oxford University Press, 1992), 5.

[9] Crittenden, *Beyond Individualism*, 131.

[10] Charles Taylor, *Sources of Self* (Cambridge: Cambridge University Press, 1989); Aladsair MacIntyre, "The Privatization of Good," *The Liberalism-Communitarianism Debate*, ed. C. F. Delaney (Latham, MD: Rowman and Littlefield, 1994).

By contrast, some liberal scholars accept the communitarian insight that liberal theory is in some way dependent upon unarticulated notions of collectivity. These scholars are interested in developing an approach that thinks through the relationship between this bounded community and the theory and practice of liberalism. Kymlicka, for instance, argues that contemporary liberals must articulate a better understanding of the political and cultural context in which liberalism functions. For Kymlicka, this means taking a more concrete look at how the liberal notion of freedom is itself culturally and socially determined. In Kymlicka's words, the "freedom which liberals demand for individuals is not primarily the freedom to go beyond one's language and history, but rather the freedom to move around within one's societal culture."[11] For Kymlicka, the choices individuals make as they pursue their discrete visions of the good life are not made in a cultural vacuum but are informed, constrained, and enhanced by their linguistic and social environment, an environment that Kymlicka refers to as a "societal culture." Unlike communitarian critics of liberalism, Kymlicka maintains that these cultures do not need to hold any substantive vision of a universal good; instead, they need only supply the emotional and cultural tools that individuals require to make informed choices.[12] To do this, societal cultures must be "institutionally embodied" in "schools, media, economy, government, etc."[13] For Kymlicka, once we understand the important role these institutionally established, societal cultures play in liberal decision making, we can better address issues of multinational or multicultural citizenship from within a liberal context.

In Kymlicka's view, that societal cultures almost always see themselves (and are defined by others) as nations is incidental. While he repeatedly acknowledges that the societies he is interested in are "typically associated with national groups" and that they "tend to be national cultures," nothing is implicitly embedded within the concept of nation that makes it necessary to the construction of societal culture.[14] In Kymlicka's argument, national identity is just another means of social identification, one more component of the glue which binds people to their own culture. "I suspect," Kymlicka observes at one point "that the causes of this attachment lie deep in the human condition, tied up with the way humans as cultural creatures need to make sense of their world, and that a full explanation would involve aspects of psychology, sociology, linguistics, the philosophy of mind, and even neurology." In sum, nothing is unique in the

---

[11] Kymlicka, *Multicultural Citizenship*, 90–91.
[12] Ibid., 92.
[13] Ibid., 76.
[14] Ibid., 75, 84.

historically constructed concept of nationality that makes it particularly suited for creating the kinds of bounded cultures that liberals, Kymlicka argues, have implicitly accepted as the "basic units of liberal political theory."[15]

In contrast, for Yael Tamir the concept of nationhood stands alone in its ability to invent and maintain the internal cohesion that Kymlicka envisions for societal culture. In *Liberal Nationalism* Tamir begins her argument with a notable communitarian critique of liberalism, drawing extensively upon the work of Sandel. Tamir suggests that although they are rarely explicit about it, most liberals imagine some sort of boundaries around the societies they theorize. As an example, Tamir points to the work of that perennial scapegoat of communitarianism, John Rawls. Tamir argues that Rawls's notion of distributive justice implies the existence of an inward-oriented national community that is necessarily "prior to justice and fairness in the sense that questions of justice and fairness are regarded as questions of what would be fair or just within a particular political community."[16] Rawls may base his theory of justice on a "love of humankind," Tamir notes, but this love never extends beyond individual states and is never used to justify a global system of distribution. Rawls, she argues, defends his limited vision of humanity by using the language of realism, by couching his argument in the "is" rather than the "ought," in the need to be practical about policy changes.

Tamir insists, however, that it is no mere coincidence of historical circumstance, no mere realist acceptance of the "is," that prompts liberal theorists to so readily accept the nation as the organizing principle of the state. Instead, she maintains that when one looks closely at the liberal agenda, one will usually find "national values" hidden not so deeply under the surface.[17] According to Tamir, the logic of nationhood is singularly capable of addressing the difficult questions of membership that liberal theory is unequipped to answer on its own. For instance, if the liberal state is nothing more than the product of human contract, as Locke argued, why not let any one who wants to voluntarily enter into that contract do so? Why not ask non-members to join? Why accept the state's current boundaries? Tamir argues that modern liberal states have drawn upon the notion of national self-determination and national identity as a means to confront these questions and avoid a more explicit discussion of demarcation. In other words, because liberal theory is ostensibly based upon the universal rights of humankind, it contains no language capable of justifying its own boundaries, of explaining why its

---

[15] Ibid., 93.
[16] Yael Tamir, *Liberal Nationalism* (Princeton: Princeton University Press, 1993), 120.
[17] Ibid., 117.

universal principles are not universally applicable, why its commitment to freedom of movement, association, and speech do not apply equally to Mexican immigrants, to Turkish guest workers, to Palestinians. Nationality provides the liberal state with the perfect idiom through which to justify its exclusivity by insisting that its terms of membership be understood in relation to a "distinct historical community" rather than "a voluntary association."[18]

This disconnect between liberalism's universal commitments and the exclusive boundaries of the nation state is not enough to dissuade Tamir that liberals cannot redeem nationalism as a political, cultural, and *communal* agenda. On the contrary, she believes with Kymlicka that nationality, like cultural affiliation, is an important part of personal identification. National societies, she argues, provide each individual citizen with the freedom to "develop without repression those aspects of his personality which are bound up with his sense of identity as a member of his community," or which allow each individual to choose his, in David Miller's words, "own plan of life."[19] In the end, she thinks that it is possible to preserve the unifying, liberating qualities of national identity by (in a un-credited return to Zimmern) uncoupling nationality from nation states. Tamir thus envisions a future in which current nation states cede authority both downward toward national minorities with regard to culture, and upward toward larger regional authorities with regard to economic policy, defense, and the environment.

Both Kymlicka and Tamir succeed in unpacking the theoretically dense connections between societal or national cultures, the fulfillment of liberal freedom, and the historical development of the liberal state. Each also concludes that liberalism must actively refashion its relationship to these cultural communities. For Kymlicka, this means developing a more diverse understanding of "multicultural citizenship"; for Tamir, it means conceptualizing a liberalized form of nationality. Neither theorist, however (despite Kymlicka's genealogical investigation of the liberal tradition's treatment of minority rights) explores historical examples of liberals who reimagined the relationship between liberalism and community. Doing this would have enabled them to see how certain constructions of this relationship not only undercut liberalism's most basic commitment to equality but also recast relations of political and economic domination as apparently natural. Perhaps nowhere is this tendency to naturalize political community better exemplified than in Murray's and Zimmern's desire to reform the British Empire through a reconceived notion of the global liberal community.

[18] Ibid., 124.
[19] Ibid., 9: David Miller, *On Nationality* (Oxford: The Clarendon Press, 1995), 47.

LIBERALISM, EMPIRE, AND SOCIAL ORDER

As this book has elaborated in detail, Murray and Zimmern consistently couched their internationalisms in terms of Liberal spirit and the relationship between this spirit and the fraternal bonds of an evolving international society. At the same time, their unwillingness to imagine the League of Nations as a super-state forced Murray and Zimmern to cast about for non-state social institutions that could actualize Liberal spirit in the world. Like the earlier idealist liberals whom they resembled in so many ways, Murray and Zimmern resolved this tension on a global level by rooting liberal internationalism in organically and naturally conceived notions of a world society, the contours of which bore an uncanny resemblance to the economic and imperial structure of the pre-war world.

The primary discursive effect of Murray's and Zimmern's naturalized approach to global community was the shadow it cast over the power relations involved in post-war imperial politics. Again, however, neither man began the 1920s a completely naive supporter of the empire. Indeed, both men were openly critical throughout their careers of imperialism (although not of the empire in theory), and each argued forcefully for imperial reform, particularly after the war. The most exploitative economic and politically repressive aspects of imperial governance, each maintained, would have to change for the empire to survive. In Murray's words, it "might be possible to hold by force India alone, or Egypt alone, or Mesopotamia alone. It is not possible to hold all three. We must govern by consent of the governed or not at all."[20] Murray argued that the empire had to either acquire the political consent of its colonies or cease to exist.

At the same time, however, Murray's works also made clear that, for him, ending colonial government was not an option and that consent in this case did not imply democracy insofar as democracy in the colonies might lead to political independence. Murray's internationalism masterfully made this apparent contradiction—between accepting the liberal idea that consent might be necessary to govern the colonies and discounting independence as a possibility—seem perfectly manageable. For Murray, liberalism itself required a moral and spiritual foundation to flourish. The foundation upon which liberal international society rested was, he maintained, embodied in a well-understood and cohesive form of cosmos or world order in which the traditional relationship between leaders and led was clearly understood. For Murray, this was not some form of imperialist propaganda but simply the way "all societies naturally organized themselves," international society included.[21]

---

[20] Murray, *The Problems of Foreign Policy*, 79.
[21] Murray, *Satanism and The World Order*, 40.

For Murray, then, the difference between those able to govern themselves and those in need of colonial protection was a *permanent* feature
of international life. By virtue of its very naturalness, its rootedness in the
logic of the cosmos, the fixed and hierarchical texture of international
society made it impossible for consent ever to imply self-government for
certain peoples. British liberals, who were simultaneously worried about
the exploitative practices of imperial governments, the real post-war possibility of colonial rebellion, and the potential inclusion of the "less mature" peoples of the world in the newly formed League of Nations, could
be comforted by Murray's apparently benign understanding of both liberalism and world order. One of liberalism's main objectives, according to
Murray's entire body of political thought, was to situate people within a
context in which they understood their duties and relationships to others.
His "theory of international duty" did precisely this at the same time it
made the bonds of duty between the world's governed and governing
appear both fixed and natural.[22] Within this world order, liberalism fit
perfectly with the logic of empire.

In his commitment to a permanent notion of international society that
was by its nature hierarchical, Murray's theory of international duty went
beyond traditional liberal justifications for social and political inequalities
and, indeed, beyond the logic of those who framed the League's system
of colonial mandates. Since Locke, liberal theorists had turned to the logic
of family to explain the apparent contradiction between liberalism's commitment to universal rights and the liberal state's reluctance to grant these
rights universally. For Locke, parents dare not give children full liberal
rights because they "are not born in this full state of equality, though they
are born to it."[23] Until they reached the age of maturity and developed
the capacity to reason, according to Locke, children had to remain under
the tutelage of their parents. Likewise, individuals who remained like children (notably women, criminals, and the insane) were similarly positioned outside the liberal polity. Toward the mid-nineteenth century, this
notion of parental guidance was expanded in the wake of imperial exploration and the rising influence of Social Darwinism to exclude not only
specific individuals but also entire populations from the reach of liberal
rights. This era was thus largely characterized by the metaphor of the
family of man, a notion best represented, according to Anne McClintock,
by the well-known colonial image of a racial family tree.[24] McClintock

---

[22] Murray, "Orbis Terrestris," 200.

[23] John Locke, *Second Treatise of Government*, par. 55.

[24] Anne McClintock, "No Longer In a Future Heaven," *Dangerous Liaisons: Gender,
Nation and Postcolonial Perspectives*, eds. Anne McClintock, Aamir Muftie, and Ella Shohat (Minneapolis: University of Minnesota Press, 1997), 91. In this family tree, Africans
appear at the bottom and Europeans occupy the highest, most evolved branches.

argues that this notion served two purposes. First, it demonstrated that different races occupied discrete positions along the road to evolutionary progress; second, it suggested that the colonial parent had a responsibility to care for the family's less mature, less evolved children. This language of maturity and tutelage also characterized the League's approach to those colonies mandated by the war.[25]

At times, Murray's own thinking on empire mirrored this developmental logic. Thus, he argued in 1925 that "with regard to the general hegemony of the white races, our Liberal position is clear. It is expressed in Article XXII of the Covenant. We do not believe in the equality of all nations; we believe rather in a certain hierarchy, no doubt a temporary hierarchy of races, or, at least, of civilizations."[26] More often, however, Murray's descriptions of global hierarchy were cast in immutable rather than temporary terms. World order was moral for Murray precisely because it wedded individuals and populations to a comprehensive, hierarchical social plan.

Historically, Murray's increasingly vehement attachment to world order throughout the 1920s and '30s makes considerable sense given the state of the empire. World War One had made it necessary for Britain to call upon its colonial citizens to fight for its cause, and in the aftermath these same colonials began claiming loudly that they deserved similar treatment in peacetime by being granted independence. Many colonial nationalists' insistence that they had met the burden of proof that qualified them as mature independent members of the world community went straight to the primary instability at the heart of nineteenth-century liberalism's evolutionary approach to empire. As Uday Singh Mehta argues, an understanding of empire that bases its moral rationale on the notion of "backwardness" and "progress" is wedded to a temporal understanding of civilization in which the past (in the form of the colonized civilization) and the present (the imperial state) not only coexist but in which

---

[25] Article XXII of the Covenant reads:

> To those colonies and territories which as a consequence of the late war have ceased to be under the sovereignty of the States which formerly governed them and which are inhabited by peoples not yet able to stand by themselves under the strenuous conditions of the modern world, there should be applied the principle that the well-being and development of such peoples form a sacred trust of civilization and that the securities for the performance of this trust should be embodied in this Covenant . . . the tutelage of such peoples should be entrusted to the advanced nations who by reason of their resources, their experience or their geographic position can best undertake this responsibility and who are willing to accept it, and that this tutelage should be exercised by them as Mandatories on behalf of the League.

Miller, *The Drafting of the Covenant*, 73.
[26] Murray, "What Liberalism Stands For," 688.

the past is normatively understood as inferior.[27] The Achilles' heel of such an ideological approach lies in the possibility that the colonized could call the civilized on their bluff by claiming that they had arrived in the present. And this was precisely what Indian and Egyptian nationalists did in 1920. Murray's response to this phenomenon seems to have been to draw, once again, on the idealist origins of his thinking by relocating the moral center of liberal imperialism away from a temporal theory of evolutionary development and toward a fixed understanding of social order, thus reconciling the universalizing ideology of liberalism with a permanent form of international hierarchy.

Murray's internationalism thus avoided the family of man metaphor, with its potentially dangerous suggestion that the colonized could, in fact, grow up. By contrast, Zimmern's internationalism drew extensively upon the language of family—without, however, using the idea of a single family of man. The power of the trope, as McClintock argues, lay in its ability to naturalize imperialist domination by situating all human beings within the putatively biological hierarchy of the family.[28] Zimmern's commitment to describing *nations* as distinct families of mankind (as opposed to understanding all humans as members of one great family) imparted a natural sheen to imperial domination in a significantly different way. At the same time, Zimmern was developing a theory of voluntary commonwealth that ultimately knit these families together into a densely idealist form of organic whole. Zimmern's approach to nationhood spoke directly to the desire of British liberals to justify imperialism during an era of nascent post-colonial revolt at the same time that his vision of a commonwealth appeared to expand the central commitments of liberal voluntarism to the colonized world.

Zimmern's interest in imperial politics began early in his career. At the turn of the century, he was already lecturing on the dangers of "financial imperialism," the idea that as states expand, they must use military means to develop markets abroad. For Zimmern, such imperialism was too narrowly financial in its purview and ultimately benefited "no more than a small number of financiers and manufacturers."[29] Later, Zimmern expanded his critique to suggest that the only way for Britain to maintain its moral grasp on the empire was to develop a more normative and proactive approach its governance. Thus he argued in 1913 that if "the British Empire is destined to endure, it will be only as the guardian of the moral welfare of its peoples. Faith in this mission alone can justify the effort to further its consolidation."[30]

---

[27] Mehta, *Liberalism and Empire*, 107.

[28] McClintock, "No Longer In A Future Heaven," 91.

[29] Bodl. MS Alfred Zimmern (135) fol.24 (early lectures, 1900–1905.)

[30] Zimmern, *Nationality and Government*, 484. This essay first appeared in 1913.

Given the idealist liberal bent of his approach to empire, that Zimmern would be drawn to the Round Table Society is hardly surprising. In his own writings, Zimmern coupled the Round Table's vision of moral imperialism with his theory of nationhood. Thus, he argued, the British Empire (or Commonwealth, depending on whether he was writing before or after 1913) embodied the inevitable political development of the world more generally. What made the empire unique and important for the twentieth-century, Zimmern maintained, was that its very existence gestured toward the evolutionary demise of the nation *as state* and the growth of international "composite states." Thus, according to Zimmern, only "those who are blind to the true course of human progress can fail to see that the day of the Nation-State is even now drawing to a close in the West."[31] The future for Zimmern was to fall to those composite states that could efficiently govern diffuse collections of nationalities—those, like the British, that were able to throw "a girdle of law around the globe."[32] Zimmern's use of the family metaphor to describe the essential nature of nationalities more generally drove this point home by effectively uncoupling nations from states. Nations were familial; they were therefore intimate, emotional, and nutritive, argued Zimmern, and in liberal terms as old as Locke's tirade against "paternal government," must not in themselves be considered political. Politics took place outside of nations (outside of families) in the state centers of colonial governance.

Zimmern's decision to depoliticize the nation (by rooting it in the familial) spoke to the exigencies of imperial and international politics both during and after the war . Even before Wilson made his famous pitch for the rights of nations to self determination, nationalism had become the *lingua franca* of marginalized people seeking political autonomy throughout the colonial world, in eastern Europe, and elsewhere. Zimmern's timing was impeccable. Precisely at a moment when colonized peoples were claiming their right to independence through nationhood, Zimmern was claiming that, as families, nations were not political. This served two related purposes. First, strikingly similar to how Bosanquet and Ritchie had imagined the relationship between the nuclear family and the moral social order, Zimmern's emphasis on the familial qualities of nations allowed him fix the moral origins of liberal internationalism in a global social network of national families. Second, it provided both imperial states and the League of Nations with the means to address issues of nationalism without having to accede to the nationalist's demands for sovereignty. If nations were primarily spiritual and familial, the appropriate response to nationalist movements, from Zimmern's perspective, was not political but cultural autonomy.

[31] Zimmern, *Nationality and Government*, 20.
[32] Ibid., 21.

At the same time, Zimmern also managed to frame his idealist conception of nations as familial communities within the context of the liberal
notion of voluntary contract. Again, however, Zimmern's take on this
was as old as liberalism itself. As the most fundamental assumption of
contract theory, "voluntarism" has long stood at the heart of liberal approaches to both social institutions and the state. Liberals as diverse as
Mill, Locke, and Green all understood the relationship between the citizen
and the state as essentially voluntary. Likewise, voluntary principles have
historically guided liberal understandings of the family.[33] Rather than arising from a preordained patriarchal order, liberal thinkers have tended to
regard the nuclear family as a voluntary commitment between a man and
a woman. In response, some feminist theorists argue that this notion of
free, voluntary union has obscured actual relations of patriarchal
power—which were hardly voluntary—within the liberal family.[34]

Implicit in Zimmern's blending of familial, national, and imperial politics is a similar slippage. As Zimmern understood it, nothing in the spiritual bonds that developed within nations was inherently exclusionary.
Rather, he argued that nationality could be voluntarily adopted, not in
the liberal sense in which a citizen explicitly or tacitly agrees to live under
the influence of a state but in the familial sense in which parents adopt
children or individuals join a family through marriage. It was thus possible to marry the nation and still feel about it as one might feel toward
one's biological family.

> National sentiment is intimate; whether it be mainly compounded of influences
> of heredity (as in Europe) or of environment, as in the older Americans, or
> whether it be something newly acquired and deliberately cherished as among
> the new arrivals, it is something that goes deep down into the very recesses of
> the being. . . . The nationality of a European and the nationality of a recent
> American may perhaps be compared to a man's relation to his parents and
> his relation to his wife. Both sentiments are intimate; both can legitimately be
> compared, in the sphere of personal relations, to the sense of nationality in the
> wider sphere of corporate relations. But the one is hereditary and the other is
> elective.[35]

Zimmern thus combined two apparently antithetical notions of family:
the liberal ideal of the family as a voluntary commitment between a man
and a woman, and a more pre-liberal understanding of the family as an

---

[33] Green, *Prolegomena to Ethics*, 232.

[34] Melissa Butler, "On Locke," *Feminist Interpretations and Political Theory*, eds. Mary
Lyndon Shanley and Carole Pateman. (University Park: Pennsylvania State University Press,
1991), 90–91; Zillah Eisenstein, *The Radical Future of Liberal Feminism* (New York: Longmans, 1981), 47–49.

[35] Zimmern, "Nationalism and Internationalism," 85.

ethical community of blood relations. At the same time, Zimmern also brought together two seemingly contradictory notions of nationhood: the liberal understanding of nationhood as something one enters into by choice, and the more German idea of Volk nationalism based on a shared ethnic parentage. In this manner, Zimmern transformed nationhood into both a voluntary and natural—liberal and organic—phenomenon.

As noted earlier, Zimmern's enthusiasm for nations as voluntary and familial institutions often elided or simply ignored internal power relationships. Zimmern argued quite forcefully in *Nationality and Government*, for example, that social injustice, racial inequality, and civic strife all found their antidotes in a growing sense of nationalism. Thus, he lauded the education of immigrants in America as a testament to the salving powers of nationality. Likewise, he argued that encouraging a sense of nationality among African Americans would eventually speak to "the thorniest of all the many thorny problems of American life."[36] Never did it occur to Zimmern to ask whether membership in a nation, as in a family, might be circumscribed by a politics based not on loving *inclusion* but on an internal form of *exclusion* (e.g., Jim Crow laws in the American south) and might be far from voluntary.

The language of voluntary consent also resurfaced within Zimmern's approach to commonwealth. Early in his career, Zimmern described the "Imperial Union" as a type of polity "less rigid than a federation but more intimate than an alliance."[37] Implicit in this idea was the notion of free union between "self governing political units." By 1928, the language of imperial union had changed; now it was the commonwealth that was both intimate and free, that combined both the characteristics of an organism and the liberal rule of law.[38] Almost ten years later, for Zimmern, consent—the actions of national actors who chose to throw in their lot together—still held together the organic qualities of the commonwealth.[39] Such an organization needed no state coercion, according to Zimmern, because at its heart it was freely cooperative.

At the same time, as with his conception of nationhood, Zimmern's notion of the commonwealth as a free union of consenting states obscured many underlying power relations between England, the "white dominions," and non-white imperial holdings. While Zimmern maintained that the British Commonwealth was a voluntary association of free and equal nations, its reality was something quite different. In actuality, it was only during a brief three-month period in 1917–18 that heads of state from

---

[36] Zimmern, *Nationality and Government*, 81.
[37] Bodl. Ms. Zimmern (135), fol. 124.
[38] Zimmern, "German Culture and the British Commonwealth," 369.
[39] Zimmern, *The League of Nations and the Rule of Law*, 282.

the white dominions were invited to participate in the creation of imperial policy.[40] Likewise, non-white dominions were easily dismissed from even the pretense of cooperative politics. Zimmern himself blithely assumed that, because they had not yet reached a stage of development in which they were capable of voluntary consent, certain national members of the empire would not be allowed to cooperate voluntarily. "I am not speaking at all of India or of our Tropical dependencies," he argued in 1905, "but of the self governing portions of the Empire."[41]

Yet at other times Zimmern seemed happy to include such imperial dependencies in his notion of commonwealth and argued that one of its strengths was its flexibility, its capacity to encompass "races and peoples at varying levels of social progress which is its peculiar task."[42] In his desire to balance liberal philosophical commitments with a hierarchical idealist politics, Zimmern maintained that the commonwealth was sometimes voluntary, sometimes familial, and sometimes both; comprised solely of white dominions able to achieve self-government, but at other times it led "non adult races" toward civilization. In essence, the language of voluntarism (and, indeed, the very language of "common"-wealth) allowed Zimmern's theory to speak to any number of competing claims: to don the mantle of liberal universalism while justifying the political exclusion of most of the world; to theorize organic cooperation while centralizing politics in the motherland; to believe in the impartial rule of law while cherishing all that was intimate in family life.

In key ways, then, Murray's and Zimmern's approaches to internationalism, along with their understandings of both imperialism and the relationship between imperial government and international organization, spoke to the incoherence of the post-war empire as well as the radical changes taking place within the international system. One can read these thinkers' internationalism as an attempt to reconcile an older system of world politics governed by the competing claims of empires with the newly emerging rationale of international cooperation organized around sovereign nation states. After World War Two and the period of decolonization that followed, Woodrow Wilson's call for "national self-determination" would finally be realized as the supreme ideology of global cooperation, and nation states (that is, nations *as* sovereign states) would emerge as those sole political units worthy of recognition by the post-war world community of nations and its most visible institution, the United Nations.[43] In this light, Murray's and Zimmern's internationalisms func-

[40] D. A. Low, *Eclipse of Empire* (Cambridge: Cambridge University Press, 1991), 37.

[41] Bodl. Ms. Zimmern (135), fol. 153.

[42] Zimmern, *Nationality and Government*, 17.

[43] Adam Watson, *The Evolution of International Society* (London: Routledge, 1992), 300–301.

tioned as a kind of transitional model for world organization in which both nationality (in distinction from state sovereignty) and *inter*nationality (in the form of the League) could exist simultaneously even as the pre-war power relationships between imperial states and their colonies were, in the words of Adam Watson, "left virtually intact."[44] In the most basic of senses, Murray's and Zimmern's work formed the intellectual backbone of an approach to liberalism and internationalism in which internationalism could coexist with imperialism. Liberals, diplomats, and state leaders from the Great Powers could have it all: internationalism without international authority and the rights of sovereignty and liberal democracy at home while denying those rights to millions elsewhere.

Conclusion: Liberalism, Natural Hierarchy, and the New Imperialism

For liberal political theorists, Murray's and Zimmern's approaches to liberalism, international community, imperialism, and social order continue to highlight the lure of the "natural." Today, scholars interested in grounding liberal assumptions of humanity more firmly in both a commitment to individual rights *and* existing forms of communal relationships still face the temptation to imagine these relationships as natural, spontaneous, national forms of communal cohesion rather than as products of political power. While the paternalistic politics of idealist liberals like Green, Bosanquet, and their colleagues also demonstrates this tendency within liberal reformism, the very boldness of Murray's and Zimmern's projects, that they literally had to *create* an international community in the absence of any historical precedent, frames this temptation in stark relief. As such, it serves as a relevant, cautionary example for thinkers like Kymlicka and Tamir.

Kymlicka, for instance, pays little attention to the existing internally constituted social relationships that make liberal "societal cultures" flourish. He is far less interested in theorizing the cultural assumptions that support those liberal states that need to develop new understandings of minority rights than he is in examining the social and cultural infrastructures of national and ethnic minority communities. He thus assumes that the liberal state *will have* liberal origins, that it will be grounded in voluntary relationships that are primarily *liberal*. Murray's and Zimmern's works on international order shine a bright light on the remarkably illiberal, even anti-liberal origins and foundations of liberal societies themselves. Kymlicka's work thus unintentionally perpetuates the liberal

[44] Ibid., 282.

conviction that its own social institutions and assumptions are both natural and, in some way, beyond reproof.

Tamir's work acknowledges that the national cultures that unify and ground liberal states are themselves based upon a logic inherently hierarchical in its simultaneous ability to exclude and include individuals based on a pre-liberal understanding of cultural belonging. But by claiming that nationalism can be refashioned and reconceived to accommodate liberalism, Tamir refuses to engage the possibility that the liberal state might actually depend on nationalism to make sense out of state power by locating that power within a continuum of political and cultural solidarity. In Margaret Canovan's words, nationalism links the liberal individual to the community by giving "cold institutional structures an aura of warm togetherness." It makes liberal democracy appear easy and natural by turning political institutions into the "kind of extended family inheritance" explicitly theorized by Zimmern.[45] By appearing natural and familial, national cultures create an illusion of inevitability and belonging that obscures the cluster of power relationships—economic and political—necessary to link state power to a "people." In addition, as Zimmern's work demonstrates so clearly, even putatively liberal "composite states" willing to cede cultural autonomy to individual nations might themselves be structured around fundamentally hierarchical imperial relationships.

This latter point is brought home in a particularly striking manner by the post–September 11 mobilization of a specifically *liberal* imperialist movement, which in its explicit linkage of liberal values to imperialist practices harkens directly back to the legitimating ideology of the interwar era. In this sense, new imperialists are in many ways bucking the anti-imperialist norm that had dominated modern liberal discourse since World War Two when the UN Charter replaced the mandate system of the League with a trusteeship council.[46] While the creation of the trusteeship council initially did little to change the behavior of colonial states, the council's focus on political independence allowed members of the UN General Assembly to take it to task for not working quickly enough to achieve this goal. Ultimately, the trusteeship council's formal commitment to independence provided anti-colonial forces within the assembly some institutional legitimacy. By 1960, these forces were able to successfully push for passage of General Assembly Resolution 1514, the Declaration

[45] Margaret Canovan, *Nationhood and Political Theory* (Cheltenham: Edward Elgar, 1996), 69.

[46] Although based on a similar principle of colonial "tutelage," the Trusteeship Council differed from the mandate system in its explicit promise to help "non-self-governing territories" achieve political independence. [James Barros, *The United Nations: Past, Present, and Future* (New York: The Free Press, 1972), 146–47.]

on the Granting of Independence to Colonial Countries and Peoples.[47] While sovereignty remained the principal requirement of membership in the UN just as it had in the League, the process of decolonization coupled with the virtual absorption of the trusteeship council into the general assembly meant that by the mid-1960s, the actual constitution of the assembly differed dramatically from the League's. Rather than an ensemble of Great Powers, their colonies, and a few independent ex-colonial nations, the UN today is constituted primarily by sovereign nation states.[48]

As a result of these changes, up until just a few years ago the idea of reconciling liberal internationalism with a benign form of empire was anathema to most liberal scholars. In the wake of the events of September 11, 2001, however, a disturbing number of self-declared liberal IR theorists, foreign affairs experts, and journalists have—with the titillating joy of naughty school boys empowered to speak the word "sex" aloud for the first time—called for a return to the organizational and moral simplicity of empire. In the pages of both scholarly journals and the popular press, thinkers like Robert Cooper, Robert Kagen, Fareed Zakaria, and Michael Ignatieff sing the praises of an American (and to a lesser degree, British) imperium emboldened with the military might and moral rectitude necessary to transform the world into a well-ordered bastion of human rights, liberal democracy, and free market economics. In so doing, these contemporary thinkers mimic many of the most disturbing aspects of Murray's and Zimmern's liberal imperialism, particularly in their relentless invocation of the need for world order.

Robert Cooper's influential essay in the Foreign Policy Center's 2002 publication *Re-Ordering the World: The Long-Term Implications of September 11*[th] is illustrative in this regard. The primary goal of Cooper's article is to reconcile what he terms the "waning of the imperial urge" among European states during the second half of the twentieth century with what he suggests is the current imperative to impose order on the chaotic politics of non-western states—what Cooper, in racist language

---

[47] Ibid., 152. The United States voted against this resolution, along with Australia, Belgium, the Dominican Republic, France, Portugal, Spain, the Union of South Africa, and the United Kingdom. In an ironic gesture of protest, the one African-American member of the U.S. delegation, Zelma Watson George, stood up and applauded as the resolution was adopted.

[48] In fact, in the years since its inception, membership in the United Nations has more than tripled, and African and Asian nations now occupy a superior numerical position within the assembly. [Peter Baehr and Leon Gordenker, *The United Nations in the 1990's* (New York: St. Martin's Press, 1994), 42]. It is always important to remember, however, that superior numbers within the assembly do not translate into a more democratic representation of African and Asian nations within the Security Council, which is still dominated by the interests of its five permanent members, the United States, Britain, France, Russia, and China.

that could have been uttered by the most sanguine of Victorian imperialists, refers to as "the jungle."[49] Cooper reconciles these competing sets of interests by positing a new, three-tiered approach to statehood that rejects the liberal imperialist language of development and maturity altogether even while remaining curiously developmental. For Cooper, the current world can best be understood as divided into pre-modern, modern, and post-modern states. In an oddly foundationalist inversion of post-modernist logic, Cooper suggests that European states have evolved to a point where they no longer desire to go to war with one another because they have become, in effect post-modern. But because they live in a world made unstable by those "more old-fashioned kinds of states outside of the continent of Europe," European states need to adopt "double standards" when dealing with states mired in modern, or even, pre-modern, forms of statehood. The danger posed by these less evolved states to the world order requires, according to Cooper, the creation of a "new kind of imperialism," one that he argues is *voluntary*.

In language that almost exactly mimics Zimmern's description of a voluntary commonwealth, Cooper's "new kind" of imperialism would be based upon voluntary participation in the world economy. If states wished to benefit from this economy, they must "open themselves up to the interference of international organizations and foreign states." Cooper contends that those pre-modern states "wishing to find their way back into the global economy and into the virtuous circle of investment and prosperity" that accompanies it will receive positive political assistance from post-modern world. Those who do not will be subject to the "rougher methods" of an earlier age. As with Zimmern, however, Cooper's liberal rhetoric of *voluntary* participation in the global economy occludes precisely the kinds of structural inequalities that Thomas Pogge's work elaborates so clearly. A deep-seated double bind is at work here, one that the smooth glissade of liberal voluntarism appears to erase. In a world tightly controlled by the demands of an increasingly transnational economy, few developing states have the option to voluntarily exit from the global market. Those "pre-modern" states that do voluntarily participate in the economy by taking advantage of the IMF and World Bank lending policies have no incentive (given the current economy's unceasing desire for cheap resources) to develop democratic polities. When these governments collapse or fail to control terrorism in a manner deemed sufficient by western states, they then lay themselves open to imperial intervention. In this context, Cooper's "virtuous cycle" looks more like a vicious cycle of authori-

---

[49] Robert Cooper, "The Post Modern State," *Re-Ordering the World: The Long-Term Implications of September 11th* (The Foreign Policy Centre, 2002). Available at http://fpc.org.uk/hotnews/full?activeid=169&tabeid=writes.

tarianism (from without and within) and poverty. His work thus ultimately illustrates the perversity of a liberal imperialism whose claims to be voluntary occlude deep, permanent divisions in the world economy.

A similar liberal sleight of hand is at work in the post–September 11 writings of Fareed Zakaria and Robert Kagan, both of whom have openly acknowledged their desire to see America's power in the world expanded in directions that are more explicitly and unapologetically imperial. Zakaria and Kagan each equate liberalism on a global level with international order, international order with American hegemony, and American hegemony with the good of the world. "America did not change on Sept 11th," argues Kagan, it "only became more itself."[50] And, using Madeline Albright's oft quoted phrase, Kagan defines America as the "indispensable nation" with powers and responsibilities that outrank all others. According to Kagan, the primary ends of a nation with as much power as the United States ought to be imperial. Along with the one ally he deems acceptable to fully participate in this endeavor (ironically, but not surprisingly, Britain), Kagan argues for a foreign policy aimed at "preserving and advancing an international liberal order in the years and decades to come."[51] If we take Kagan at his word we should assume that the benefits of this liberal order are themselves beyond question, particularly when compared to the images of insupportable chaos Kagan associates with, for instance, the possibility that America might fail to take up the imperial mantle and "hand over" the responsibility for rebuilding a post-war Iraq to the United Nations. "Either the United States does what it takes to succeed in Iraq," argued Kagan in an article for the *Weekly Standard* in September 2003, "or we lose in Iraq. And if we lose, we will leave behind us not blue helmets but radicalism and chaos, a haven for terrorists, and a perception of American weakness and lack of resolve in the Middle East and reckless blundering around the world."[52] Fareed Zakaria adopts a similar tone when discussing the perceived necessity of American imperial power. "In principle," he argued in March 2003, "American power is not simply good for America; it is good for the world. . . . Other countries are simply not ready or able, at this point, to take on the challenges and burdens of leadership."[53]

[50] Robert Kagan, *Of Paradise and Power: America and Europe In the New World Order* (New York: Alfred A. Knopf, 2003), 85.

[51] Robert Kagan, "The Healer," *The Guardian*, March 3, 2003. Available at http://www.guardian.co.uk/print/0,3858,4616744–103680,00.html.

[52] Robert Kagan, "America's Responsibility," *The Weekly Standard*, September 15, 2003. Available at http://www.ceip.org/files/publications/2003–09–15-Kaganwklystandard.asp.

[53] Fareed Zakaria, "The Arrogant Empire," *Newsweek*, March 24, 2003. Available at http://www.fareedzakaria.com/articles/newsweek/032403.html.

Zakaria and Kagan also hold in common an instrumental approach to liberalism that allows them to deflect some of the less comfortable aspects of their call for a new imperialism. Both men couch the current state of American hegemony in terms of historical accident: this is simply a situation that America finds itself in. American presidents, argues Zakaria, have been "slow to embrace their imperial destiny"—but embrace it they must for the good of the world.[54] Kagan and Zakaria also acknowledge that to make their imperial mission as free of conflict as possible, the United States must learn to be more cordial to its allies, particularly its European allies. The United States, argues Kagan, ought to "pay its respects to multilateralism and the rule of law and try to build some international political capital for those moments when multilateralism is impossible."[55] In other words, America needs to at least humor some of the rest of the world to justify its occasional but necessary forays into unilateral action. Zakaria is even more blatant in his belief that the primary aim of American diplomacy ought to be to "make the world comfortable with its power."[56] And nothing serves the purpose of making the world more comfortable with American hegemony than a stated commitment to liberal ends—the proliferation of democracy, civilization, and open markets. Indeed, Zakaria even goes so far as to suggest that the United States should emulate the rhetoric of turn-of-the-century British liberal imperialists as it strives to legitimate its power in the world.[57]

True to the styles of Murray and Zimmern, Kagan and Zakaria also inoculate themselves from the potential consequences of this kind of stated commitment to liberal ends, a commitment that might, at least rhetorically, require the United States to live out the full implications of liberal universalism and abide by international law. Both men argue that a deep gulf separates the reality of U.S. political, economic, and military power and the ideals of liberalism. They posit this situation as regrettable but unavoidable, and thus establish a false moral dichotomy between the choices we would like to make and those we must make. No one is really responsible for current state of world affairs; rather, the gap between reality and ideals presses us to act in certain ways. "The problem lies neither in American will or capability," argues Kagan, "but precisely in the inherent moral tension of the current international situation."[58] Zakaria makes a similar move through an analogy to the British Empire at the turn of

---

[54] Fareed Zakaria, "Our Way," *The New Yorker*, October 14, 2002. Available at http://www.fareedzakaria.com/articles/nyer/101402.html.

[55] Kagan, *Of Paradise and Power*, 103.

[56] Zakaria, "The Arrogant Empire."

[57] Zakaria, "Our Way."

[58] Robert Kagan, "Power and Weakness," *Policy Review* 113 (2002). Available at http://www.policyreview.org/JUN02/kagan_print.html.

the century. British imperialists, Zakaria argues, were consistently faced with a deep, and in the end, overwhelming tension between their power in the world and their liberal ideals. "This is a historic lesson that should interest Americans today," he argues "as we contemplate our own lofty ideals and immense power."[59]

Both men thus transform a real discrepancy between the ideals of liberalism and the behavior of imperial states into an inherency, an unavoidable moral conflict. This then allows them to have their cake and eat it too—to claim affinity for a set of liberal ends while reluctantly supporting a foreign policy that denies these ends to millions, and to claim a kind of moral helplessness in the face of world instabilities while denying all responsibility for creating these instabilities in the first place. Zakaria's and Kagan's stated commitments to liberalism as read through their theory of inevitable conflict amount to an act of erasure. Gone is any analysis of the current economic or political circumstances that generate the kind of world they both believe to be in such desperate need of order. Gone also is any sense of historic accountability on the part of imperial powers, past and present.

One would hope that Michael Ignatieff, as a historian, might be more sensitive to this issue of accountability, that he might critically engage the role the United States and other world powers played in creating the political instabilities that frame the human rights abuses he cares so passionately about. Unfortunately, Ignatieff's approach to the relationship between liberalism and empire casts a penumbra similar to Kagan's and Zakaria's. In his seminal article for the *New York Times Magazine* in January 2003, "The American Empire: The Burden," Ignaieff argues that the ethical principles that inspired the move toward decolonization in Africa and Asia after the Second World War—human rights and self-determination—have now come into conflict with each other, privileging the latter over the former.[60] Ignatieff argues that only a renewed and reinvigorated "humanitarian" imperialism can remedy the current "vacuum of chaos and massacre" that characterizes the political situations in many collapsing former colonial states. In a recent elaboration on this new form of empire (what he refers to as "empire lite"), Ignatieff acknowledges as ironic that someone like himself—a "liberal believer" in the ideas of human equality so implicit in the concept of self-determination—should advocate the creation of a "new humanitarian empire, a new form of

---

[59] Fareed Zakaria, "The Previous Superpower," *New York Times*, July 27, 2003. Available at http://www.fareedzakaria.com/articles/nyt/072703.html.

[60] Michael Ignatieff, "The American Empire: The Burden," *New York Times Magazine*, January 5, 2003. Available at http://www.cid.harvard.edu/cidinthenews/articles/nyt-010503.html.

colonial tutelage" but argues that this renewed paternalism is itself the result of the failed project of self-determined nation-building in former colonies. However right the liberal principle of self-determination might be, he maintains, "the political form in which they are realized—the nationalist nation building project—so often fails to deliver them."[61] As a result, what should have been a post-colonial age characterized by free, equal, and self-governing states has mutated into "an age of ethnic cleansing and state failure."[62]

Ignatieff's "empire lite" leaves the concerned liberal with only two alternatives to humanitarian crises: self-determination (with all its attendant baggage of "ethnic cleansing and state failure") or reluctant imperial tutelage. By positing these two alternatives as the only viable solution to chaos and genocide, Ignatieff situates his argument within ahistorical space. While the nation state model may indeed be deeply flawed, Ignatieff's analysis fails to account for the a variety of other circumstances that have destabilized political society within many post-colonial states, including structural inequalities in the world economic system and Western powers' consistent (often illegal and violent) political intervention in the political processes of post-colonial states. Ignatieff's treatment of the American campaign in Afghanistan is particularly vacuous in this regard. In Afghanistan in 2001, Ignatieff argues, the United States saw first hand how dangerous a seemingly remote "collapsed" state could be. He argues that circumstance pressed the United States into acting imperially (reluctantly, of course) to bring order to the region.[63] While Ignatieff concedes that the Afghanis should be allowed "some degree" of self-determination, he also insists that in all new imperial situations the "real power" must remain in Washington. But this imperial formula neglects to account for Washington's culpability in generating the current political instabilities within Afghanistan by financing the efforts of fundamentalist Islamic groups to overthrow the Soviets throughout the 1980s. Philosophically and morally, Ignatieff's position is untenable insofar as it refuses to place any responsibility on the United States for contributing to the political collapse of Afghani state, instead placing the blame for this collapse entirely on characteristics seemingly inherent to the project of post-colonial nation building itself.

More than this, however, Ignatieff's liberal imperialism refuses to acknowledge its own deeply anti-liberal assumptions by clinging tenaciously to a set of liberal goals. The liberal "moral premises" of anti-imperial-

---

[61] Michael Ignatieff, *Empire Lite: Nation Building in Bosnia, Kosovo, and Afghanistan* (London: Vintage, 2003), 122.

[62] Ibid., 133.

[63] Ignatieff, "The American Empire."

ism—that "all peoples should be equal and peoples should rule them-selves"—are all well and good, argues Ignatieff, but they have been thwarted by post-colonial nationalizing movements that subvert human rights. Thus, Americans and their European allies have to be willing to sacrifice liberal "moral premises" and deny certain peoples equality in situations of state collapse and/or genocide. What Ignatieff fails to ac-count for, however, is that every modern Western state, at one time, went through a similar project of nation-building. To now declare the entire project untenable for some peoples while insisting that imperial states maintain all the rights and privileges of sovereign statehood at its core implies that some people are responsible enough to shoulder the burdens of sovereignty while others are not. The language of colonial tutelage might imply (as it supposedly did for the drafters of the League of Na-tion's mandate system) that this double standard is only temporary, a mere bump along the rocky road to mature statehood. But Ignatieff's own analysis of nation-building suggests quite strongly that post-colonial peo-ples are incapable of sustaining this political project. If Ignatieff had wanted to mount a radical critique of self-determined nationhood—a commendable goal—to preserve a liberal commitment to equality, he would have had to argue for a thoroughgoing examination of *all* self-determined nations. Instead, Ignatieff has opted for what amounts to a good old-fashioned liberal imperialism that refuses to acknowledge its own commitment to what are, in fact, fixed hierarchical assumptions about the world.

This is profoundly ironic. Ignatieff clearly does not want his notion of "empire lite" to mimic the "old European imperialism" with all of its racist and Social Darwinist rhetoric and economic exploitation. And yet Ignatieff's insistence that the only realistic and humane response to hu-manitarian crises is for the Unites States to "create a global order" through a new and improved form of empire implicitly binds him to a paternalistic politics that echoes the liberal imperialism of an earlier era.[64] Perhaps the most important thing that Murray's and Zimmern's notions of global order have to teach us in this regard is that such notions, even when articulated by liberal reformists, are difficult to sustain without an implicitly hierarchical vision of the social, a notion that relegates entire populations to the pre-liberal status of subjects rather than citizens.

This book insists that we view Murray's and Zimmern's commitment to a hierarchical global order as both a critical mirror for thinkers like Tamir and Kymlicka—thinkers interested in theorizing the relationship between liberalism and community—and as a warning to contemporary liberal imperialists. Murray's and Zimmern's work ultimately suggests

[64] Ibid.

that the underlying contours of liberal communities, domestic and global, may very well be based on a exclusive rationale that stands in stark distinction from their own professed commitment to universalism. Each man's sustained approach to international society also demonstrates how a liberalism that consciously sets out to theorize community can vitiate its own most important conventions by equating liberal values with a social order whose assumed interest in those values then obscures the very economic and power relationships that constitute the community in the first place.

But the response to Murray's and Zimmern's example should not be theoretical and political paralysis. Rather, liberals committed to thinking community ought to engage in a process that embeds Murray's and Zimmern's ethical projects within a dense critique of power by analyzing the relationship between liberal freedom and its communal context while simultaneously remaining cognizant of how this context might naturalize inequalities. When liberals are once again throwing their weight behind new and improved forms of imperialism, the time is ripe to take Zimmern's desire to create "one single body politic, which will be the whole world" to its own radical conclusions, to theorize in the context of world power relations a global polity that unflinchingly commits itself to the principle of human equality rather than empire.[65]

[65] Zimmern, "The Problem of Collective Security," 18.

Bibliography

Anderson, Benedict. *Imagined Communities*. 2nd ed. London: Verso, 1991.

Angell, Norman. "Pacifism Is not Enough." *Problems of Peace: Lectures Delivered at the Geneva Institute of International Relations: 1934*. Oxford: Oxford University Press, 1935.

Avineri, Shlomo. *Hegel's Theory of the Modern State*. Cambridge: Cambridge University Press, 1972.

Baehr, Peter, and Leon Gordenker. *The United Nations in the 1990s*. New York: St. Martin's Press, 1994.

Balibar, Etienne, and Immanuel Wallerstein. *Race, Nation, Class*. London: Verso, 1991.

Band, D. C. "The Critical Reception of English Neo-Hegelianism in Britain and America, 1914–1960." *The Australian Journal of Politics and History* 23(2) (1980).

Barkan, Elexar. *The Retreat of Scientific Racism: Changing Concepts of Race in Britain and the United States Between the World Wars*. Cambridge: Cambridge University Press, 1992.

Barnes, Harry. *World Politics in Modern Civilization: Contributions of Nationalism, Capitalism, Imperialism, and Militarism to Human Culture and International Anarchy*. New York: Alfred A. Knopf, 1930.

Barnet, Richard, and John Cavanagh. *Global Dreams: Imperial Corporations and the New World Order*. New York: Simon and Schuster, 1995.

Barnett, Correlli. *The Collapse of British Power*. Amherst, NY: Humanities Press, 1986.

Barros, James. *The United Nations: Past, Present ,and Future*. New York: The Free Press, 1972.

Barthes, Roland. "The Great Family of Man." *Mythologies*. New York: Hill and Wang, 1972.

Basch, Linda, Nina Glick Schiller, and Christina Stanton Blanc. *Nations Unbound: Transnational Projects, Postcolonial Predicaments and Deterritorialized Nation-States*. Berlin: Gordon and Breach, 1994.

Beitz, Charles. *Political Theory and International Relations*. Princeton: Princeton University Press, 1970.

Bell, David. "The Revolution of Moore and Russell: A Very British Coup?" *German Philosophy Since Kant*. Ed. Anthony O'Hear. Cambridge: Cambridge University Press, 1999.

Bellamy, Richard. *Liberalism and Modern Society: An Historical Argument*. University Park: Pennsylvania State University Press, 1992.

———. *Victorian Liberalism*. London: Routledge, 1990.

Beloff, Max. *Britain's Liberal Empire: 1897–1921*. 2nd ed. London: Macmillan, 1987.

Benhabib, Seyla. "On Hegel, Women, and Irony." *Feminist Interpretations of G.W.F. Hegel.* Ed. Patricia Jagentowitz Mills. University Park: Pennsylvania State University Press, 1997.

Bentley, Michael. *The Liberal Mind, 1914–1929.* Cambridge: Cambridge University Press, 1977.

Biagini Eugenio. *Citizenship and Community: Liberals, Radicals, and Collective Identities in the British Isles, 1865–1931.* Cambridge: Cambridge University Press, 1996.

Bosanquet, Bernard. "Charity Organization and the Majority Report." *International Journal of Ethics* 20 (1910).

———. *A Companion to Plato's Republic.* New York: Macmillan, 1895.

———. "The English People: Notes on National Characteristics." *International Monthly* 3 (1901).

———. *The Introduction to Hegel's Philosophy of Fine Art.* London: Kegan Paul, Trench, 1886.

———. *The Philosophical Theory of the State.* 8th ed. London: Macmillan, 1958 [1889].

———. *Science and Philosophy.* New York: MacMillan, 1927.

———. *Social and International Ideals.* (1917) Freeport, NY: Books for Libraries, 1967.

———. "Socialism and Natural Selection.". *The British Idealists.* Ed. David Boucher. London: Cambridge University Press, 1997 [1895].

Boucher, David, and Andrew Vincent. *A Radical Hegelian: The Political and Social Philosophy of Henry Jones.* New York: St. Martin's, 1994.

———. "British Idealism, the State, and International Relations." *Journal of the History of Ideas* 55 (1994).

———. *The British Idealists.* Cambridge: Cambridge University Press, 1997.

Bradley, Francis Herbert. *Appearance and Reality: A Metaphysical Essay.* Oxford: The Clarendon Press, 1930.

———. *Essays on Truth and Reality.* Oxford: The Clarendon Press, 1914.

———. "Ideal Morality." *Ethical Studies.* 2nd ed. Oxford: The Clarendon Press, 1927.

Bramstei, Ernest. "Apostles of Collective Security: The LNY and its Functions." *The Australian Journal of Politics and History* 13 (1967).

Brand, Carl. *The British Labour Party: A Short History.* Stanford: Stanford University Press, 1964.

Buck-Morss, Susan. "Passports." *Documents* 3 (1993).

Bull, Hedley. *The Anarchical Society.* New York: Macmillan and Columbia, 1977.

Bull, Hedley, and Adam Watson. *The Expansion of International Society.* London: Oxford University Press, 1984.

———. "The Twenty Years' Crisis Thirty Years On," *The International Journal* 24(4) (1969).

———. "The Theory of International Politics, 1919–1969." *The Aberystwyth Papers: International Politics, 1919–1969.* Ed. B. Porter. Oxford: Oxford University Press, 1917.

Burchill, Scott, and Andrew Linklater. *Theories of International Relations.* New York: St. Martin's Press, 1996.

Burns, Cecil. "The Activity of Mind." *Proceedings of the Aristotelian Society* 26 (1926).

———. "The Contact of Minds." *Proceedings of the Aristotelian Society* 23 (1923).

———. *Democracy: Its Defects and Advantages.* London: George Allen and Unwin, 1929.

———. "Ethical Principles of Social Reconstruction." *Proceedings of the Aristotelian Society* 17 (1916–17).

———. *International Politics.* London: Methuen, 1920.

———. *The Growth of Modern Philosophy.* London: Sampson Low, 1909.

———. "The Making of the International Mind." *International Journal of Ethics,* 1926. *From Readings in Public Opinion: Its Formation and Control.* Ed. Brooke Graves. New York: D. Appleton, 1928.

———.*The Metaphysical Theory of State.* 6th ed. (New York: Barnes and Noble, 1960).

———. *The Morality of Nations: An Essay on the Theory of Politics.* London: University of London Press, 1916.

———. "Nationalism and Internationalism: The Education of Public Opinion." *Problems of Peace: Lectures Delivered at the Geneva Institute of International Relations: 1926.* Oxford: Oxford University Press, 1927.

———. *The Philosophy of Labour.* London: Oxford University Press, 1925.

———. *Political Ideals.* Oxford: Oxford University Press, 1919.

———. "The State and Its External Relations." *Proceeding of the Aristotelian Society* 26 (1915–16).

———. "When Peace Breaks Out." *International Journal of Ethics* 26 (1915–16).

———. *The World of States.* London: Headley Bros., 1917.

Burrow, J. W. *Evolution and Society.* Cambridge: Cambridge, University Press, 1970.

Butler, Judith. *Subjects of Desire: Hegelian Reflections in Twentieth-Century France.* New York: Columbia University Press, 1987.

———. "Universality in Culture." *For Love of Country.* Ed. Martha Nussbaum. Boston: Beacon Press, 1996.

Butler, Melissa. "On Locke." *Feminist Interpretations and Political Theory.* Eds. Mary Lyndon Shanley and Carole Pateman. University Park: Pennsylvania State University Press, 1991.

Caird, Edward. "Individualism and Socialism." *The British Idealists.* Ed. David Boucher. Cambridge: Cambridge University Press, 1997 [1897].

———. *Lay Sermons and Addresses.* Glasgow: James Maclehose and Sons, 1907.

Canovan, Margaret. *Nationhood and Political Theory.* Cheltenham: Edward Elgar, 1996.

Cap and Gown (1906). Bodl., G.A. Oxon. 4 to 219(16).

Carr, Edward. *The Twenty Years Crisis, 1919–1939: An Introduction to the Study of International Relations.* 9th ed. London: Macmillan, 1961.

Clarke, Peter. *Liberals and Social Democrats.* Cambridge: Cambridge University Press, 1978.

Claude, Inis. *Swords into Plowshares: The Problems and Progress of International Organization.* New York: Random House, 1956.

Collingwood, R. G. *An Autobiography.* London: Oxford University Press, 1939.

Collini, Stefan. *Liberalism and Sociology.* Cambridge: Cambridge University Press, 1979.

Conca, Ken, "Environmental Protection, International Norms, and State Sovereignty." *Beyond Westphalia? State Sovereignty and International Intervention.* Eds. Gene Lyons and Michael Mastanduno. Baltimore: The John Hopkins University Press, 1995.

Constantine, Stephen. "Britain and the Empire." *The First World War in British History.* New York: St. Martin's Press, 1995.

Cooper, Robert. "The Post Modern State." *Re-Ordering the World: The Long-Term Implications of September 11th.* The Foreign Policy Centre, 2002. Available at, http://fpc.org.uk/hotnews/full?activeid=169&tabeid=writes.

Copleston, Frederick. *A History of Philosophy.* vol. 8, part 2. New York: Doubleday, 1962.

Crittenden, Jack. *Beyond Individualism: Reconstituting the Liberal Self.* Oxford: Oxford University Press, 1992.

Dangerfield, George. *The Strange Death of Liberal England.* New York: Capricorn, 1935.

de los Angeles Torres, Maria. "Transnational Political and Cultural Identities: Crossing Theoretical Borders." *Borderless Borders: U.S. Latinos, Latin Americans, and the Paradox of Interdependence.* Eds. Frank Bonilla, Edwin Melendex, Rebecca Morales, and Maria de los Angeles Torres. Philadelphia: Temple University Press, 1998.

Deslandes, Paul. " 'The Foreign Element': Newcomers and the Rhetoric of Race, Nation, and Empire in 'Oxbridge' Undergraduate Culture, 1850–1920." *Journal of British Studies* 37 (1998).

Dickinson, G. Lowes. *The Autobiography of G. Lowes Dickinson, and Other Unpublished Writings.* Ed. Dennis Proctor. London: Duckworth, 1973.

Gerard, Degroot. *Blighty: British Society in the Era of the Great War.* London: Longmans, 1996.

Den Otter, Sandra. *British Idealism and Social Explanation: A Study in Late Victorian Thought.* London: The Clarendon Press, 1996.

———. "Thinking in Communities: Late Nineteenth-Century Liberals, Idealists and the Retrieval of Community." *The Age of Transition: British Politics 1880–1914.* Ed. E.H.H. Green. Edinburgh: Edinburgh University Press, 1997.

Disch, Lisa. "Publicity-Stunt Participation and Sound Bite Polemics: The Health Care Debate 1993–94." *Journal of Health Politics, Policy, and Law* 21 (1996).

Dockrill, Michael, and J. Douglas Goold. *Peace Without Promise.* Hamden, CN: Archon Books, 1981.

Doty, Roxanne. "Sovereignty and the Nation." *State Sovereignty as a Social Construct.* Eds. Thomas Biersteker and Cynthia Weber. Cambridge: Cambridge University Press, 1996.

Dunbabin, J. P. "The League of Nations' Place in the International System." *The Historical Association.* Oxford: Blackwell, 1993.

Dunn, Seamus, and Thomas Hennessey. "Ireland." *Europe and Ethnicity.* Eds. Seamus Dunn and T. G. Fraser. London: Routledge, 1996.

Dyson, Ken. *The State Tradition in Western Europe*. Oxford: Oxford University Press, 1980.

Dworkin, Ronald. "Liberal Community." *Communitarianism and Individualism*. Eds. Shlomo Avineri and Avner De-Shalit. Oxford: Oxford University Press, 1992.

Egerton, George. "Feminism, Family and Community." *Feminism and Community*. Eds. Penny Weiss and Marilyn Friedman. Philadelphia: Temple University Press, 1995.

———. *Great Britain and the League of Nations: Strategy, Politics, and International Organization, 1914–1919*. Chapel Hill: North Carolina University Press, 1978.

Eichengreen, Barry. *Golden Fetters: The Gold Standard and the Great Depression, 1919–1939*. Oxford: Oxford University Press, 1995.

Eisenstein, Zillah. *The Radical Future of Liberal Feminism*. New York: Longmans, 1981.

Eichenberger, Clark. *The U.N.: The First Ten Years*. New York: Harper and Bros., 1955.

Fisher, H.A.L. *An Unfinished Autobiography*. Oxford: Oxford University Press, 1940.

Foreman-Peck, James. *A History of the World Economy: International Economic Relations Since 1850*. Totowa, NJ: Barnes and Noble, 1983.

Fortner, Robert. *International Communication: History, Conflict, and Control of the Global Metropolis*. Belmont, CA: Wadsworth, 1993.

Foucault, Michel. "Nietzsche, Genealogy, History." *The Foucault Reader*. Ed. Paul Rabinow. New York: Pantheon, 1984.

Freeden, Michael. *Liberalism Divided*. Oxford: The Clarendon Press, 1986.

———. *Minutes of the Rainbow Circle, 1894–1924*. London: Offices of the Royal Historical Society, University College London, 1989.

———. *The New Liberalism: An Ideology of Social Reform*. Oxford: The Clarendon Press, 1978.

———. "The New Liberalism and its Aftermath." *Victorian Liberalism*. Ed. Richard Bellamy. London: Routledge, 1990.

Gellner, Ernest. *Nations and Nationalism*. Ithaca: Cornell University Press, 1983.

George, Lloyd. "Some Considerations for the Peace Conference before They Finally Draft their Terms." *Mirror of the Past: A History of Secret Diplomacy*. Ed. Konni Zilliacus. New York: Current Books, 1946.

Getzler, Israel. "Soviets as Agents of Democratization." *Revolution in Russia: Reassessments of 1917*. Eds. Edith Rogovin Frankel, Jonathan Frankel, and Baruch Knei-Paz. London: Cambridge University Press, 1992.

Gillis, John. *For Better, For Worse: British Marriages, 1600 to the Present*. Oxford: Oxford University Press, 1985.

Gilpin, Robert. *The Political Economy of International Relations*. Princeton: Princeton University Press, 1987.

Goldman, Lawrence. *Dons and Workers: Oxford and Adult Education Since 1850*. Oxford: Oxford University Press, 1995.

Goldman, Wendy. *Women, the State and Revolution: Soviet Family Policy and Social Life, 1917–1936*. Cambridge: Cambridge University Press, 1993.

Golman, Kjell. *The Logic of Internationalism*. London: Routledge, 1994.

Gramsci, Antonio. *Selections from the Prison Notebooks*. New York: International Publishers, 1971.

Green, Thomas Hill. *Lectures on the Principles of Political Obligation*. London: Longmans, Green, 1963.

———. *Prolegomena to Ethics*. Oxford: Oxford University Press, 1884.

———. *The Works of Thomas Hill Green*. Ed. R. L. Nettleship. London: Longmans, Green, 1906. 3 vols.

Guibernau, Montserrat. *Nationalisms: The Nation-State and Nationalism in the Twentieth Century*. London: Polity Press, 1996.

Gupta, Akhil. "The Song of the Nonaligned World: Transnational Identities and the Reinscription of Space in Late Capitalism." *Cultural Antrhopology* 7(1) (1992).

Gurr, Ted Robert, and Barbara Harff. *Ethnic Conflict in World Politics*. Boulder: Westview, 1994.

Haldar, Hiral. *Neo Hegelianism*. London: Heath Cranton, 1927.

Hankin, G. T. "The Cinema House as a Centre of International Political Education." *Intercine* (May, 1931).

Harris, Frederick Philip. *The Neo-Idealist Political Theory*. New York: Kings Cross, 1944.

Harrison, Brian. *Separate Spheres: The Opposition to Women's Suffrage in Britain*. New York: Holmes and Meier, 1978.

Harvie, Christopher. *The Lights of Liberalism*. London: Allen Lane, 1976.

Hegel, G.W.F. *Grudlinien der Philosophie des Rechts*. Leipzig: Verlag von Felix Meiner, 1911.

———. *Introduction to the Philosophy of History*. Trans. Leo Rauch. Indianapolis: Hacket, 1988.

———. *Lectures on the Philosophy of World History*. 7th. ed. Trans. H. B. Nisbet. Cambridge: Cambridge University Press, 1989.

———. *Logic*. 3rd ed. Trans. William Wallace. Oxford: The Clarendon Press, 1989.

———. *Phenomenology of Mind*. Trans. J. B. Baillie. New York: Harper and Row, 1967.

———. *Philosophy of Right*. Trans. T. M. Knox. Oxford: Oxford University Press, 1967.

Hetherington, H.J.W., and John Muirhead. "The Conception of a Unitary Social Order." *Proceedings of the Aristotelian Society* 18 (1917–18).

———. *Social Purpose: A Contribution to a Philosophy of Civic Society*. London: Allen and Unwin, 1918.

Hinton, James. *Labour and Socialism: A History of the British Labour Movement, 1867–1947*. Amherst: University of Massachusetts Press, 1983.

Hobhouse, Leonard T. *Democracy and Reaction*. London: Fisher Unwin, 1904.

———. *Liberalism*. London: Williams and Norgate, 1911.

———. *The Metaphysical Theory of the State*. 6th ed. New York: Barnes and Noble, 1960.

———. "Physical, Biological and Psychological Categories." *Proceedings of the Aristotelian Society* 18 (1917–18).

Hobsbawm, Eric. *Nations and Nationalism Since 1780*. Cambridge: Cambridge University Press, 1993.

Hobson, J. A. *Confessions of an Economic Heretic*. London: George Allen and Unwin, 1938.

———. *The Crisis of Liberalism: New Issues of Democracy*. London: P. S. King and Son, 1909.

———. *Democracy after the War*. London: George Allen and Unwin, 1918.

———. "The International Mind." *Towards International Government*. London: Garland, 1971.

Hollis, Martin, and Steve Smith. *Explaining and Understanding International Relations*. Oxford: The Clarendon Press, 1990.

Hollis, Patricia. *Women in Public: The Women's Movement 1850–1900*. London: George Allen and Unwin, 1979.

Huttenback, Robert. *The British Imperial Experience*. New York: Harper and Row, 1966.

Ignatieff, Michael. "The American Empire: The Burden." *New York Times Magazine*, Jan. 5, 2003. Available at http://www.cid.harvard.edu/cidinthenews/articles/nyt-010503.html.

———. *Empire Lite: Nation Building in Bosnia, Kosovo, and Afghanistan*. London: Vintage, 2003.

Inis, Claude, *Swords into Plowshares: The Problems and Progress of International Organization*. New York: Random House, 1956.

Johnston, G. A. *Citizenship in the Industrial World*. London: Longmans, Green, 1928.

———. *International Social Progress: The Work of the International Labour Organization of the League of Nations*. London: George Allen and Unwin, 1924.

Jones, Henry. "The Social Organism." (1883) *The British Idealists*. Ed. David Boucher. Cambridge: Cambridge University Press, 1997.

Jourdain, Margaret. "Some Recent Literature Upon a League to Enforce Peace." *International Journal of Ethics* 28(1) (1917).

Jowett, Benjamin. *Dialogues of Plato*. vol. 3. Oxford: The Clarendon Press, 1871.

Kagan, Robert. "America's Responsibility." *The Weekly Standard*, September 15, 2003. Available at http://www.ceip.org/files/publications/2003–09–15-Kagan wklystandard.asp.

———. "The Healer." *The Guardian*, Monday, March 3, 2003. Available at http://www.guardian.co.uk/print/0,3858,4616744–103680,00.html.

———. *Of Paradise and Power: America and Europe In the New World Order*. New York: Alfred A Knopf, 2003.

———. "Power and Weakness." *Policy Review* 113 (2002). Available at http://www.policyreview.org/JUN02/kagan.html.

Kant, Immanuel. "Perpetual Peace." *Kant's Political Writings*. Ed. Hans Reiss. Cambridge: Cambridge University Press, 1970.

Kendle, John. *The Round Table Movement and Imperial Union*. Toronto: University of Toronto Press, 1975.

Kennan, George. *American Diplomacy, 1900–1950*. London: Secker and Warburg, 1952.

Kennedy, Paul. *The Rise of the Anglo-German Antagonism, 1860–1914.* London: Allen and Unwin, 1980.

Kenwood, A. G. *The Growth of the International Economy, 1820–1989.* London: George Allen and Unwin, 1983.

Kingsely, Susan Kent. *Sex and Suffrage in Britain, 1860–1914.* Princeton: Princeton University Press, 1987.

Kirk, Neville. *The Growth of Working Class Reformism in Mid-Victorian England.* Urbana and Chicago: University of Illinois Press, 1985.

Knutsen, Torbjorn. *A History of International Relations Theory.* Manchester, UK: Manchester University Press, 1997.

Kramnick, Isaac, and Barry Sheerman. *Harold Laski: A Life on the Left.* New York: Penguin, 1993.

Kupchan, Charles. "Nationalism Resurgent." *Nationalism and Nationalities in the New Europe.* Ithaca: Cornell University Press, 1995.

Kymlicka, Will. "Language Rights and Political Theory." *Annual Review of Applied Linguistics* 23 (2003).

———. "Liberalism and Minority Rights." *Ratio Juris* 12 (1999).

———. *Multicultural Citizenship.* Oxford: Oxford University Press, 1995.

———. *Politics in the Vernacular.* Oxford: Oxford University Press, 2001.

Langland, Elizabeth. *Nobody's Angels: Middle Class Women and Domestic Ideology in Victorian Culture.* Ithaca: Cornell University Press, 1995.

Laski, Harold. "The Apotheosis of the State." *The New Republic,* July 22, 1916.

———. *Authority in the Modern State.* New Haven: Yale University Press, 1919.

———. *Democracy in Crisis.* Chapel Hill: University of North Carolina Press, 1933.

———. "The Economic Foundations of Peace." *The Intelligent Man's Way to Prevent War.* Ed. Leonard Woolf. London: Victor Gollancz, 1933.

———. *Foundations of Sovereignty and Other Essays.* Free Port, NY: Books for Libraries Press, 1921.

———. *A Grammar of Politics.* London: Allen and Unwin, 1963, 1938.

———. "International Government and National Sovereignty." *Problems of Peace: Lectures Delivered at the Geneva Institute of International Relations: 1926.* Oxford: Oxford University Press, 1927.

———. "The Personality of the State." *The Nation,* July 22, 1915.

———. *Politics.* Philadelphia: J. B. Lippincott, 1931.

———. "Preface." *The Dying Peace.* Vigilantes (Konni Zilliacus.) London: The New Statesman and Nation, 1933.

———. *The Rise of European Liberalism: An Essay in Interpretation.* London: Allen and Unwin, 1936.

———. *The State in Theory and Practice.* New York: Viking, 1935.

Latane, John, ed. *Development of the League of Nations Idea; Documents and Corresepondence of Theodore Marburg.* New York: Macmillan, 1932.

Laybourn, Keith. *Britain on the Breadline: A Social and Political History of Britain Between the Wars.* Gloucester: Alan Sutton, 1990.

———. *A History of British Trade Unionism: 1770–1990.* Gloucester: Alan Sutton, 1992.

League of Nations. Information Section. *An Illustrated Album of the League of Nations*. Geneva: League of Nations Press, 1925.

———. "The League of Nations and The Press: International Press Exhibition, Cologne, May–Oct. 1928." Geneva: League of Nations Press, 1928.

———. League Document A.74.1938.VII. *Records of the Nineteenth Ordinary Session of the Assembly, Minutes of the Sixth Committee*. Geneva : League of Nations Press, 1920–1938.

Lebedev-Polyansky, P. I. "Revolution and the Cultural Task of the Proletariat." *Bolshevik Visions*. Ed. William G. Rosenberg. Ann Arbor: University of Michigan Press, 1990 [1918].

Lebow, Richard Ned. *White Britain and Black Ireland: The Influence of Stereotypes of Colonial Policy*. Philadelphia: Institute for the Study of Human Issues, 1976.

Leigh, Robert. "The Mass Communications Inventions and International Relations." *Technology and International Relations*. Ed. William Fielding Ogburn. Chicago: University of Chicago Press, 1949.

Lenin, Vladimir Ilyich. "Socialism and the War." *The Lenin Anthology*. Ed. Robert Tucker. New York: Norton, 1975 [1914].

Lewis, Jane. *Women in England: 1870–1950*. Bloomington: Indiana University Press, 1984.

Linklater, Andrew. "Rationalism." *Theories of International Relations*. Eds. Scott Burchill and Andrew Linklater. New York: St. Martin's Press, 1995.

Lloyd-Jones, Hugh. "Gilbert Murray." *American Scholar*. 51 (1) (1981–82).

Locke, John. "Second Treatise on Government." *Locke: Political Essays*. Ed. Mark Goldie. Cambridge: Cambridge University Press, 1997.

Lois-Dop. "The Role and the Purpose of the International Cinematographic Institute." *Intercine* 1 (1929).

Long, David, and Peter Wilson. *Thinkers of the Twenty Years Crisis*. Oxford: The Clarendon Press, 1995.

Low, D. A. *Eclipse of Empire*. Cambridge: Cambridge University Press, 1991.

MacIntyre, Aladsair. "The Privatization of Good." *The Liberalism-Communitarianism Debate*. Ed. C. F. Delaney. Latham, MD: Rowman and Littlefield, 1994.

MacKillop, I. D. *The British Ethical Societies*. Cambridge: Cambridge University Press, 1986.

Malkki, Lisa. "Citizens of Humanity: Internationalism and the Imagined Community of Nations." *Diaspora* 3 (1) (1994).

Mandell, Edward, and Charles Seymour, eds. *What Really Happened At Paris*. New York: Charles Scribner's and Sons, 1921.

Markwell, D. J. "Sir Alfred Zimmern Revisited: Fifty Years On." *Review of International Studies* 12 (1986).

Marrin, Albert. *Nicholas Murray Butler*. Boston: Twayne, 1976.

Mason, Michael. *The Making of Victorian Sexuality*. Oxford: Oxford University Press, 1994.

McClintock, Anne. "Family Feuds: Gender, Nationalism, and the Family." *Feminist Review* 44 (1993).

———. *Imperial Leather: Race, Gender and Sexuality in the Colonial Contest*. London: Routledge, 1995.

McClintock, Anne. "No Longer in a Future Heaven." *Dangerous Liaisons: Gender, Nation and Postcolonial Perspectives*. Eds. Anne McClintock, Aamir Muftie, and Ella Shohat. Minneapolis: University of Minnesota Press, 1997.

McKim, Robert, and Jeff Mahan, eds. *The Morality of Nationalism*. Oxford: Oxford University Press, 1997.

Mehta, Uday Sing. *Liberalism and Empire*. Chicago: University of Chicago Press, 1992.

Mehta, V. R. "The Origins of English Idealism in Relation to Oxford." *Journal of the History of Philosophy* 13 (2) (1975).

Messinger, Gary. *British Propaganda and the State in the First World War*. Manchester: Manchester University Press, 1992.

Mill, John Stuart. "Considerations on Representative Government."

———. "The Subjection of Women." *Essays on Sex Equality: John Stuart Mill and Harriet Taylor Mill*. Ed. Alice S. Rossi. Chicago: University of Chicago Press, 1970.

Miller, David. *On Nationality*. Oxford: The Clarendon Press, 1995.

Miller, David Hunter. *The Drafting of the Covenant*. vol. 1. New York: G. P. Putnam's Sons, 1928. 2 vols.

———. *The Geneva Protocol*. New York: Macmillan, 1925.

Minow, Martha, and Mary Lyndon Shanley. "Revisioning the Family: Relational Rights and Responsibilities." *Reconstructing Political Theory: Feminist Perspectives*. Eds. Mary Lyndon Shanley and Uma Narayan. University Park: Pennsylvania University State Press, 1997.

Mintz, Steven. *A Prison of Expectations: The Family in Victorian Culture*. New York: New York University Press, 1983.

Moore, G. E. "The Nature of Judgment." *Mind* 8(30) (1899).

Morgan, Lloyd. "A Concept of the Organism, Emergent and Resultant." *Proceedings of the Aristotelian Society* 27 (1926–27).

Morgenthau, Hans, and Kenneth Thompson. *Politics Among Nations*. 6th ed. New York: Alfred A. Knopf, 1985.

———. *Principles and Problems of International Politics*. New York: Knopf, 1950.

Morrow, John. "British Idealism, German Philosophy, and the First World War." *Australian Journal of Politics and History* 28(3) (1982).

Mosse, George. *Nationalism and Sexuality: Middle Class Morality and Sexual Norms in Modern Europe*. Madison: University of Wisconsin Press, 1985.

Muirhead, John. "The Family." *Ethical Democracy: Essays in Social Dynamics*. Ed. Stanton Coit. London: Grant Richards, 1900.

———. *The Platonic Tradition in Anglo Saxon Philosophy: Studies in the History of Idealism in England and America*. New York: Macmillan, 1931.

———. "What Imperialism Means." *The British Idealists*. Ed. David Boucher. Cambridge: Cambridge University Press, 1997 [1900].

Murray, Gilbert. "Epilogue." *The Evolution of World Peace*. Ed. F. S. Marvin. Oxford: Oxford University Press, 1933.

———. *The Five Stages of Greek Religion*. New York: Columbia University Press, 1925.

——. *From the League to the U.N.* Westport: Greenwood Press, 1988.

——. "Herd Instinct and the War." *The International Crisis in its Ethical and Psychological Aspects.* Oxford: Oxford University Press: 1915.

——. The Gilbert Murray Papers. Bodl. MS. Gilbert Murray, Boxes 1, 3, 11, 133, 189, 241, 242, 391, 418, 419, 436, 489, 500, adds. 11.

——. *A History of Ancient Greek Literature.* New York: Appleton, 1897.

——. *The League of Nations and the Democratic Idea.* Oxford: Oxford University Press, 1918.

——. *The League of Nations Movement: Some Recollections of the Early Days.* London: David Davies Memorial Institute of International Studies, Thorney House, 1955.

——. "The League of Nations Union Policy: An Address Delivered at a Meeting of the General Assembly of the League of Nations Union, Dec. 19, 1924." League of Nations Union; 1924.

——. *Liberalism and the Empire.* London: R. Brimpley Johnson, 1900.

——. *Liberality and Civilization.* New York: Macmillan, 1938.

——. "National Ideals: Conscious and Unconscious." *Essays and Addresses.* London: George Allen and Unwin, 1921.

——. *The Ordeal of This Generation: The War, the League and the Future.* London: George Allen and Unwin, 1929.

——. "The Problem of Nationality." *Proceedings of the Aristotelian Society* 20 (1919–1920).

——. *The Problems of Foreign Policy.* Boston: Houghton Mifflin, 1921.

——. *Proceedings of the British Academy,* vol. 26. London: Humphrey Milford Amen House, 1940.

——. *Satanism and the World Order.* London: George Allen and Unwin, 1920.

——. *The Schools of Europe.* London: League of Nations Union, 1935.

——. "Self-Determination of Nationalities." *International Affairs* 61 (1922).

——. "A Survey of Recent World Affairs." *Problems of Peace: Lectures Delivered at the Geneva Institute of International Relations: 1932.* Oxford: Oxford University Press, 1933.

——. *An Unfinished Autobiography.* London: Allen and Unwin, 1960.

——. "The Value of Greece to the Future of the World." *The Legacy of Greece.* Ed. R. W. Livingston. Oxford: Oxford University Press, 1921.

——. "What Liberalism Stands For." *Contemporary Review* 128 (1925).

——. "The World and the League: An address delivered at the Annual Meeting of the League of Nations Union General Council by Professor Gilbert Murray, L.L.D., D.Litt., June 17th, 1924." League of Nations Union, 1924.

Murray Butler, Nicholas. *The International Mind: An Argument for the Juridical Settlements of International Disputes.* New York: Shares Scribner's Sons, 1913.

Nader, Ralph. "WTO Means Rule by Unaccountable Tribunals." *The Ralph Nader Reader.* New York: Seven Stories Press, 2000.

Naff, Alixa. *Becoming American: The Early Arab Immigrant Experience.* Philadelphia: University of Pennsylvania Press, 1985.

The Nation. "A Liberal in a Muddle." *The Nation.* London, England; November 23, 1918.

Nicholson, Linda. *Gender and History: The Limits of Social Theory in the Age of the Family*. New York: Columbia University Press, 1986.

Nicholson, Peter. *The Political Philosophy of the British Idealists*. Cambridge: Cambridge University Press, 1990.

Nixon, Rob. "Of Balkans and Bantustans: 'Ethnic Cleansing' and the Crisis in National Legitimation." *Transition* 50 (1993).

Northcroft, D. M. *Women At Work in the League of Nations*. London: Wadsworth, the Rydal Press, 1927.

O'Brien, Mary. "Hegel: Man, Physiology, and Fate." *Feminist Interpretations of G.W.F. Hegel*. Ed. Patricia Jagentowitz Mills. University ParkA: Pennsylvania State University Press, 1997.

Oslander, Andreas. "Rereading Early Twentieth Century IR Theory: Idealism Revisited." *International Studies Quarterly* 42 (1998).

Ostrower, Gary. *The League of Nations From 1919–1929*. Garden City Park, NY: Avery, 1996.

Pateman, Carol. *The Disorder of Women: Democracy, Feminism, and Political Theory*. Stanford: Stanford University Press, 1989.

Patrick, James. *The Magdalen Metaphysicals: Idealism and Orthodoxy at Oxford, 1901–1945*. Macon, GA: Mercer, 1985.

Peterson, Spike. *Gendered States: Feminist (Re)visions of International Relations Theory*. Boulder: Lynn Reinner, 1992.

Pettman, Jan. *Worlding Women: A Feminist International Politics*. London: Routledge, 1996.

Philips, Gordon. *The Rise of the Labour Party:1893–1931*. London: Routledge, 1992.

Pogge, Thomas. "Creating Supra-National Institutions Democratically: Reflections on the European Union's 'Democracy Deficit.'" *The Journal of Political Philosophy* 5(2) (1997).

———. "Economic Justice and National Borders." *Revision* 22(2) (1999).

———. "Moral Universalism." *Politics, Philosophy and Economics* 1(1) (2002).

Polanyi, Karl. *The Great Transformation*. Boston: Beacon Press, 1944.

Pollak, Gustav. *International Minds and the Search for the Restful*. New York: The Nation Press, 1919.

Powers, James. *Years of Tumult: The World Since 1918*. New York: Norton, 1932.

Prakash, Gyan. "Postcolonial Criticism and Indian Historiography." *Dangerous Liaisons: Gender, Nation and Postcolonial Perspectives*. Eds. McClintock, Aamir Muftie, and Ella Shohat. Minneapolis: University of Minnesota Press, 1997.

Pugh, Martin. *The Making of Modern British Politics*. New York: St. Martin's Press, 1982.

Purvis, June. *Hard Lessons: The Lives and Education of Working-class Women in Nineteenth-Century England*. Minneapolis: University of Minnesota Press, 1989.

Putnam, Hilary. "Must We Choose?" *For Love of Country*. Ed. Martha Nussbaum. Boston: Beacon Press, 1996.

Quigley, Carroll. *The Anglo-American Establishment: From Rhodes to Clivenden*. New York: Books in Focus, 1981.

Ratcliffe, S. K. *The Story of South Place*. London: Watts and Co., 1955.

Rawls, John. *Justice as Freedom*. Cambridge: Harvard University Press, 2001.

———. *Political Liberalism*. New York: Columbia University Press: 1993.

Ray, James Lee. *Global Politics*. Boston: Houghton Mifflin, 1979.

Ree, Jonathan. "Internationality." *Radical Philosophy* 60 (1992).

Rich, Paul. "Reinventing Peace: David Davies, Alfred Zimmern and Liberal Internationalism in Interwar Britain." *International Relations* 16 (2002).

Richter, Melvin. *The Politics of Conscience: T. H. Green and His Age*. Cambridge: Harvard University Press, 1964.

Ritchie, David. "Darwin and Hegel." *Proceedings of the Aristotelian Society* 1 (1891–2).

———. *Darwinism and Politics*. London: Swan Sonnechshein and Co., 1891.

———. "Ethical Democracy: Evolution and Democracy." *Ethical Democracy, Essays in Social Dynamics*. Ed. Stanton Coit. London: G. Richards, 1900.

———. *Natural Rights: A Criticism of Some Political and Ethical Conceptions*. 3rd ed. London: George Allen and Unwin, 1916.

———. "The One and the Many." *Philosophical Studies*. London: Ed. R. Latta, 1905.

———. *The Principles of State Interference*. London: Swan Sonnenschein, 1891.

———. "Social Evolution." *Studies In Political and Social Ethics*. London: Swan Sonnenschein, 1902.

Robbins, Peter. *The British Hegelians*. London: Garland, 1982.

Rose, Mary. "Britain and the International Economy." *The First World War in British History*. Eds. Stephen Constantine, Maurice W. Kirby, and Mary Rose. London: Edward Arnold Press, 1995.

Rose, Sonya. *Limited Livelihoods: Gender and Class in Nineteenth-Century England*. Berkeley: University of California Press, 1992.

Rosenberg, Justin. *The Empire of Civil Society*. London: Verso, 1994.

Rosenthal, Joel. *Righteous Realists: Political Realism, Responsible Power, and American Culture in the Nuclear Age*. Baton Rouge: Louisiana State University Press, 1991.

Russell, A. K. *Liberal Landslide: The General Election of 1906*. Hamden, CN: Archon Books, 1973.

Russell, Bertrand. *Autobiography*. London: George Allen and Unwin, 1967.

Said, Edward. *Culture and Imperialism*. New York: Vintage Books, 1994.

Sandel, Michael. "The Procedural Republic and the Unencumbered Self." *Communitarianism and Individualism*. Eds. Shlomo Avineri and Avner De-Shalit. Oxford: Oxford University Press, 1992.

Sassen, Saskia. *Globalization and Its Discontents*. New York: The New Press, 1998.

Schmidt, Brian. "Lessons from the Past: Reassessing the Interwar Disciplinary History of International Relations." *International Studies Quarterly* 42 (1998).

———. *The Political Discourse of Anarchy*. Albany: State University of New York Press, 1998.

Schmidt, Ernst Gnther. "Ulrich Von Wilamowitz-Moellendorff to Sir Alfred Zimmern on the Reality of Classical Athens." *Philologus* 2 (1989).

Schmitt, Bernadotte Everly. *England and Germany, 1740–1914*. Princeton: Princeton University Press, 1918.

Serge, Victor. *Year One of the Russian Revolution*. London: Pluto Press, 1992.

Seth, Andrew. "Man's Place in the Cosmos." *The British Idealists*. Ed. David Boucher. Cambridge: Cambridge University Press, 1997 [1897].

Sharpe, Allen. "The Genie that Would Not Go Back Into the Bottle; National Self Determination and the Legacy of the First World War and the Peace Settlement." *Europe and Ethnicity*. Eds. Seamus Dunn and T. G. Fraser. London: Routledge, 1996.

Sifry, M. L., and C. Cerf. *The Gulf War Reader: History, Documents, Opinions*. New York: Times Books, 1991.

Siebert, Rudolf. *Hegel's Concept of Marriage and the Family*. Washington, DC: University Press of America, 1979.

Simai, Mihaly. *The Future of Global Governance*. Washington, DC: United States Institute for Peace Press, 1994.

Smith, Steven. *Hegel's Critique of Liberalism*. Chicago: University of Chicago Press, 1989.

Smith, Malcolm. "The War and British Culture." *The First World War in British History*. Eds. Stephen Constantine, Maurice W. Kirby, and Mary Rose. London: Edward Arnold Press, 1995.

Sobel, Russel. "The League of Nations Covenant and the United Nations Charter, An Analysis of Two International Constitutions." *Constitutional Political Economy* 5(2) (1994).

Soffer, Reba. "Nation, Duty, Character and Confidence: History at Oxford, 1850–1914." *The Historical Journal* 30(1) (1987).

Soloway, Richard. *Demography and Degeneration: Eugenics an the Declining Brithrate in Twentieth-Century Britain*. Chapel Hill University of North Carolina Press, 1995.

Spencer, Herbert. *Data of Ethics*. New York: William Allison, 1879.

———. *The Evolution of Society; Selections from Herbert Spencer's Principles of Sociology*. Chicago: University of Chicago Press, 1967.

Stapleton, Julia. *Englishness and the Study of Politics: The Social and Political Thought of Ernest Barker*. Cambridge: Cambridge University Press, 1994.

Stansky, Peter, ed. *The Left and the War: The British Labour Party and World War I*. Oxford: Oxford University Press, 1969.

Steichen, Edward. "Introduction." *The Family of Man: The Greatest Photographic Exhibition of all Time—503 pictures from 68 Countries*. New York: Museum of Modern Art, 1955.

Steiner, Zara. *The League of Nations in Retrospect*. New York: Walter de Gruyter, 1983.

Stoler, Ann. "Making Empire Respectable: The Politics of Race and Sexual Morality in Twentieth-Century Colonial Cultures." *Dangerous Liaisons: Gender, Nation and Postcolonial Perspectives*. Eds. Anne McClintock, Aamir Muftie, and Ella Shohat. Minneapolis: University of Minnesota Press, 1997.

———. *Race and the Education of Desire*. Durham: Duke University Press, 1995.

Suganami, Hidemi. *The Domestic Analogy and World Order Proposals*. Cambridge: Cambridge University Press, 1989.

Sylvester, Christina. *Feminist Theory and International Relations in a Post Modern Era*. Cambridge: Cambridge University Press, 1994.

Tamir, Yael. *Liberal Nationalism*. Princeton: Princeton University Press, 1993.

———. "The Right to National Self-Determination as an Individual Right." *History of European Ideas* 16 (1993).

———. "Two Concepts of Multiculturalism." *Journal of Philosophy of Education* 29 (1995).

Taylor, Charles. *Hegel*. Cambridge: Cambridge University Press, 1975.

———. *Sources of Self*. Cambridge: Cambridge University Press, 1989.

Thompson, John. *Russia, Bolshevism, and the Versailles Peace*. Princeton: Princeton University Press, 1966.

Thompson, Kenneth. *Fathers of International Thought: A Legacy of Political Theory*. Baton Rouge: Louisiana State University Press, 1994.

Thomson. J.A.K. *Proceedings of the British Academy*. vol. XLIII. Oxford: Oxford University Press, 1957.

Toynbee, Arnold. *Acquaintances*. Oxford: Oxford University Press, 1967.

———. *Civilization on Trial*. Oxford: Oxford University Press, 1948.

———. *Janus at Seventy Five*. Oxford: Oxford University Press, 1964.

———. *Nationality and the War*. London: J. M. Dent and Sons, 1915.

Turner, Frank M. *The Greek Heritage in Victorian Britain*. New Haven: Yale University Press, 1981.

———. "The Triumph of Idealism in Victorian Classical Studies." *Contesting Cultural Authority: Essays in Victorian Intellectual Life*. Cambridge: Cambridge University Press, 1993.

Vanderpool, Harold. *Darwin and Darwinism: Revolutionary Insights Concerning Man, Nature, Religion, and Society*. Lexington, MA: Heath, 1973.

Vasquez, John. *The Power of Power Politics, A Critique*. New Brunswick: Rutgers University Press, 1985.

Vincent, Andrew, and Raymond Plant. *Philosophy, Politics and Citizenship*. London: Basil Blackwell, 1984.

Watson, Adam. *The Evolution of International Society*. London: Routledge, 1992.

Weber, Cynthia. *Simulating Sovereignty: Intervention, the State, and Symbolic Exchange*. Cambridge: Cambridge University Press, 1995.

Weeks, Jeffrey. *Sex, Politics, and Society: The Regulation of Sexuality Since 1800*. London: Longmans, 1989.

Wellek, Rene. *Immanuel Kant in England, 1793–1938*. Princeton: Princeton University Press, 1931.

Wells, H. G. *In the Fourth Year: Anticipations of a World Peace*. New York: Macmillan, 1918.

West, Francis. *Gilbert Murray: A Life*. New York: St. Martin's Press, 1984.

Whitehead, Annie, Clara Connolly, Erica Carter, and Helen Crowley. "Editorial." *Feminist Review: Nationalism and National Identities* 44 (1993).

Wilson, Duncan. *Gilbert Murray OM, 1866–1957.* Oxford: The Oxford Clarendon Press, 1987.

Wilson, Peter, "The Myth of the 'First Great Debate'." *Review of International Studies* 24 (1998).

Wilson, Trevor. *The Downfall of the Liberal Party, 1914–1935.* Ithaca: Cornell University Press, 1966.

Winkler, Henry. *The League of Nations Movement in Great Britain: 1914–1919.* New Brunswick: Rutgers University Press, 1952.

Wolfe, Willard. *From Radicalism to Socialism: Men and Ideas in the Formation of Fabian Socialist Doctrines, 1881–1889.* New Haven: Yale University Press, 1975.

Wolin, Sheldon. "Collective Identity and Constitutional Power." *The Presence of the Past: Essays on the State and the Constitution.* Baltimore: Johns Hopkins University Press, 1989.

Wood, Allen. *Hegel's Ethical Thought.* Cambridge: Cambridge University Press, 1990.

Wright, Quincy, *Neutrality and Collective Security.* Chicago: Chicago University Press, 1936.

Yearwood, Peter. " 'On the Safe and Right Lines': The Lloyd George Government and the Origins of the League of Nations, 1916–1918." *The Historical Journal* 32 (1989).

Young, Crawford. "The Dialectics of Cultural Pluralism: Concept and Reality." *The Rising Tide Of Cultural Pluralism: The Nation State At Bay?* Ed. Crawford Young. Madison: University of Wisconsin Press, 1993.

Zakaria, Fareed. "The Arrogant Empire." *Newsweek*, March 24, 2003. Available at http://www.fareedzakaria.com/articles/newsweek/032403.html.

———. "Our Way," *The New Yorker*, October 14, 2002. Available at http://www.fareedzakaria.com/articles/nyer/101402.html.

———. "The Previous Superpower." *New York Times*, July 27, 2003. Available at http://www.fareedzakaria.com/articles/nyt/072703.html.

Zastoupil, Lynn. *John Stuart Mill and India.* Stanford: Stanford University Press, 1994.

Zerilli, Linda. *Signifying Woman: Culture and Chaos in Rousseau, Burke, and Mill.* Ithaca: Cornell University Press, 1994.

Zilliacus, Konni. *Mirror of the Past: A History of Secret Diplomacy.* New York: Current Books, 1946.

Zimmern, Alfred. The Alfred Zimmern Papers. Bodl. MS Alfred Zimmern, Boxes 5, 7, 11, 16, 82, 85, 135, 136.

———. *America and Europe and Other Essays.* London: Oxford University Press, 1929.

———. *The British Commonwealth in the Post-War World; a Lecture Delivered at Trinity College, Oxford, on 6 May, 1925.* London: Oxford University Press, 1926.

———. "Capitalism and International Relations." *Some Ethical Aspects of International Relations.* Oxford: Oxford University Press, 1917.

———. "The Development of the International Mind." *Problems of Peace: Lectures Delivered at the Geneva Institute of International Relations*. Oxford: Oxford University Press, 1926.

———. *The Economic Weapon in the War Against Germany*. London: Allen and Unwin, 1918.

———. *Education and International Good Will; the Sixth Earl Grey Memorial Lecture, Delivered at King's Hall, Armstrong College, New Castle-On-Tyne, on April 25, 1924*. Oxford: Oxford University Press, 1924.

———. "The Ethics of Empire." *The Round Table* (June 1913) 484–501.

———. *Europe in Convalescence*. London: Mills & Boon, 1922.

———. *From the British Empire to the British Commonwealth*. London: Longmans, 1941.

———. The Future of Democracy. *The University of Buffalo Studies* 8(2) (1930).

———. "German Culture and the British Commonwealth." *The War and Democracy*. Eds. R. W. Seton Watson, J. Dover Wilson, Alfred E. Zimmern, and Arthur Greenwood. London: Macmillan, 1928.

———. *The Greek Commonwealth: Politics and Economics in Fifth-Century Athens*. 7th ed. Oxford: Oxford University Press, 1961 [1911].

———. "The Influence of Public Opinion on Foreign Policy." *Problems of Peace: Lectures Delivered at the Geneva Institute of International Relations: 1928*. Oxford: Oxford University Press, 1929.

———. "Introduction." *The New Germany: Three Lectures by Ernst Jackh*. Oxford: Oxford University Press, 1927.

———. "The League and International intellectual Co-operation." *Problems of Peace: Lectures Delivered at the Geneva Institute of International Relations: 1926*. Oxford: Oxford University Press, 1927.

———. *The League of Nations and the Rule of Law, 1918–1935*. London: Macmillan, 1936.

———. *Learning and Leadership: A Study of the Needs and Possibilities of International Intellectual Co-operation*. Geneva: Intellectual Co-operation Section, League of Nations Press, 1927.

———. "Liberty, Democracy, and the Movement Towards World Order." *Problems of Peace: Lectures Delivered at the Geneva Institute of International Relations: 1935*. Oxford: Oxford University Press, 1936.

———. *Modern Political Doctrines*. London: Oxford University Press, 1939.

———. "Nationalism and Internationalism." *The Prospects of Democracy*. London: Chatto and Windus, 1929 [1923].

———. *Nationality and Government*. New York: Robert M. McBride, 1918.

———. "The New International Outlook: Two Lectures at the Fenton Foundation of the University of Buffalo, Delivered in November, 1926." *The University of Buffalo Studies* 5(1) (1926).

———. "Political Thought," *The Legacy of Greece*. Ed. R. W. Livingston. Oxford: Oxford University Press, 1921.

———. "Preface," *University Teaching of International Relations: A Record of the Eleventh Session of the International Studies Conference, Prague, 1938*. Paris: International Institute of Intellectual Co-operation, League of Nations, 1939.

Zimmern, Alfred. "The Problem of Collective Security." *Neutrality and Collective Security*. Ed. Quincy Wright. Chicago: Chicago University Press, 1936.

———. "Progress in Government." *Progress and History*. Ed. Francis Sydney. New York: Books for Libraries Press, 1916.

———. *Quo Vadimus? A Public Lecture Delivered on 5 February 1934*. Oxford: Oxford University Press, 1934.

———. *The Reorganization of Industry: Papers by Professor A. C. Pigou, Arthur Greenwood, Sidney Webb, and A. E. Zimmern*. London: Active Printing Society, 1916.

———. *Spiritual Values and World Affairs*. Oxford: Oxford University Press. 1939.

———. "The Study of International Relations, An Inaugural Lecture, Delivered Before the University of Oxford, 20, Feb., 1931." Oxford: The Clarendon Press, 1931.

———. *The Third British Empire; Being a Course of Lectures Delivered at Columbia University, New York*. London: Oxford University Press. 1934.

———. "Was Greek Civilization Based on Slave Labour." *Solon and Croesus and Other Greek Essay*. Freeport, NY: Books for Libraries Press 1968 [1928].

Ziring, Lawrence. *The Middle East: A Political Dictionary*. Santa Barbara: ABC-CLIO, 1992.

Index